INNER MASTERY,
OUTER IMPACT

INNER MASTERY, OUTER IMPACT

How Your Five Core Energies
Hold the Key to Success

HITENDRA WADHWA, PhD

hachette
BOOKS

New York

Hachette Go, an imprint of Hachette Books
Hachette Book Group
1290 Avenue of the Americas
New York, NY 10104
HachetteGo.com
Facebook.com/HachetteGo
Instagram.com/HachetteGo

First Edition: June 2022

Hachette Books is a division of Hachette Book Group, Inc.

The Hachette Go and Hachette Books name and logos are trademarks of
Hachette Book Group, Inc.

The publisher is not responsible for websites (or their content) that are not
owned by the publisher.

Print book interior design by Jeff Williams

Library of Congress Cataloging-in-Publication Data
Names: Wadhwa, Hitendra, author.
Title: Inner mastery, outer impact : how your five core energies hold the
   key to success / Hitendra Wadhwa.
Description: First edition. | New York, NY : Hachette Go, [2022] | Includes
   bibliographical references. | Summary: "Columbia Business School
   professor and founder of the Mentora Institute shares how to have your
   outer success reflect your inner core, based on his popular course,
   "Personal Leadership and Success.""– Provided by publisher.
Identifiers: LCCN 2021051706 | ISBN 9780306827860 (hardcover) | ISBN
   9780306827884 (ebook)
Subjects: LCSH: Success. | Self-realization. | Leadership. | Conduct of
   life.
Classification: LCC BF637.S8 W23 2022 | DDC 158.1–dc23/eng/20211109
LC record available at https://lccn.loc.gov/2021051706

ISBNs: 9780306827860 (hardcover), 9780306827884 (ebook)

Printed in the United States of America

LSC-C

Printing 1, 2022

To my mother,
for the wisdom in her love,
and my late father,
for the love in his wisdom

CONTENTS

INTRODUCTION

꒰ ꒱

You will never have a greater or lesser dominion than
that over yourself.

—*Leonardo da Vinci*

THE EXPERIENCE I WILL NEVER FORGET

One day, in the pre-internet age, I drove from my home in Palo
Alto to Yosemite National Park upon the invitation of two
friends who were camping there. This was going to be my first time at
Yosemite. I had not seen any photos of the park, so I had no idea what
to expect. It was dark by the time I reached its gates. I was greeted by
park rangers and given a map. A long and winding road took me to
the valley within. As I drove the final stretch, a blanket of peace fell
over me. My spirit began to soar, and my thoughts became clearer.
Nature—with its gurgling brooks, rustling leaves, and starlit sky—was
casting a spell. I arrived at my friends' campground in the pitch of
darkness and was soon happily asleep, imagining we were in a lush
meadow surrounded by hills. When I awoke and walked out of my
tent at dawn the next morning, I was instantly awestruck. Towering,
steep, barren rock formations shooting up toward the skies from
everywhere, a waterfall roaring down from one of the mountains, the
color green taking on a thousand hues, and vistas upon vistas—it was

nature at its rapturous best. I had no idea this was the paradise I had entered the night before and so casually slept in. The sheer splendor of Yosemite Valley was breathtaking, and the feelings of grandeur and beauty it evoked have never left me. I recall feeling like I was in the presence of something divine.

Now you have opened this book to go on a drive of your own, with me as your guide. Our path may be a bit rugged and sometimes winding, and we may not see much of anything for a while. But what if I told you that there is a wealth of peace, wisdom, love, and joy that awaits you at our destination, your Inner Core? That whatever glimpses you get along the way, the little insights and inspirations, are but a drop in the grand ocean that lies in wait at the very center of your being? That this Core already exists within you, ready to offer its treasures whenever you awaken to its presence? That discovering it will be even more awe inspiring than arriving in Yosemite Valley? I have struggled to find a way to put this promise in words, so instead I thought of sharing the feeling of transcendence I experienced that magical morning at Yosemite. Let our journey begin.

MY BREAKTHROUGH MOMENT

On one fateful day in the classroom, I finally figured out what I wanted to be when I grew up. It wasn't a professor who helped me get there; it was a student. You see, I was the professor.

My search for a lifelong passion had already taken me down three paths—mathematics, management consulting, and entrepreneurship—by the time I joined the Columbia Business School faculty in 2004. It was now December 2005, and I was wrapping up my fall semester course on marketing strategy. I had developed a strong bond with my students, and recognizing that I might not see them again after the course ended, I felt a keen desire to impart to them the most valuable guidance I could. So before concluding my final lecture, I shared three personal stories and the lessons I'd learned from them. After class, a student, Min-Jun, came up to me and said,

"Professor, thank you for your time with us this semester. But most of all, thank you for your personal stories today. Those were for me the most valuable learnings from the course."

I was happy, and dumbstruck. Through this parting comment, Min-Jun had confirmed what I'd long felt as a nagging suspicion—that there was a big hole in what we were teaching at business school. We were teaching how to grow a startup, a product, an investment, or a new business idea to its full potential. But we were not teaching how to grow your own self to your full potential. We were teaching how to direct others, change others, motivate others, influence others, and inspire others. But we were not teaching how to direct yourself, change yourself, motivate yourself, influence yourself, and inspire yourself. We were teaching how to lead everyone else, but not how to lead yourself.

"Hitendra," I told myself that day, "this is what you want to research and teach in the years ahead."

Eighteen months later, after I had conducted extensive research, delivered a series of seminars, and built a whole new curriculum, Columbia allowed me to take a professional leap by formally offering a new course called Personal Leadership and Success. For both me and Columbia this was a radical experiment. As I prepared to deliver my first class in the course in the summer of 2007, my mind retraced the steps that had brought me to this point.

OUTER ME, INNER ME

I was ten years old when I came across the story of the Indian emperor Ashoka. He ascended to the throne after killing his brothers. As king, he waged war upon bloody war to bring other kingdoms under his subjugation, building a vast empire that swept across the Indian subcontinent. But that is not why he is revered by the people of India.

One day, Ashoka stepped on the battlefield to witness the ravages of war. As he saw the wounded and the dead, the wailing widows and the orphans, his heart melted. He realized the folly of his ways and committed to never waging another war. He still planned to pursue success, but not the kind of success he had chased until that moment. He spent the rest of his life using his wealth to serve his people and propagate spiritual understanding throughout his kingdom. It is this reformed Ashoka—not the rapacious Ashoka—who reigns supreme in the hearts of Indians more than two thousand years after his death. He is commonly known as Ashoka the Great.

When I was a ten-year-old, my fascination with Ashoka stemmed from neither his former ferocity nor his latter nobility, but rather from his capacity to transform himself, in one short life, from one to the other. It made me wonder. Do I, too, possess seeds of remarkable transformation within myself? What is the greatest version of me that I could be?

Ever since then, I have had a deep and abiding interest in exploring the highest achievements in human life, and the inner and outer steps we can take to get there. India, the country of my birth, provided fertile soil for such tilling. It was in this land that timeless truth-seekers forged the discipline of yoga, which cultivates the potential we all possess for perfection in action, thought, feeling, and spirit. It was in this land that a privileged prince renounced his luxuries and slipped out of his palace to embark on a lifelong quest for enlightenment, transforming himself into the Buddha. It was in this land that a remarkable lineage of ten spiritual teachers distilled the notion of an ideal life into the simple, devotional, and service-oriented faith of Sikhism. And it was in this same land where another great faith, Jainism, perfected nonviolence into a discipline that could be practiced not only with other humans, but with all living beings; not only in action, but also in speech, thought, and intention. India has from ancient times sought to map the contours of human potential, only to discover that there are no limits to it at all.

And whenever Indian civilization has encountered the prickly strands of foreign faiths, it has happily woven their finest threads into its own spiritual fabric. The Sufis, practitioners of a mystical branch of Islam, brought their intoxicating poetry and music to India, illuminating the human heart's capacity for a pure, universal, ever-expanding form of love, and fostering an even more mystical path by fusing their faith with India's. Mahatma Gandhi's epochal movement against British rule was as deeply influenced by Christ's teachings of love and forgiveness and the American Transcendentalists' teachings of civil disobedience as by the Hindu prophet Krishna's teachings of nonattachment to the fruits of one's labor. Perhaps it is this spiritual immersion that moved Martin Luther King Jr., on his sole visit to India, to say, "To other countries I may go as a tourist, but to India I come as a pilgrim."

For me, growing up in India was like partaking every day in a sumptuous feast of spirit. From childhood on, thanks to the retreats my family attended and the spiritual literature on my father's bookshelf, I developed certain inner and outer routines of my own—an irregular meditation practice, late-night conversations with the universe, and a sampling of world scriptures, philosophies, and truth-seekers' journeys—that made me keenly aware of a life beyond the material and the everyday.

In high school, I dove avidly into the study of psychology to advance what I'd learned of human nature from faith and philosophy. I thought this might be the route to the transformation I was seeking. But I struggled to connect with the subject. At that time, in the 1980s, psychology was focused on the darkness within us and not the light—on schizophrenia, depression, and trauma, not genius, joy, and flourishing. So I gave up on my plan to major in psychology in college. I made the exploration of my highest potential a quiet, inner pursuit, while on the outside I got swept up in a swirl of ambition to excel and succeed. By my mid-thirties, I had graduated with an MBA and a PhD, worked as a management consultant, founded and led (and two years later, much humbled, bore witness to a fire sale of) a Web 1.0 tech startup in Silicon Valley, and taken on a teaching career at Columbia Business School. From the outside, I was inhabiting a gilded world. But from within, I had a gnawing feeling that my life might hurtle toward its final act without my ever having come close to living it.

So I unsheathed the soul-searching swords I had acquired over the years—meditation, writing, reflection, retreats, and conversations with truth-seeking monks—and sent them to battle with that ultimate question, "What should I do with my life?" The answer was vague at first. It took a few years to come into sharper relief, but when it did, it was resoundingly clear. I wanted to dissolve the boundaries between my inner life and outer life, and translate my passion for pursuing my highest potential into a teaching that could help others approach their own. Case closed. I had finally, with my hair now more salt than pepper, figured out what I wanted to be when I grew up. After my excursions into mathematics, consulting, and entrepreneurship, I had come back full circle to the same question that I had been so drawn to as a ten-year-old: What is the highest peak one can scale in a well-trekked life?

But in summer 2007, while I was awaiting news on the enrollments in my Personal Leadership and Success course, I had to wonder: Did other people share that questing spirit? How many Columbia MBAs would find it worthwhile to take such a class?

Right from its inaugural semester, Personal Leadership and Success ended up being oversubscribed, and multiple sections were added over time. The parallel tracks of my inner and outer journeys were now finally converging. My private passion became my public profession.

Over the last fifteen years, at Columbia and at the Mentora Institute, which I founded in 2011 to further disseminate these teachings to organizations worldwide, twenty thousand participants across forty-plus countries—including senior executives, managers, entrepreneurs, investment bankers, doctors, consultants, MBA students, school superintendents and principals, the formerly incarcerated, social workers, church ministers, undergraduates, high-schoolers, and retirees—have gone through a version of this class and applied its lessons to their life and work. During this period, I've experienced the truth in the statement "When one teaches, two learn." The questions, challenges, insights, and real-life stories these participants have shared have not simply enriched my teachings—they have enriched me. And for that, I tip my hat to each of them.

GUIDES ON OUR JOURNEY

My goal in this book is to help us find universal laws of human nature that can guide us to our true nature—our highest potential—and to demonstrate that when we live in harmony with these laws, we create the conditions for outer success and impact. We will arrive at these laws by studying the common ground that is emerging between ancient wisdom, drawn from the great scriptures, and the science of human nature, drawn from psychology, psychotherapy, neuroscience, sociology, behavioral economics, and medicine. When you come across statements like "Science has shown . . . ," "Research shows . . . ," or "A scientific experiment . . . ," you will find corresponding references in the Sources section at the end of the book. I have benefited greatly from the dialogs and partnerships I've had over the last sixteen years with leading experts on the fast-evolving science of human nature, including David Burns, Dan Siegel, Richie Davidson, Angela Duckworth, Albert Bandura, Carol Dweck, Amy Edmondson, James Doty, Jamil Zaki, and Scott Barry Kaufman. I also offer stories from the lives of participants who have taken my classes and workshops that exemplify the principles in this book.* Occasionally, I share my own personal journey.

And finally, I draw from my research of transformative figures from history—people who have led storied lives, pursued noble causes, and inspired others to achieve great things. When we hear anecdotes from the lives of those who inspire us, we unconsciously start to walk in their shoes. We are transported to their time and place, and their story becomes our story. We start to bring them into

---

* When I use only a first name for a former participant, it means the name has been changed to preserve the person's confidentiality. When I use both a first and last name, it is the individual's real name.

our world to inform and inspire our own choices. Research shows that in your day-to-day moments, if you bring a role model to mind who exemplifies a certain quality you are inspired by, you are more likely to act out that quality yourself. If, for instance, you admire your mother for her compassion, then if you think of your mother when you are interacting with someone in need, you are more likely to act compassionately.

An individual doesn't have to be perfect for them to inspire us or be worthy of emulation. Arya shared the following story in one of my workshops:

> I worked very hard for two years in my early twenties to get selected for the coveted civil service in my country. I was devastated when I didn't make it. I became depressed and lost all motivation to pursue a career. After a few months, I started to notice that my dog, Pluto, was becoming blind. He would walk around the house bumping into objects, struggling to get to his food bowl or to the family. And yet I noticed he did not lose his zest for life–he continued to wag his tail all the time and walk around friskily. It woke me up. "If Pluto can be so inspired to seize each day even while he is losing his sight," I asked myself, "then how can I be losing my motivation over this one setback? I still have so much of life ahead of me!" Pluto cured me of my depression.

Pluto did not need to be perfect to inspire Arya. Heck, he didn't even need to be a human being.

In Part Two of the book I will showcase the Inner Mastery, Outer Impact journeys of five inspiring figures from history: Eleanor Roosevelt, Abraham Lincoln, Nelson Mandela, Mother Teresa, and Gandhi. On the surface, there's not much in common between these people and you. They lived in different times, played different roles, and likely had different personalities from you. And yet if you expand your thinking about them, you will see that they were, like you and me, on a human journey. They had their dreams, like we have ours.

They had their failings and failures, like we have ours. There were a lot of things not in their control. And yet they kept going and growing, and that's what made the paths they took increasingly luminous over the course of their lives. I hope to show you some of the small steps these five individuals took.

But there is an even more central member of our cast I want to introduce to you now.

THE MOST IMPORTANT HERO IN YOUR LIFE

Take a moment to identify your favorite hero.

You likely haven't cited the most important hero in your life—the one who Ben, a successful finance professional in his late thirties, introduced to my executive MBA class one day. Here is Ben's story:

> When I was fourteen, I got struck by cancer. I was a fighter, and I was able to fight it off with the help of the right therapies. It was a tough period, but I came out victorious. I returned to school and gradually picked up the pieces of my life. It felt good to beat cancer.
>
> Then, at sixteen, the cancer came back. This time, I felt totally sapped of spirit and energy. Another round of cancer therapies started, and I just couldn't muster up the strength to fight again. This time cancer was winning.
>
> One day, my mother took my hand in her hand and looked lovingly into my eyes. "Son, I want to tell you a story about your father. Everything you know about him has come through my stories since he died before you were born, and this is one story I have not shared with you so far. It was my birthday, and he came home with a big smile on his face. He had a surprise for me, he said. We got in our car and he drove me up the highway. We stopped at a car dealership. And then it dawned on me. He was going to buy me the car of my dreams! This was the car I had dearly wanted for so long. He had been saving up for it quietly, and now he was going to give me this beautiful birthday gift. I was so happy that day.

"We returned to our old car, for he wanted us to drive home sitting together in the same car. We were pulling the new car with some chains attached to the bumper of our old car. As we were driving down the highway, the chains started to loosen up a bit, so he stopped the car on a side lane and got out to fix it. Then, suddenly, BANG! I looked back in horror. A truck had crashed into our new car from the back, and your father had been crushed in between our old car and the new one. He was dead. I have never shared with you before the circumstances of his death, and now you know.

"I was in shock, and I felt a deep sense of despair. I opened the door, and I was about to walk into the highway, intent on getting hit by a passing vehicle so that I, too, would be dead. There was no point living any more.

"And then I felt this little kick in my womb. It was you. It was as though you were telling me, 'Mom, don't take your own life. I know this is a terrible thing to happen. You have lost your husband, and I my father, and we will always grieve our loss. But we will survive, and one day we will even thrive. So stay back here with me, and keep your hope alive.'

"Son, that day, you were my hero. You saved me from taking my own life. And ever since then, you have been my hero. There have been so many times when I have leaned on you for wisdom and strength and grace. And today," she said, squeezing my hand, "I again need you to be my hero. I want you to stay in this fight. I want you to win again. I want you to be back in the arena of life and grow into the wonderful man I have seen in you from the time you were not even born."

This story, and my mother's appeal, was like a bolt from the blue. I found a surge of strength within me. I kept my spirits high. I regained my hope for the future. And I survived cancer, for a second time. It has never returned, and I have been healthy ever since.

I share this story today because I want all of you to know that just as I have been a hero in my mother's life, you, too, are a hero in some people's lives. You owe it to them to be your best self, to fight the good fight, to approach your highest potential.

I came to Columbia thinking it was my responsibility to shine a light for my students on the big questions in life, only to discover, through stories like Ben's, that this light is already present within us all. This inner light is what all the great ones have sought, within themselves and within humanity. At the height of America's gravest national crisis, the Civil War, as President Lincoln faced fierce criticism from all corners of the country, he once reflected, "It is my ambition and desire to administer the affairs of the government [such] that if at the end I should have lost every other friend on earth, I shall at least have one friend remaining and that one shall be down inside of me."

It is my hope that by the end of the journey we are on in this book, you, too, will form an abiding kinship with the most important hero in your life: the friend down inside you, your own true self.

Part One

THE MAP

⤛⚿⤜

AT THE VERY CENTER OF THE SUN IS WHAT SCIENTISTS call its core. The core represents only 1 percent of the sun's volume. Remarkably so, this 1 percent is responsible for 99 percent of the energy the sun generates.

What if this were true of you as well? What if, at the very center of your being, lay your Inner Core, and this 1 percent of you was responsible for 99 percent of your potential, or perhaps even more?

Chapter 1

A LIFE WELL LIVED

‑⸮‑

Man naturally desires, not only to be loved, but to be lovely; or to be that thing which is the natural and proper object of love. . . . He desires, not only praise, but praiseworthiness; or to be that thing which, though it should be praised by nobody, is, however, the natural and proper object of praise.

—*Adam Smith*

ALFRED'S WAKE-UP CALL

Alfred was a scientist, engineer, inventor, and businessman who by the time he was fifty-five had invented a very important technology, patented it, commercialized it for use in many industries, and become immensely wealthy. By all conventional measures, Alfred was a success. But one day in 1888 his comfortable world was shaken when he woke up to read his own obituary in the newspapers. The newspapers reported him dead; in actuality, it was his twin brother, Ludwig, who had died the previous day.

But what was even more of a shock to Alfred was to read what a French newspaper wrote about him. Under the headline "The Merchant of Death Is Dead," the obituary said, "The man who was responsible for killing more people faster than ever before, died yesterday."

Alfred's invention was dynamite, and it was being deployed in construction and mining but also in warfare. Alfred was shocked to realize that this was how the world was going to remember him. He began pouring his energy and wealth into creating the legacy he wanted for himself, the legacy we actually remember him for: the Nobel Prizes that are awarded to, according to Alfred's will, "those who, during the preceding year, have conferred the greatest benefit to humankind."

For the Alfred in our story is none other than Alfred Nobel.

Eight years after reading his own obituary and changing his life's direction, he was dead—truly dead. Few people in the world today remember him for what he did to earn the moniker "the merchant of death"; most remember him for what he created in the final stage of his life: the institution of the Nobel Prize. Never believe it is too late to turn your life in the direction of the legacy you wish to leave.

But what Alfred Nobel achieved represents only half the glory you can pursue. Bronnie Ware's story reveals the other half.

WHEN THE CURTAIN FALLS

A palliative care nurse, Bronnie wrote a blog in 2009 in which she shared a powerful finding about her experiences in caring for the dying during their last few weeks. She had made it a practice, over the years, to ask them, "What is your biggest regret in life?" and her blog was about the five most common regrets of the dying. What do you think is number one on that list?

Let me first tell you what it is not. It is not, like what most people imagine, "I wish I had worked less," or "I wish I had spent more time with family," or "I wish I had been more successful," or "I wish I could leave behind a better legacy."

Instead, it is "I wish I'd had the courage to live a life true to myself, not the life others expected of me."

It is as though you have been toiling, year upon year, to be an accomplished actor on the stage of life, under the watchful gaze of an audience whose validation you ardently seek—an audience that includes your parents, siblings, partner, children, friends, mentors, associates, superiors, the media, and the community. The curtain falls and you stride back onstage, hoping for a standing ovation, but as you take your final bow and the crowd fades away, you suddenly realize that there is only one person whose applause you have hungered for—yourself.

Alfred Nobel's path was the path of outer success, one that at the time of his passing would have made the world proclaim, "This was a life well lived!" But Bronnie Ware points us to the path of inner success, one that at the time of your passing would make *you* proclaim, "This was a life well lived!"

Consciously or unconsciously, we are all seeking both inner and outer success. When we experience an alignment between our outer ambitions and our inner self, we feel energized, committed, at peace, fulfilled, integrated, understood, and validated for who we are. Our inner and outer worlds are in harmony.

But finding that harmony requires work.

LIFE'S BIG BOUT: OUTER VERSUS INNER

Many of us struggle to balance the demands of the world with the desires of our own heart. We live with family members we feel emotionally distanced from; we feel disengaged from our job but fearful about trying out a new path; we feel the pressure to conform to others' expectations even though they do not make sense to us or seem downright wrong. The waters of life are often muddy, and our spirit strains to be in full bloom.

Some of us deal with these dilemmas by splitting life into two parallel tracks, seeking to live authentically in our personal sphere while chasing earthly glory on the outside. When we do this, we never fully occupy either space. That's how I was operating in my teens and twenties.

Others divide life into two phases. Phase one is the here-and-now pursuit of outer accomplishment in which we strive to earn a lot of money, achieve success at work, outshine our peers, and find security and validation. Phase two is the "sometime in the future" pursuit of inner success—becoming the people we want to be. I have witnessed this approach in some of my MBA students. In their quest for relevance and rewards, they see no option but to go after the most coveted and highly paid careers, even when they care little for the organization they will work for, the customer they will serve, or the product they will be making or marketing. They promise themselves that once their outer hungers have been fed, they will feed their inner yearnings and become their true selves.

But too often the compromises struck in phase one become a way of life, and the years speed by without the person ever finding time to explore and express those deeper yearnings. Before they know it, the end is in sight, a palliative care nurse like Bronnie is holding their hand, and they realize, through the nurse's questions, that they pawned their soul and never went back to reclaim it.

Some of you may be thinking, "That's not me! I am always true to myself. I do and say what I wish. I don't suppress my feelings. I won't sacrifice my authenticity at the altar of outer success." I applaud you if that's who you are. But the pursuit of inner success might come at its own cost: the price of diminished earthly rewards. In being unapologetically true to our self, we may end up hurting, disappointing, or antagonizing others, leading to strained relationships and lost opportunities. Doors may shut because people in our personal and professional circles feel that we are not attuned to their needs, not flexible or collaborative in our approach. And even if we attain power and influence, we may be feared, perhaps respected, but not admired or loved.

It may seem that inner and outer success are doomed to be in conflict, that we must choose between them. The more we focus on getting other people's approval and pursuing success based on their rules, the less we feel true to ourselves; the more we pursue our own agenda and freely express ourselves, the less open we are to striking compromises to gain other people's support, and the less worldly success we enjoy.

Investor Warren Buffett has put it this way: "The big question about how people behave is whether they've got an Inner Scorecard or an Outer Scorecard." Or, as he puts it, what if you had to choose between being the best investor in the world, even though the world thinks you are the worst, or being the worst investor in the world, even though the world thinks you are the best? Which would it be for you—inner or outer?

How distressing to have to strike such a Faustian bargain! Could we not have them both? Let's go back and look at Buffett for a moment. He has reflected, "[My dad] was a hundred percent Inner Scorecard guy. . . . He taught me how life should be lived," and "As you move along in your career, you always want to consider your Inner Scorecard—how you feel about your own performance and success. You should worry more about how well you perform rather than how well the rest of the world perceives your performance."

These are not mere words. By all accounts, Buffett has lived with an inner scorecard. After graduating from Columbia Business School, he made many contrarian moves that put him at odds with convention. He ran his investment business from Omaha, Nebraska, not Wall Street; he made an immense fortune but lives till this day not in a mansion but in the same home that he bought in 1958; he didn't succumb to the temptation to invest in internet and telecom stocks during the Web 1.0 stock market boom (and subsequent bust), even when critics like Harry Newton, publisher of *Technology Investor* magazine, in early 2000 were claiming, "Warren Buffett should say, 'I'm sorry.' How did he miss the silicon, wireless, DSL, cable, and biotech revolutions?"; he resisted the financial world's fascination with day trading and chose instead to focus on stocks that promise long-term value creation. And he has donated most of his money to social causes.

It has been through his commitment to inner success—to being true to himself and following his own inner code—that Warren Buffett has achieved extraordinary outer success. He is not just the most successful investor on the planet and one of its richest inhabitants; he is almost universally admired and loved, both by those in his inner circle and by the world at large. Go figure.

Inner and outer success do not have to compete with each other. My goal in this book is to help you pave a path in life so that, at curtain fall, your audience *and* you will jointly proclaim, "Bravo! This was a life well lived."

Chapter 2

THE PURSUIT OF SUCCESS

⤞

Break into the peace within
Hold attention in stillness
And in the world outside
You will ably master the ten thousand things.

—*Lao Tzu*

HOW GANDHI CAPTIVATED THE BRITISH

During a visit to Britain in 1931, Gandhi spoke eloquently before the House of Commons for two hours. Eknath Easwaran has described what happened next:

After he had finished, the London reporters clustered excitedly around Gandhi's secretary, Mahadev Desai. "How is it," they demanded, "that he is able to speak so well for such a long time without any preparation, without any prompting, without even any notes?"

Desai replied, "What Gandhi thinks, what he feels, what he says, and what he does are all the same. He does not need notes." Then he added smiling: "You and I, we think one thing, feel another, say a third, and do a fourth, so we need notes and files to keep track."

What a beautiful statement. What a resonant idea. What a perfect definition of inner success.

In what situations, in work and elsewhere, do you feel true to yourself, so that what you think, feel, say, and do are in perfect harmony? When do you *not* feel this way? What limits you in those situations?

It is tempting to believe that being true to yourself involves simply flipping an on/off switch. In fact, it is more of a journey. Here's why.

OUR AGE OF INDIVIDUALISM

In centuries past, we lived more for others than for ourselves. Potentates, priests, and patriarchs prescribed and proscribed our roles in society. What we did, what we ate, what we wore, how we danced, how we grieved, how we loved—every bead of our life's necklace was picked for us, not by us. Your path was not *your* path, but a well-paved and well-trodden road on which you were meant to march to an orderly beat based on your station in life. If you fell out of line, woe be to you! You were then a black sheep, a heathen, an outcast, a renegade, a rebel, a witch, a deranged mind, possibly possessed by the devil, and certainly headed for eternal damnation. You would thus deservedly be castigated, ostracized, exorcised, excommunicated, exiled, imprisoned, conquered, enslaved, or maybe even impaled.

Then came the Age of Enlightenment, bringing with it a new-found respect for individual freedom. The French Revolution paved the way for people to depose monarchies in favor of republics and democracies. A nation called the United States of America loftily proclaimed that it was every individual's birthright to enjoy "life, liberty and the pursuit of happiness," an ideal that it is still perfecting in practice. People in many regions of the world today are shedding the shackles of conformity, rebelling against social restrictions that limit their freedom of thought, speech, and action. The human spirit will no longer be enchained. Today, if there are two roads that diverge in the wood and you take the one less traveled, you are a hero, not a heathen.

But this freedom to be yourself has come at a grave cost. We are witnessing disturbing levels of stress, depression, loneliness, estrangement, chronic disease, suicide, conflict, and addiction in society today, even among those we might have considered the most free—the young, the high income, the educated, the famous, the tech visionaries. "The mass of men," Henry Thoreau observed, "lead lives of quiet desperation." Why is this age of free expression leading us not up a mountain of joy but down a valley of despair? It is as though, as Winston Churchill said, "The power of man has grown in every sphere except over himself."

THE WAR WITHIN

The root of this problem is the mistaken idea that you are being true to yourself when you give free expression to your thoughts, feelings, values, personality, and desires. By indulging whatever urge arises within us, we entangle ourselves in the web of instant gratification. We may feel authentic, validated, and free in the moment, but over time we grow increasingly trapped in our impulses, habits, and weaknesses, which keep us far from our full potential. Science has shown that our long-term outcomes—in terms of health, happiness, high performance, and harmony in relationships—become highly compromised when we habitually choose immediate over delayed gratification.

The figures from history who have inspired us understood that there were times when it was critical that they rein in their thoughts, feelings, and desires rather than allow them full expression. Take Abraham Lincoln. He was president of the United States when the nation went to war with itself. As commander in chief of the Union army, in the days before telecommunications, Lincoln stayed in constant contact with his generals through letters sent back and forth by messengers from the White House to the battlefront. He used the letters to counsel, coax, and, where needed, castigate the generals. In one such letter to General Hooker, Lincoln wrote, "During

Gen. Burnside's command of the Army, you . . . thwarted him as much as you could, in which you did a great wrong to the country. . . . I much fear that the spirit which you have aided to infuse into the Army, of criticizing their Commander, and withholding confidence from him, will now turn upon you." In a letter to General Meade he wrote, "I do not believe you appreciate the magnitude of the misfortune involved in Lee's escape. He was within your easy grasp, and to have closed upon him would, in connection with our other late successes, have ended the war. As it is, the war will be prolonged indefinitely. . . . Your golden opportunity is gone, and I am distressed immeasurably because of it."

Historians have discovered myriad such letters in which Lincoln criticized his generals for their conduct of the war. But, remarkably, many of these letters were unsigned and unsent. Discovered in Lincoln's presidential desk in the White House after his passing, they are aptly called Lincoln's hot letters. (The one to General Hooker was signed and dispatched to its recipient, while the one to General Meade was unsigned and unsent.)

Why did Lincoln write hot letters that were never sent to the intended audience? Perhaps he recognized as he was writing that he was in the grip of anger and it would be better to sleep on things, to look the missive over in the morning when he was calmer and better able to operate with wisdom. Perhaps he realized that by expressing himself so freely he might demoralize the recipient or alienate them at a time when he desperately needed their commitment and their loyalty.

By not sending those letters, was Lincoln being false to himself? Or was he in fact being *more* true by reining in thoughts and feelings that might have been counterproductive to his goals? Are there times in your life when you have felt, thought, said, or done something in the heat of the moment that you later regretted? When you might in fact have been more true to your values and purpose if you had restrained yourself from expressing those sentiments?

In posing these questions it seems that I am dismantling the Gandhian view that we're true to ourselves when our thoughts and feelings are aligned with our actions. I assure you that the Gandhian view will be redeemed as we proceed. But let's acknowledge that before you and I can aspire to be true to our self, we need to first establish what our "self" really is. When you say, "I want to be true to myself," which "self" are you referring to? For I will confess that I have many selves.

A part of me wants to please others; another part wants to please myself. I call these my please-others self and my please-me self. Then there is my indulgent self, my disciplined self, my habitual self, my aspirational self. And I've only just begun. These different selves all clamor for my attention, every moment of every day. Should I express the frustration or anger I feel toward someone, or should I bite my tongue because I know that venting what I am feeling may backfire? Should I linger indulgently in bed, or whip myself into disciplined action? Should I procrastinate on a task I find tedious, or stick with it to serve my team?

I invite you to pause for a minute and take an honest look inside yourself. Do you not at times feel like there's a war going on within, that you are listening to a cacophony of conflicting entreaties from your many selves? How can you be true to your "self" when you have multiple parts within you jostling for influence?

The path to inner success lies in discovering your true self and manifesting it in your every thought, feeling, word, and action. This requires you to become an inner warrior, to vanquish the many false selves that are holding your true self hostage. When you allow one of your false selves to seduce you, it may not bother you in the moment—in fact, it might actually feel good to gratify an impulsive desire, feeling, or thought—but one day you will wake up to regret that you did not live a life true to the truest part of you.

What is your true self? I offer that it is your Inner Core—the space of highest potential within you, your best self. When you operate from your Core, you are free from ego, attachments, blinding beliefs, limiting habits, and insecurities. You are at peace with yourself. It reflects the purest part of who you are and your noblest intentions. If you're like most of us, you sometimes operate from your Core, sometimes drift away from it, and sometimes (sigh) veer far, far away. And yet that part of who you are is always there for you to come back to and connect more deeply with.

You may have heard or used phrases like "I like Peter's energy" or "That individual just didn't bring the right energy to the meeting." Everything we do—our thoughts, emotions, speech, and behavior—is fueled by our energy. My research has revealed that all of us possess, in that space of highest potential within, five Core Energies. We experience a powerful shift when we start to activate and express these energies in everything we do.

YOUR FIVE CORE ENERGIES*

Purpose: Pursue a purpose-driven path in life, paved with values, with goals as your milestones.

Wisdom: Uncover and embrace the truth in all matters, and direct your emotions and thoughts in the service of your Purpose.

Growth: Each day, grow your inward connection with your Core and your outward expression of it in all you do.

Love: Take joy in others' joy, and find success in their success.

Self-Realization: Be centered in your tranquil and joyful spirit within.

We discuss these five energies—how you can activate them to arrive at your Core—in Part Two of the book.

NO FORMULA FOR OUTER SUCCESS

But what about outer success?

---

* Purpose, Wisdom, Love, and Self-Realization align well with the popular view that our whole self consists of body, mind, heart, and spirit. These four energies also align well with yoga's four main paths—karma yoga, gyana yoga, bhakti yoga, and raja yoga. Growth enables us to cultivate the other four energies.

Here is a sobering realization: there is no teacher, no teaching, no path that can guarantee outer success. After all, can anyone guarantee that I will never sustain a debilitating injury? That a recession, war, or pandemic will not upend my career ambitions? That all through my life I will enjoy the company of loving family and friends? That the whimsical winds of public opinion will never blow against me? So much of what shapes outer success is about timing, events, people, and other forces beyond our direct control. But while no one can guarantee outer success, we can create the conditions that maximize the likelihood of our attaining it. And we do that when we embrace the call of leadership.

"Leadership?" you may wonder. "What does that have to do with me?"

LEADERSHIP ISN'T
AN OUTER DISPENSATION

This is how the game is played. First, you must go through the grind, for it is a rite of passage. Then you climb the ladder and acquire power and authority, step by step. A bigger team, a greater budget, a loftier title. Don't be shattered if you still don't make it, since there is only room for a few at the top. But if you master the rules of the game and play it well, and if the roll of the dice favors you, one day you will be invited into the inner circle, perhaps even given the keys to the corner office. It is then that you may rejoice as you finally cast away your role as a follower. You are now a leader. The world has validated what you suspected all along—that you are special.

I understood leadership this way when my peers and I graduated from MIT's Sloan School of Management to launch our careers. I know better now. I know now that it is not power and authority that make you a leader; it is leadership, when practiced the right way, that makes power and authority flow to you. That's what we learn from Babette's story.

Babette, an organic chemist, was doing drug research at a lab. Her boss was a well-regarded scientist but also a very temperamental man. After taking some coaching from a renowned psychotherapist,

Dr. David Burns, on how to engage better with her boss, Babette one day walked into his office to find out what he thought of a research paper they were coauthoring. He told her that he had thrown it in the wastebasket because it was the "worst piece of rubbish" he'd ever seen. The paper represented months of arduous research. Babette replied,

> Gordon, I'm not a bit surprised that you thought the paper was rubbish. To be honest, I had the exact same feeling when I was writing it. I felt like I was rambling on and on. I'm always amazed when I read your papers because they're so incredibly clear and lucid. That's actually one of the reasons I wanted to work with you and why I was so excited when you offered me a position last fall. The results of our research could be extremely important, and I know that if the paper were well written, it might make a tremendous impact. The paper may be beyond repair, but I'm wondering if you might have any suggestions about how I could make it better. I want to learn as much from you as I possibly can.

Gordon's mood seemed to instantly improve, and he pulled the paper from the wastebasket. As he looked it over, he pointed out problems that needed to be addressed and offered ideas about other fixes Babette could make. Subsequently she not only was able to publish the paper in a top journal in her field, but also received a major award for their research.

In this situation, who was leading, and who was following?

Leadership isn't an outer dispensation—it is an inner choice. We lead by seeking to have the maximum positive impact within our sphere of influence. The traditional view encourages you to advance your career so you can maximize your moments of leadership. The view I am proposing encourages you to advance your *character* so you can maximize the leadership in your moments.

My student Stacey shared the following story with our MBA class.

When I was thirteen, I had a health problem and had to be taken to the hospital. It was determined that I needed surgery, which was scheduled for the week after. I was to stay in the hospital during this time so they could monitor my condition. But on the second day, the physician knocked on the door of my room and asked to speak with my father. They both left the room to have a conversation.

What ensued between them was not made known to me at that time, but my father shared it many years later with me. The physician told my father that he had two pieces of bad news. One, they would need to perform the surgery that very evening—he had determined it would not be safe to wait a week. And two, because of a medical issue I had, they would not be able to give me anesthesia, so the surgery would need to be performed without it.

I did not know about this conversation, because it happened outside the room. What I did experience was what happened next. My father returned to my room, beaming with a smile. "My dear Stacey, you know that surgery they were to do on you? Well, I have two pieces of good news for you. The first is that the doctor says you can actually have that surgery *today*—he does not need to wait a week. So you'll recover over the next three days and then will be back at home instead of waiting another week. And the second good news is that they have been observing you at this hospital, and you are the bravest teenager they have seen! They don't even believe you need any anesthesia when he performs the surgery. It may hurt a little here and there, but you'll get through it fine, because you're so brave. I am so proud of you."

I do not know how I went through the surgery that day, but my father's words and beaming smile had a lot to do with it. There was pain, but I wasn't going to let it matter because I was after all the bravest teenager in that hospital's history. Only years later did I learn what the doctor had actually told my father.

In striving to stay calm when the doctor broke the news to him, in transcending his own fear and pain about what his daughter was going to have to go through, in finding a way to spark courage in his daughter, was Stacey's father merely living—or leading? And in opening up to her father's invitation to go on a hero's journey rather than dismissing his message, in taking on the challenge of proving that she was in fact possessed of remarkable mettle, was Stacey merely living or was she leading?

What if we approach all life moments as leadership moments?

WHEN OTHERS DON'T DO THEIR PART

Now, you might say, "That's cool. But it takes two to tango. In Stacey's story, her father did the right thing, and she did the right thing. It doesn't always work that way. There are times when I am doing my part, but the other party isn't doing theirs. How can I lead when the other party isn't doing what they should?"

I understand. I went through an experience like that as a first-year associate at McKinsey. I was staffed on a consulting engagement for a biotech client. My team included our manager, Sheila, another associate, Jeremy, and a business analyst, Martin.* Within one week, it was clear to me that as a manager, Sheila was a disaster. She never smiled, she kept to herself, and she acknowledged our presence only when she needed to give instructions or review our work. She did not invite us into important meetings, nor did she update us on key developments on the project. I vividly remember an occasion when I finally got a chance to present my work to a senior McKinsey director who was spending a rare, prized half hour with us. This was going to be my moment. Our audience with him was all I thought of for forty-eight hours. As I launched into my presentation, Sheila stared at me unblinkingly, pursed her lips, and made a rapid circling gesture with her forefinger. My very soul was pierced by her searing message: "Speed up, Hitendra! This is a senior director you are speaking to.

---

* The names have been changed to protect the innocent—and the guilty.

He has no time to waste. Do you really need to explain that pie chart to him in this much detail? He can read and think *very* fast. C'mon, be quick!" My moment of glory was over in a flash.

Jeremy and I bided our time on that project grudgingly, envious of the many fellow associates who had, by sheer luck, been assigned to more caring managers. The project finally wrapped up and we were able to move on to a less tortured future.

But something else was going on there. Martin, the business analyst on our team, acted quite differently than Jeremy and me. He walked into the team room each day and instantly lifted our spirits with his broad smile and infectious humor. He would approach Sheila, speak to her in a soothing voice, perk her up by finding something to appreciate about her, then nudge her toward the behavior he was seeking. *Could Sheila make sure to include him in the client meeting where his research was going to be reviewed? Wouldn't it be great if Sheila updated the team on Wednesday as soon as she learned about a certain decision on the project? Why not hold a celebratory team dinner next week now that we have reached a major milestone?*

While Jeremy and I stewed over all the imperfections we saw in Sheila's management style and wondered why we deserved this, Martin took active steps to make the most of a bad situation. Martin didn't have better behaviors than me or Jeremy—he had better beliefs. I discovered that over dinner one day with him, when we both dropped our guards a bit and had a heart-to-heart chat.

"Martin," I said, "Sheila is a terrible manager. C'mon, you know it."

"I know what you are saying, Hitendra. Like you, I wish things were different."

"Then what gets you to accept her callous attitude toward us? You are so nice to her all the time!"

"Well, here's how I see it. I only intend to be at McKinsey for two years before I go for my MBA. I don't want the ten weeks on this project to be a waste. I want to make the most of it. So I look for ways to get what I think we all need from her."

"And you do that so well, Martin. Were you just born with this gift?"

He became quiet. I could see I had stirred him at a deep level.

"Hitendra, growing up as an African American, I learned early that some people won't have the right attitude toward you. If you wait for those people to change, you might end up waiting forever. So I started to take a keen interest in people, in what makes them tick, in how they perceive and react to me, and in what I can do to get a desired result from them. That's helped me in life to get the most out of others, and that's all I've been doing here. You could, too, if you wanted to. It works."

During those ten weeks, Martin had taken full responsibility for producing the outcome he wanted by creatively working to get the best out of Sheila. In contrast, I had been sulking, waiting for the project to end because I felt I was entitled to a good manager. Jeremy and I thought we were the wise ones, Jeremy with his MD and me with my PhD, but it was this freshly minted college grad who demonstrated over that short period the secret to success in an imperfect world. You can wait until people reform themselves, if they do, or you can take personal responsibility to do your best to bring out the best in them.

Over time, I came to realize that Sheila's heart had been in the right place. She genuinely wanted to help me and the team, but her deeply reclusive nature got in the way. She conducted a performance review for me at the end of the project, and there I saw how caring, insightful, and fair she was at her Core. Now and then, when I find myself overcommunicating in sharing my ideas with someone, Sheila's finger-twirl plays like a TikTok video in my head and alerts me to be more mindful of my audience's time. I am grateful for this part of her that has become a part of me.

When we define leadership as *the discipline of bringing out the best in ourselves and the best in others in all situations, in the pursuit of a common positive purpose*, then all life's moments become leadership moments. Because why wouldn't we always want to bring out our best—and why wouldn't we want to bring out the best in others too? If we approach life this way, then we have created the conditions for outer success. This is the best we can do. The rest is chance, or fate. It's mathematical.

MY TODDLER TEACHER

One day in 2003, my one-year-old daughter, Mrinalini, while sitting on my lap, casually dropped a glass she was holding. Orange juice splashed all over our rug like a Jackson Pollock painting. "Oh no! Why on Earth would you do that?" I exclaimed in a tone of dismay and frustration. I recovered my composure a few seconds later— after all, she was just a toddler. But it was too late. Mrinalini had burst into tears, deeply shaken by the fierce look she saw on my face in those fateful few seconds.

"Why would she break down like this just because of a momentary lapse from me?" I wondered. Then the realization came. At her tender age, she viewed me not simply as her father; I was her *world*. When I lost my cool, history may record it as a transient meltdown of a flawed but caring father, but to her, the entire world had come crashing down, and she didn't have any clue how long it would last or whether I'd ever recover.

I was deeply touched, embarrassed, regretful. I worked hard to step up my game in the days that followed, striving to stay unshakably serene in her presence. Life was teaching me that if I wanted my daughter to thrive in a safe, secure, and supportive world, I had to start by *being* that safe, secure, and supportive world for her.

I realized that this same dynamic is present in other relationships as well. If you are a professor who has a strong rapport with your students, they will look up to you, and your every microexpression will have an amplified effect. As an executive, your subordinates will be similarly sensitive to your every behavior. So I have learned that I must be very mindful of my emotions and the way they get unintentionally expressed in fleeting moments, especially in situations where I hold some form of power or influence over others. By striving to become a better parent, I have gained wisdom that can make me a better professor and a better executive. (I'm still working on it.)

Life lessons are leadership lessons. When you grow as a human being, you grow as a leader.

PUBLIC MOMENTS, PRIVATE MOMENTS

As Lisa, an executive, stood in the ordering queue at a Starbucks next to her office, she noticed that the woman in front of her was carrying an attractive designer handbag. She exclaimed appreciatively, "What a beautiful bag—is this part of the new Louis Vuitton line?" The woman turned her head to shoot a dismissive look toward Lisa, as though saying, "Don't bother me!" Without a word, she resumed facing forward. Lisa felt miffed, but she shrugged it off, and a few minutes later, latte in hand, returned to her office.

Soon there was a knock on her door. It was her next appointment—a candidate she was interviewing for an open position in her group. She looked up from her desk to see a startled face. The candidate at the door was none other than the woman with the Louis Vuitton handbag. Just imagine how this woman may have felt about her earlier conduct as she stood now face-to-face with Lisa. Perhaps at Starbucks she had been feeling stressed about something, or mentally rehearsing her lines for the interview. Who can say? Regardless of her mitigating circumstances, as she entered Lisa's office she must have deeply regretted not being at her best when Lisa had inquired about her bag.

Leadership isn't a formal suit you put on to go out and perform in the spotlight. It is a fundamental value that guides you to approach every role, public and private, personal and professional, with the intent of operating from your Core, your true self, and seeking to have the greatest impact. If life moments are leadership moments, and life lessons are leadership lessons, and life roles are leadership roles, then, I offer, life *is* leadership.

WHAT IS OUR "BEST"?

How can you bring out your best? What is your "best"? One way to approach the question is by compiling a list of qualities that you should master—qualities that experts will tell you are critical to success in life and work, qualities that successful people exhibit. Here are some that are often cited:

- Be **adaptive**! The world is changing fast, and you must change with it. And be **tenacious** too! Have the grit to keep fighting the good fight.

- Be an **extrovert**! When you project warmth and energy and enthusiasm, you draw people toward you. And be an **introvert** as well! Listen mindfully, empathize with others, and understand them.

- Be a **risk taker**! Innovate, embrace failure, step out of your comfort zone. Don't stay stuck in the same groove. And be a **risk manager** too! Do not bet the farm. Anticipate problems and be prepared for them.

- Be a **visionary**! Take giant leaps and have your head in the skies. And be **pragmatic** too! Keep your feet planted firmly on the ground.

- Be **decisive**! Don't let hesitancy or paralysis prevent you from taking timely action. And be **patient** as well! You can't pluck the fruit without first sowing the seeds and watering the plant.

- Be **connected**! Gather ideas from others. Build your network. Don't each lunch alone. And **disconnect** too! Practice solitude and reflection—that's what the great ones do.

- Be **agreeable**! Listen to others and find common ground with them. Be **assertive**, too! Have the courage to express uncomfortable truths and stand your ground.

This isn't even a complete list, for we could keep going on and on. To put it simply, to succeed in our fast-paced, ever-changing, uncertain, and complicated world, you need to be *everything—and the complete opposite.* The right behavior totally depends on the situation you are in.

The idea of being everything and the complete opposite may sound inauthentic and unachievable. And yet I have found that those who have left a luminous mark on history have practiced this seeming contradiction, changing their behavior from moment to moment, embracing complexity and paradox, holding opposites in balance within themselves. Josiah Holland, one of Abraham Lincoln's earliest biographers, wrote, "The writer has conversed with multitudes of men who claimed to know Mr. Lincoln intimately; yet there are not two of the whole number who agree in their estimate of him. The fact was that he rarely showed more than one aspect of himself to one man. He opened himself to men in different directions." Holland goes on to recount the different qualities people attributed to Lincoln: "A very ambitious man." "Without a particle of ambition." "One of the saddest men that ever lived." "One of the jolliest men that has ever lived." "The most cunning man in America." "Has not a particle of cunning in him." "A leader of the people." "Always led by the people." "Cool and impassive." "Susceptible to the strongest passions."

Everything—and the complete opposite. When we pause to think about it, the concept starts to make sense. Lincoln was president at a time when his nation was in crisis. He needed to display an acute understanding of the different high-stakes situations he was thrust into and adapt his behavior accordingly, without letting his personality or predilections limit his effectiveness.

But something else was also operating in Lincoln. His friend and law partner for twenty years, William Herndon, observed, "His pursuit of the truth . . . was indefatigable. . . . Lincoln loved truth for its own sake. . . . He saw all things through a perfect mental lens." Lincoln operated from a steady Core within. He leaned into outer chaos from a place of inner harmony. And that is the thesis I want to offer you—that when you have mastered your inner game, you become free to play your best outer game. The key to success lies within—in operating from your Inner Core.

Your Inner Core brings the clarity of mind you need to analyze issues objectively and make enlightened choices. It frees you from habitual modes of thought and from confining personality traits and attachments, so your choices can be guided not by ego or insecurity but by your commitment to your purpose and values. It creates a space between the triggers you experience—the disappointing email, the challenging question from a colleague at a meeting—and your response to those triggers, empowering you to act with intention rather than instinct. It grounds you on the inside and then empowers you to act in the most impactful way on the outside. You bring out your best when your behavior is the outer expression of your Core Energies: Purpose, Wisdom, Growth, Love, and Self-Realization.

And if this is true of you, it is true of everyone. To get the best out of others, you need to help them activate their Core. When you are operating from your Core and they from theirs, together you form a Common Core. In that moment everyone experiences a deep resonance, not just in what they are saying or doing but in what they are feeling, thinking, and valuing on the inside. Reflect on moments like this—when you and another individual, you and your family, you and your team, you and an audience felt a kind of fusion of spirit, as though there were only one heart beating in the room. Such occasions may be rare, but they are real. And magical.

Usually, when we strive to do well at something, we assess ourselves by asking, "Am I saying the right thing, doing the right thing?" Our speech and action are the outer metrics we use to measure our performance. But there are inner metrics we can use as well.

INNER PERFORMANCE METRICS

Am I operating from my Inner Core? Am I . . .

Committed to my Purpose? (Purpose)

Calm and receptive to the truth? (Wisdom)

Curious and open to learnings that help me further activate and express my Core in all I do? (Growth)

Connected with all who cross my path, and all I serve? (Love)

Centered in my tranquil and joyful spirit within? (Self-Realization)

And am I doing my best to help others operate from their Inner Core as well, by assisting them in being committed, calm, curious, connected, and centered?

Getting to this level of mastery may seem intimidating. But there's much to be optimistic about. When we sift through findings across a range of scientific fields—positive psychology, the psychology of ultimate concerns, emotional intelligence, cognitive behavioral therapy, acceptance and commitment therapy, altruism, neuroplasticity, gratitude, influence, motivation, self-esteem, self-efficacy, mindfulness, empathy, growth mindset, and more—the conclusion is clear: within each of us lies vast, untapped potential to rewire our brains over time, to become more and more anchored in our authentic self, and to help others get there too.

Instead of pursuing myriad paths to learn how to be "everything and the complete opposite," I invite you to translate your quest for success into one simple goal: to learn to operate from your Inner Core in all you do.

HOW CAN WE EXCEL AT LEADERSHIP?

For many years, I puzzled over how the people I've researched—Gandhi, Eleanor Roosevelt, Steve Jobs, Lincoln, Mother Teresa, and others—became good at leadership. After all, they held remarkable sway over people. Well, first, let me tell you how they *didn't* get there.

Lincoln had only one year of schooling. Eleanor Roosevelt's education didn't advance beyond high school. Mother Teresa joined a nun order at the age of eighteen. Jobs dropped out of college. Mandela and Gandhi obtained law degrees, but both were, of their own confession, indifferent students. Quite evidently, these people didn't take any leadership classes or executive workshops. And perhaps that isn't a bad thing, for the reason I now explain.

Experts have organized the discipline of leadership into competencies, and then developed classes to teach each competency to aspiring leaders. *How to have difficult conversations. Build trust. Give feedback. Coach others. Inspire others. Change others' behavior.* And more.

But this approach to teaching leadership frequently leads to the "learning-doing" gap. Participants attend a class, get some training on a competency, but then aren't able to effectively translate their intellectual understanding into an embodied practice in real life. Experts have believed that to close this gap they need to develop better training or get learners to be more motivated. But my research shows that this approach has some fundamental limits, and is in need of a major upgrade. Here's why.

In the conversation that Babette, the chemist, had with Gordon, her boss, she gently turned his mood around and won him over to helping her improve the research paper so they could send it out for publication. Take a moment to go back and reread what she said, to refresh your memory. Then tell me this: In that dialog, was she having a difficult conversation with him? Building trust with him? Giving him feedback? Coaching him? Inspiring him? Influencing him? Changing his behavior?

Wasn't she doing all the above? And that, too, in a mere thirty-five seconds!

So then does it make sense to see these as separate competencies? If Babette had taken a separate class on each of these skills, read a different book, or consulted a different expert, well, then, which toolkit or book or expert would she have pulled out to guide her conversation with Gordon? If you approached your growth as a leader one competency at a time, you're unlikely to get to a place where you fully embody the discipline. And even if you acquired mastery over multiple skills, you'd never be able to execute seven of them in a half-minute exchange the way Babette did. This competency-based approach was a practical first step to take in the twentieth century as we started to understand and map out the domain of leadership, but now we know a lot more about the science of human nature. So it is time to give this approach a graceful burial.

Lincoln once said, "That some achieve great success is proof to all that others can achieve it as well." The fact that some people with limited formal education have been able to figure out the equations of leadership on their own means that a radically simple and intuitive approach to leadership must exist—we just need to find it. Let me show you where I believe it's been hiding.

THE MISSING CORE

When we find that we're not good at handling difficult conversations, or influencing others, or inspiring a team, perhaps these aren't as distinctive a set of challenges as they appear but are symptoms arising from the same root cause. *The root cause is an inability to activate the Core in yourself or others.* Our research at Mentora reveals that this is what great leaders are adept at: forming a deep, resonant bond with people by activating one or more of the five Core Energies in themselves and others in all situations. You can do so as well.

The first step is to activate one or more of the Core Energies in your own self. The more you operate from your Core, the more freedom you will have to choose how you show up in every situation. Instead of being locked in by your impulses, habits, emotions, distorted thoughts, limiting beliefs, personality, or ego, you will be committed, calm, curious, connected, and centered.

Core Energies are infectious, so when you activate them in yourself, others around you will get stirred as well. That is why when people were in Gandhi's presence, they felt very calm. In Mother Teresa's presence, very compassionate. In Steve Jobs's presence, very creative. In Churchill's presence, very courageous. In Mandela's presence, very conciliatory. Inner mastery engenders outer impact.

Once you're anchored in your Core, you can then focus on helping others anchor in theirs. But there's something even more foundational you need to do first, and it relates to the greatest leadership lesson I've learned from Steve Jobs.

Steve entered a world where high-tech products abounded with features but had poor design and usability. Think of a personal computer with a thick user manual, or a mobile phone with thirty buttons. Businesses at that time believed that technology couldn't be made easy to use or elegant in design, and that consumers only cared about features and low price. Steve took a contrarian position, obsessing over the simplicity and design of Apple products and then offering them at premium prices. His vision showed early promise, but then came crashing down when Apple floundered. In 1994, while he was out of Apple, he was asked in an interview with *Rolling Stone* magazine if he still believed in the limitless potential of technology. Jobs answered, "Oh sure. It's not a faith in technology. It's a faith in people . . . that they're basically good and smart, and if you give them tools, they'll do wonderful things with them." Jobs said he believed that people "care about things that are beautifully conceived and well made."

Jonathan Ive, Apple's chief designer, later reflected on a conversation he had with Jobs close to the end of Jobs's life—about whether they had been successful. "I think Steve felt a vindication. . . . It wasn't a vindication of 'I'm right' or 'I told you so.' It was a vindication that restored his sense of faith in humanity. Given the choice, people do discern and value quality more than we give them credit for." In another reflection, Ive has shared how he believes consumers "will sense the care that went into [making beautiful products]. . . . I do believe [people] are capable of discerning far more than [they] are capable of articulating."

Steve Jobs was able to peer into a certain nook within our souls. There, he saw an appreciation for simplicity, perfection, beauty, and creativity. Many of us may not have been aware that these qualities existed within us, which is why he wasn't interested in using market research to ask people what they wanted. But unlike most business owners of that era, he had faith that when the time came, people would intuitively gravitate toward products that express these attributes. His faith in us has today transformed the world, much beyond Apple, as businesses embrace design thinking—a commitment to going beyond features and price to designing products in the most appealing and intuitive way.

The most critical work we can do after anchoring ourselves in our Core is to, quietly in our heart, recognize the Core in everyone. Even if they don't yet see it in themselves, or if they have drifted far away from it, *we* see it in them, and *we* strive to draw it out of them. Because, like Steve Jobs, we have an unquestioned faith in the ennobling qualities present in every individual's deepest self.

Once we start to recognize the true self in others, we need to find a way to activate it in them. Over the last ten years, Mentora's research team and I have analyzed more than a thousand conversations, speeches, meetings, and other interactions that inspiring leaders have had with their colleagues, audiences, opponents, partners, friends, family, and more. We've discovered something remarkable: rather than using elaborate frameworks, toolkits, or checklists, these leaders use simple actions to activate the five Core Energies in others.

In Babette's brief response to Gordon, for example, she used five actions:

1. **Disarm (to express Wisdom):** She started by agreeing with Gordon on something. She did not agree with him that the paper was useless—only that the writing was not at his level. Finding something to agree with disarms an individual.

2. **Appreciate (to express Love):** She shared her admiration for Gordon's writing. This helped her foster a warm, positive emotional energy between them.

3. **Fuse opposites (to express Wisdom):** Even while accepting that the *writing* was subpar, she got Gordon to recognize that the *research* they had done was excellent.

4. **Appeal to values (to express Purpose):** She highlighted how the paper would have a great impact on the scientific community if it were well written—something she knew he would value.

5. **Create a growth partnership (to express Growth):** She asked Gordon to guide her on how she could improve her writing.

These are *simple* actions. After all, it took Babette an average of seven seconds to execute each of them (thirty-five seconds, five actions). Perhaps that is why inspiring leaders have never needed formal leadership training. Warren Buffett once shared, "You don't need to have extraordinary effort to achieve extraordinary results. You just need to do the ordinary, everyday things exceptionally well." Although these actions are "ordinary," to have the right impact they need to be done "exceptionally well." For instance, take Babette's second action, appreciate. Imagine if while she was appreciating Gordon's writing abilities on the outside, she was feeling and thinking something quite different on the inside, like, "He's so pompous about his writing!" Or "Why does he care so much about the writing? This isn't a college textbook. It's a research report!" Or "What a grouchy man! We've gotten such great results over this last year, and all he cares about is the grammar!"

If that were the case, then it's quite possible that Gordon would have sensed from her tone of voice and facial expressions that her appreciation was not genuine. Even if she'd fooled Gordon into believing that she meant it, if a disconnect between what she was saying on the outside and what she was thinking and feeling on the inside became a regular thing for her, she would over time have started to feel increasingly disconnected and unfulfilled at work. So, to appreciate Gordon, Babette first had to look inside herself to find something she genuinely admired him for. Only then did she earn the right to appreciate him on the outside.

In this way, your every action starts by first being an *inner* action. You have to activate the right energy on the inside by moving your feelings, thoughts, and intention to the right place, anchored in your Core. Once you've achieved this, you can more naturally express the same energy on the outside, as an *outer* action, to help move the other party's feelings, thoughts, and behavior to the right place. Leadership thus becomes a series of inner and outer actions to bring out the best in ourselves and others. In the past, leadership training has essentially ignored the inner action that has to precede the outer.

In putting your five Core Energies into action, do not lean on any expert to give you a fixed, definitive guide to which actions to use and in what sequence. You will want to choose for yourself which energies to express when, and which actions to use to express those energies, because there are factors in the unique conditions you face that no expert would have knowledge of: your goals in a given situation, your past history with the other party, the level of urgency you face, the mood in the room, your personal style, who else is listening to the exchange, what the other person responds well to, and so on. The wisdom we need to become great at bringing out the best in ourselves and others resides within each of us, and it can be accessed through the four steps outlined in the box titled "Leading from Your Core."

LEADING FROM YOUR CORE

1. Choose the Core Energy you want to activate in yourself and others. Pick a suitable action to express the energy. An action isn't an elaborate behavior; it's often something you can execute in a few seconds.

2. Execute the action from the very essence of your being. Make sure that what you think, feel, and intend on the inside are harmonized with what you say and do on the outside.

3. Stay keenly attuned with what is unfolding around you and within you. Choose your next action based on your intention and on how you see people acting and reacting.

4. Experiment and learn your way into which actions to use and how to execute them, paying attention to the effect they have in different situations. Add new actions to your repertoire over time.

The more you strive to operate from your Core in this way, the more authentic you will feel on the inside, and the more agile you will be on the outside.

SMALL STEPS, BIG LEAPS

In Mentora Institute's leadership development programs, we typically train clients in twenty-five actions (four to six actions per Core Energy). How effective could you be if you learned to activate the Core Energies in yourself and others through a set of actions like this? Turns out, a *lot*. Here's the math.

Let's define a "behavior" to be an action path consisting of five actions.

Behavior = Action 1 → Action 2 → Action 3 → Action 4 → Action 5.

For example, in her dialog with Gordon, Babette engaged in the following action path:

Babette's behavior = Disarm → Appreciate → Fuse opposites → Appeal to values → Establish a growth partnership.

If you learn ten actions like these, how many different behaviors (action paths) could you execute? The answer is sixty-five thousand. Fifteen actions would yield more than half a million behaviors. And twenty-five actions would yield more than eight million!* Five Core Energies and twenty-five actions is all it takes, in effect, to be nearly "everything and the complete opposite."

A biochemistry textbook tells us, "The stunning variety of living systems belies a striking similarity. The common use of DNA and the genetic code by all organisms underlies one of the most powerful discoveries of the past century—namely, that organisms are remarkably uniform at the molecular level." We encounter this idea everywhere: incredible diversity on the outside, remarkable uniformity on the inside. Countless liquids, solids, and gases, built from only 118 or so elements. A vast array of books and words, using the same twenty-six letters of the alphabet. Millions of melodies, played from just twelve notes in the Western musical scale. And now, a wide range of behaviors, built from a few actions. Mastering leadership is simple when you focus on learning one action at a time. And yet with every such small step, you are taking a big leap in expanding the set of behaviors (action paths) you can select from.

This approach to leadership does impose one demand on us: the need to be humble. To recognize that regardless of what heights we have scaled in life, the next step in our advancement may lie in learning, practicing, and applying a few simple actions that we

---

* Here's the math. The first action can be any of the twenty-five, the second any of the remaining twenty-four, and so on, leading to the number 25×24^4, which is > 8 million. In this model, an action can be used multiple times in an action path, but not successively.

don't presently possess in our leadership repertoire. Perhaps you are an executive. Would you have the humility to take the small step of learning to **affiliate** more meaningfully with your people—even through the simple act of injecting a warm smile into every interaction? Perhaps you are a parent. Would you have the humility to take the small step of learning to **understand** your child's unspoken thoughts and feelings before you act? Perhaps you are an irate customer. Would you have the humility to take the small step of learning to **practice unconditional respect** even as you are fiercely disagreeing with the customer service representative?

THE ESSENCE OF MAN

Winston Churchill always sought to be in the middle of the action. He was keen to participate in every battle Britain fought in his lifetime, if not as part of the military, then as a journalist covering the action or as a leader commanding the course of the war. At the age of twenty-one, he traveled to Cuba to observe its war of independence, and then he joined with Spanish troops to suppress independence fighters. Two years later, he was at it again, participating in battles in northwest India. He used his contacts with the British prime minister to get assigned to a war in Egypt and then in Sudan. He once gave skin from his arm for a graft for an injured officer—talk about having skin in the game. Later he participated in the Boer Wars in South Africa, where he was caught by the enemies and became a prisoner of war, only to plot and execute his own escape. During World War I, he was a cabinet minister in charge of the British navy. He resigned this position after a disastrous battle in Gallipoli, Turkey. So what did he do next? Join the army as a major and proceed to the battlefront.

Now imagine Churchill, a man of action, doing his final act. It is the year 1955. With age catching up to him, he has announced his resignation as prime minister and has been asked to deliver some parting words of guidance to his colleagues in Parliament. This is his opportunity to impart whatever wisdom he has learned over his long lifetime. What would you say if you were Churchill?

With the carriage waiting outside to whisk him away from the theater of public life where he had played a front-stage role for over half a century, Churchill's message was this: "Man is spirit."

This is a remarkable statement. Notice the word "spirit." Spirit is what lies beyond our senses, thoughts, and feelings. Spirit is pure. Spirit is tranquil. Spirit is in harmony with the truth. And Churchill is telling his colleagues that this is the essence of humanity—your true self, or what I am calling your Inner Core.

Now notice the word "man." Churchill is not focusing on himself, or his colleagues, or the British people, or their allies. He has chosen a word that embraces all humanity in its sweep (for in his time, the word "man" was commonly used to denote humankind). By telling his colleagues that they are spirit, he is urging them to seek out their essence. By instructing them that *all* people are spirit, he is encouraging them to see the essence in everyone.

Finally, notice the word "is." Churchill is not saying "You will become," or "You can become." You are already spirit.

Chapter 3

WAYS OF KNOWING

⚘

Truth resides in every human heart, and one has to
search for it there, and to be guided by truth as one
sees it.

—*Mahatma Gandhi*

THE LAWS THAT BIND US

St. Augustine wrote, "People travel to wonder at the height of
mountains, at the huge waves of the sea, at the long courses of
rivers, at the vast compass of the ocean, at the circular motion of the
stars; and they pass by themselves without wondering." Pause for a
moment to wonder about your own self. What exactly is your true
nature, your Inner Core? And how can you access it?

You might say, "Here is how I define my Inner Core. And here
is how I connect with it." And then I might ask you, "But what if
there's more to your Core than you believe, or a more effective way
to get there?" Then you might say, "Hitendra, this is *my* Core, and *my*
way to get there. I am free to do it my way, and you are free to do it
your way." But the fact is, we are not free. There are right and wrong
answers to these questions, and we will only succeed if we figure out
and abide by the right answers. Here's why.

Scientists have sought to decipher the mysteries of the physical world by formulating laws that govern its behavior. These laws are timeless and universal. They distill nature to its essence and provide the method behind its perceived madness; without these laws, nature seems raw, chaotic, untamed, mysterious, and out of control, but with the laws, nature becomes something we can understand and harness for the good of all.

Isaac Newton explained the mysteries of motion by zeroing in on four variables: mass, position, time, and force. With a few masterful strokes of his pen, Newton postulated laws of motion that have enabled us to explain, predict, and control moving bodies. The laws of motion launched the Industrial Revolution and birthed life-changing inventions ranging from the steam engine to the jet engine. It is because nature is governed by laws that Albert Einstein once reflected, "My scientific work is motivated by an irresistible longing to understand the secrets of nature."

Just as there are laws of nature, there are laws of human nature.* These laws, too, are timeless and universal, holding true across generations and civilizations. They tell us who we are at our Core, and how we can access that part of ourselves. When we operate in accord with these laws, we maximize the conditions for happiness, health, harmony in relationships, and high performance.

You may rebel at the idea that there are "laws" you must conform to. Does this mean one has to abandon one's own personality, temperament, thoughts, and feelings, and reduce oneself to being an obedient servant to something imposed on us from the outside? Where is the personal freedom in that?

Let me explain it this way. If you met me in my office right now, and you wished to stand up and pace the room, that is your right, and I would not judge you for it. If you wished to bang your head against the wall, that, too, is your right, and I would not judge you for it. But

---

* Newton himself was not destined to discover the laws of human nature. He once said, "I can calculate the motion of heavenly bodies, but not the madness of people."

Newton's third law of motion states that every action has an equal and opposite reaction, and this will allow me to predict, without judgment, yet with clarity and conviction, that you will soon experience a headache. You are free to choose an action, but once you take that action, you are no longer free to choose its consequences. It is therefore wise to operate in harmony with the laws of nature.

And it is similarly wise to operate in harmony with the laws of human nature. For in your pursuit of success, what if there are things you are thinking, feeling, valuing, or doing that are metaphorically like banging your head against a wall? Then you will experience a headache, metaphorical or otherwise. You are always free to do as you deem fit, but the laws of human nature will bind you to certain consequences based on your actions—consequences that will impact your happiness, health, relationships, and performance.

HOW I GOT WHACKED BY A LAW OF HUMAN NATURE

"Your roller bag is too big. You need to zip up the expandable part," the airline employee instructed me. Earlier that morning, I had placed three immaculately ironed shirts in my suitcase for a business trip to Chicago. I had unzipped the expandable section to make sure the shirts didn't get wrinkled. But then came this command from the airline employee who was checking our boarding passes as we entered security.

"Oh no," I thought, "she can't make me do this!" So I hustled, reading her name off her badge. "I'll make sure my bag fits in the aircraft, Rita. If I can't fit this bag in the storage space above my seat, I will zip it when I get there. I do not want to do it right now because it will wrinkle my shirts. I'm on a business trip."

Rita was not impressed. "You need to zip up this bag."

"What will then happen to my shirts?" I looked beseechingly at her two colleagues. Perhaps one of them would jump in and help me. But they stood sphinx-like. So I turned my attention back to her. "Look, Rita, you were not listening to what I said. I will zip up the bag in the aircraft, if needed. There is no point doing it here. I just got my shirts ironed."

"Do it now. You will not be flying today with this bag if you do not zip it up."

"Really? You will stop me from flying because of this? I wish to speak to your manager."

"I can't allow you to advance in this line. Please step aside."

I wanted to win, so badly. "OK, have it your way. I won't enter this line—I'll find *another* line and I'm sure the staff there will be more reasonable." I scanned the terminal for another security line whose staff would treat my shirts with R.E.S.P.E.C.T. There was only one other line, and it was just a few yards away. But the staff there had witnessed the unfolding spectacle and were already shaking their heads. "Sir," one of them said, "we can't allow you to go into this line like this. Do as Rita says. Zip your bag."

I threw up my hands in despair, capitulated to their command, and zipped my bag. My shirts were crushed—and with them, for that moment, my spirit too.

I have replayed this episode in my mind many times—the dogged hero, the foolish villain, the heated clash, the final surrender. Rita always emerges as the dogged hero—and I the foolish villain. After all, she was just doing her job by enforcing what must have been the airline's new policy for carry-on bags to be of a certain maximum size. On the other hand, my behavior was ludicrous. Why did I respond as I did? Because I got triggered.

We all slip into a triggered state at times, in which we experience a heightened level of anger, anxiety, frustration, or some other emotion. Then we are no longer centered in our Inner Core. We are our own worst enemy—our judgment is clouded, and we think, say, or do things we will likely not be proud of the next day. This is a law of human nature. Sometimes in my dealings with people I forget this law, or worse still, I deliberately cast it aside because I feel my triggered state is justified. *Lydia is so unreasonable! Michael deserves a piece of my mind! I won't allow them to trample over me!* For a few minutes, I feel like a lion uncaged, but then the law gives me a whack, like the one I got from Rita. I whine. I sigh. I smile. I marvel at the exactitude of the law. I am reminded that I have the freedom to choose my actions, but not their consequences.

In this sense, if we wish to discover and approach our Inner Core, we have no choice. We need to conform to the laws of human nature. Gandhi wrote, "There is an orderliness in the universe, there is an unalterable law governing everything and every being that exists or lives."

THE TRUTH SHALL SET YOU FREE

You might say, "OK, even if I accept that we are all subject to certain laws of human nature, they feel so constrictive. They will cramp my style." But think of artists, musicians, and dancers. They have to conform to laws of optics, acoustics, and motion. And yet once they have mastered those laws, they have infinite latitude in expressing their creativity, individuality, and passion to create works of astounding beauty, all emerging from the artist's mastery of the natural laws. In the same way, attuning ourselves to the laws of human nature does not stifle us—it strengthens us. It does not cage us—it gives us wings. It does not muzzle our voice—it helps us hone its timbre. When we act in concert with these laws, we connect with our true self, and we are then free to express our thoughts, feelings, desires, and values, because we have done the work of bringing them into alignment and harmonizing them with the world around us.

When I ask people what sources have taught them the most about their true nature, I get a variety of answers that can be organized into three ways of knowing: science, experience, and faith. But here is one thing I want to offer. If you only engage with these three sources in their outer forms, you run the risk of never fully discovering truth. We need to supplement outer science with inner science, outer experience with inner experience, and outer faith with inner faith. As we open up to this inner dimension of knowing, we discover that in the ultimate analysis there is only one source—one true teacher—whom we can trust to help us realize our true nature. Who that is you will discover at the end of this chapter. Don't jump ahead.

OUTER SCIENCE: ITS POWER AND PERILS

Science formulates hypotheses, runs experiments, collects observations, and draws fact-based conclusions. In recent years, the science of human nature has advanced in powerful ways. In the past, psychologists focused almost exclusively on mental maladies like depression and schizophrenia. Today they have turned their attention from human suffering to human flourishing. There is now a boom in research on topics like gratitude, grit, and giving; mindfulness, mindsets, and meaning; charisma, compassion, and creativity. Compelling findings are emerging on what it takes for people to live happy and healthy lives, thrive in relationships, and achieve peak performance at work. Neuroscientists have developed advanced instrumentation like fMRI to map brain networks associated with different behaviors, thoughts, and feelings. Now we have a way to investigate the hardware of human potential—neurons forming and performing, firing and wiring—and to study how our physical health and well-being are linked to our thoughts, beliefs, emotions, and lifestyle. Sociology is going through a distinct shift in favor of evidence-based policies—rather than conceptual models—to guide social change. Behavioral economics has made valuable contributions to our understanding of the pitfalls in human reasoning and how they can be surmounted to improve decision-making. The tree of scientific knowledge about human nature is coming into full bloom, and we will pluck actively from its many branches in this book.

Yet science has its limits. Its discoveries and teachings keep evolving as we learn more. The underlying laws of human nature do not change, but science's understanding of them does. In recent times, for instance, the field of psychology has been going through a "replication crisis" in which serious doubts have been cast on a number of its findings because the experimental results generated by the original researcher could not be subsequently reproduced by other psychologists. By one estimate, more than half of psychological experiments have failed to replicate. Further, the studies that have failed replication are much more likely to be widely cited—in other words, are the ones we are much more likely to learn about. That should give us some pause in the degree to which we can lean on the science of human nature at this stage of its evolution. These challenges to the scientific enterprise are a humbling reminder that while the ideal of science is objective, scientists ultimately are human, prone to pitfalls in their reasoning and motivations, just like the rest of us. Charles Sidney Burwell, when he was dean of Harvard Medical School, once candidly said to his students, "Half of what we are going to teach you is wrong, and half of it is right. Our problem is that we don't know which half is which."

Besides, science still lacks the tools to study certain aspects of human nature. For example, meditation is an ancient and highly effective discipline, discovered by unknown truth-seekers thousands of years ago. In the past, there was limited interest in meditation among scientists, both because existing instruments couldn't measure subtle changes in the brain, and because of skepticism about its value. After all, if you were an ambitious, can-do, success-driven individual, why would you sit down, become still, close your eyes, and do essentially "nothing"? Today, however, scientists have instrumentation advanced enough to measure subtle changes in the brain. They have opened up to take an interest in this practice, and so an explosion of scientific findings are now detailing the benefits of meditation. But even this bustling science is still playing catch-up to what has long been known by practitioners of certain spiritual traditions. Thirty years ago, if you had leaned exclusively on science, you would have never considered meditation a pathway to advancing your potential. Your entire life might have gone by without science revealing this powerful, beautiful truth to you. What other powerful, beautiful truths might science be failing to reveal to us today?

In my own investigation of human potential, I learned about an advanced and ancient meditation technique, Kriya Yoga, from the Self-Realization Fellowship lessons of Paramahansa Yogananda, known as the founding father of yoga in the West. Yogananda's teachings have been a central force in my life. Kriya Yoga works with a subtle form of life energy that flows within your body, called prana. (In ancient Chinese wisdom, it is called *chi.*) Kriya teaches you to direct the flow of prana within your spine and brain in ways that make you experience increasingly deeper states of peace, joy, and love. Prana is likely not detectable by today's scientific tools. Does that mean prana does not exist? In centuries past, scientific instruments were not advanced enough to detect the invisible forces of electricity and magnetism, yet none of us would claim that they didn't exist back then. I do not want to wait for science to advance its technology to validate or invalidate the presence of prana, for I may be dead by the time that happens. When science hasn't progressed enough yet, what is a truth-seeker to do? Become, I would offer, your own inner scientist.

INNER SCIENCE: OUR PERSONAL LAB

Scientists run experiments on "mice and men" in outer laboratories. In turn, we can run experiments on ourselves in our inner laboratory. The outer lab requires evidence from the five physical senses, but the inner lab can draw additional data directly from our feelings, thoughts, and intuition. Truth-seekers have in centuries past pursued inner experiments to accelerate their knowing. Several centuries ago, for example, one man actively investigated pathways to his Inner Core. He took on certain forms of austerity, including minimal eating and breath control, but got no meaningful results. He concluded that this kind of physical deprivation was not helping him realize his true nature. He abandoned one experiment, then began another. Eventually he took on the practice of meditation and a path of balanced living, succeeded at his goal, and became the Buddha. The rest is history, some of it still in the making.

By 2002, it had become clear to me that I needed to invest in my inner life, so I decided to put Yogananda's teachings of Kriya Yoga to test. I formulated three hypotheses: if I pursued these teachings with commitment and devotion, I would (1) experience the presence of prana within me, (2) learn to direct its flow, and (3) feel increasing peace, love, and joy from within as a consequence. I went into my inner laboratory, performed my experiment, and collected my observations. Within weeks, I started to experience the early effects of Kriya. That gave me the confidence to continue, and over time the experience became more tangible, more profound, and more consistent. Today, no outer scientist will be able to convince me that Kriya Yoga is unscientific just because they cannot yet measure prana; my own inner scientist continues to collect daily observations about the existence and benefits of prana flow. No neuroscientist will convince me that, when it comes to human nature, the only part of the body worth studying is the brain, because I have experienced the rewards of also cultivating awareness in the "heart chakra," a nerve bundle located next to the human heart. Outer science has taken some steps in the last twenty years to compile evidence on the benefits of breathing practices that form a part, but not the whole, of the Kriya method. I am glad I did not wait for this evidence to accrue before becoming my own inner scientist.

OUTER EXPERIENCE: LIFE IS A CLASSROOM

A student, Navid, shared the following story in my executive MBA class:

> When I was a boy, my family moved to another town, and I had to be enrolled in a new school. The bullies in the school came after me; they would insult me, push me around, even beat me up. I was strong physically, but there were too many of them, so I couldn't win a fight with them. I was struggling. My mother noticed my struggles and told me, "You have to use your mind." That made a light bulb go off in my head. I started to do small favors for people at school. These people started to support me, and soon the bullies were forced by my new supporters to pull

back. I learned through that experience that it is better to win hearts than to win fights.

It is better to win hearts than to win fights. We all acquire insights about human nature from our experiences in life. We do not even have to be limited to our own experience; we can learn much about human nature through observing the experiences of others. I used to believe that anyone in poor health would be in such discomfort that all they would be able to do is focus on their own condition. Then I heard a story from one of my students, Tanya:

> My father and I had a very special relationship. He was a deeply caring person, frequently asking me if I'd eaten my lunch that day. In my twenties, I saw his health decline—he had Parkinson's. I could see that he was having difficulty speaking. Even then, he would call me at the office every day and ask, "Have you eaten lunch today?" On some days, these calls came in the morning, and I would tell him, "Dad, it's only ten a.m.!"
>
> I was with him on his last day. He was struggling to breathe, had not eaten for a few days, and his last words to me were "Have you eaten today?" Even in his final moments, he was teaching me how much we can care for others regardless of what our own condition is.

After hearing her story, I have started to see so much more potential in what humans can do in moments of pain and suffering.

Life is a classroom. We learn about human nature from our outer experiences, and we accelerate our growth when we open ourselves up to learning from other people's experiences.

A TALE OF TWO REVOLUTIONARIES

Consider the remarkably parallel trajectories of Martin Luther King Jr. and Malcolm X. Both were African Americans born in the 1920s. Both had fathers who were politically active Baptist ministers, and both became ministers themselves. Both dedicated themselves to the same cause—the fight for racial justice in America in the 1950s and 1960s. Both were powerful speakers, casting a hypnotic spell on their audiences. And both lost their lives to assassins—each at the cruelly young age of thirty-nine.

And yet these similarities belie a stark difference in their paths. King was a beacon of light and love, forging a nonviolent movement that stirred America's conscience and shook up its laws. Malcolm saw white America as evil, stoked rage among African Americans, and evangelized a fight for justice "by any means necessary." How could two people emerge from such similar roots, pursue such similar ambitions, and yet follow such opposing paths?

Martin recalled his early family life this way: "My home situation was very congenial. I have a marvelous mother and father. I can hardly remember a time that they ever argued (my father happens to be the kind who just won't argue) or had any great falling out. These factors were highly significant in determining my religious attitudes. . . . The first twenty-five years of my life were very comfortable years. If I had a problem, I could always call Daddy. Things were solved. Life had been wrapped up for me in a Christmas package."

Malcolm X described his childhood this way: "My memories are of the friction between my father and mother. They seemed to be nearly always at odds. Sometimes my father would beat her." He also reflected, "My father was also belligerent toward all of the children, except me. The older ones he would beat almost savagely if they broke any of his rules. . . . Nearly all my whippings came from my mother."

Malcolm's father was killed in a suspected hate crime when Malcolm was six years old. After that, his family struggled, and "there were times when there wasn't even a nickel and we would be so hungry we were dizzy." Ultimately, Malcolm's mother was put in a mental asylum, and he was moved into foster care.

After a tough childhood, Malcolm started to shine as a student. Once he told a white teacher that he was interested in pursuing law as a career, and the teacher told him that as a black person he might want to consider carpentry instead. At that point, Malcolm dropped out of school. In a few years, he had devolved into a life of petty crime in the streets of Harlem, culminating in his being sentenced to a prison term when he was twenty-one. Prison became a crucible for Malcolm's personal transformation. In his own words: "Stumbling is not falling." "To have once been a criminal is no disgrace. To remain a criminal is the disgrace." "I don't think anybody ever got more out of going to prison than I did. In the hectic pace of the world today, there is no time for meditation, or for deep thought. A prisoner has time that he can put to good use. I'd put prison second to college as the best place for a man to go if he needs to do some thinking. If he's motivated, in prison he can change his life."

What Malcolm read and thought about in prison caused him to turn against the white race as a whole. He emerged from prison a man committed to fighting racism, and he became a powerful force of empowerment in the black community. But for twelve years after prison, Malcolm continued to be blindsided by his sweeping indictment of all white people.

Martin Luther King Jr. also had bitter encounters with racism early in his life. He related a story in his autobiography about a white friend he played with as a child of five:

> [He] told me one day that his father had demanded that he would play with me no more. I never will forget what a great shock this was to me. I immediately asked my parents about the motive behind such a statement. We were at the dinner table when the situation was discussed, and here for the first time I was made aware of the existence of a race problem. I had never been conscious of it before. . . . I was greatly shocked, and from that moment on I was determined to hate every white person. As I grew older and older this feeling continued to grow.

But Martin, unlike Malcolm, changed his mind a few years later when he started to work on racial justice in college. "We had many white persons as allies, particularly among the younger generation.

I had been ready to resent the whole white race, but as I got to see more of white people, my resentment was softened, and a spirit of cooperation took its place."

INNER EXPERIENCE: OUR QUIET REPORTER

Malcolm X saw himself as a truth-seeker. "Despite my firm convictions, I have been always a man who tries to face facts, and to accept the reality of life as new experience and new knowledge unfolds it. I have always kept an open mind, which is necessary to the flexibility that must go hand in hand with every form of intelligent search for truth." And yet he shrugged off the positive attitudes and behaviors from white people that he encountered on a number of occasions after his release from prison.

Alex Haley, who collaborated with Malcolm on the writing of his autobiography, reflected in the epilogue,

> The first time I ever heard Malcolm X speak of Handler [a white reporter], whom he had recently met, he began, "I was talking with this devil"—and abruptly he cut himself off in obvious embarrassment. "It's a reporter named Handler, from the *Times*"— he resumed. Malcolm X's respect for the man steadily increased, and Handler . . . was an influence upon the inner Malcolm X. . . . "He's the most genuinely unprejudiced white man I ever met," Malcolm X said to me. . . . I saw Malcolm X too many times exhilarated in after-lecture give-and-take with predominantly white student bodies at colleges and universities to ever believe that he nurtured at his core any blanket white-hatred. "The young whites, and blacks, too, are the only hope that America has," he said to me once. "The rest of us have always been living in a lie." . . . One day in his car, we had stopped for the red light at an intersection; another car with a white man driving had stopped alongside, and when this white man saw Malcolm X, he instantly called across to him, "I don't blame your people for turning to you. If I were a Negro I'd follow you, too. Keep up

the fight!" Malcolm X said to the man very sincerely, "I wish I could have a white chapter of the people I meet like you." The light changed, and as both cars drove on, Malcolm X quickly said to me, firmly, "Not only don't write that, never repeat it. Mr. Muhammad would have a fit."

Haley's account gives us glimpses of Malcolm's inner experience—of embarrassment when he called a white reporter a devil, of feeling exhilarated when he connected with young students, white and black, and of his instinctual desire to connect with white people who supported the civil rights movement. If Malcolm had paused and paid attention to those stirrings, he would have realized the truth that was hidden from him in plain sight: that there were many white people who shared his pain and wished to see a more equal society. But when such feelings surfaced, he swiftly turned away from them and reanchored himself in his monolithic view of the "white devil."

Winston Churchill once shared the following remark about a colleague; it could apply to any of us in our less illuminated moments: "Occasionally he stumbled over the truth, but hastily picked himself up and hurried on as if nothing had happened." If we truly want to learn from experience, we have to stay alert to feelings that arise within as we go through life. These inner responses provide valuable hints about our true nature and our place in the world.

KNOWING ME, KNOWING YOU

We reflected earlier on how we can all learn from the experiences of others. Once you start paying attention, you realize that it is not only the *experiences* of others but the *experiencing* of others that can enrich your understanding of your true nature. The most valuable lessons I have learned have come from my interactions with certain truth-seekers across cultures. When I am in the company of such individuals, I have always felt uplifted, peaceful, joyful. All my concerns and burdens fall by the wayside, and my heart swells with love. I feel a great sense of purpose and a connection with what truly matters to me. It is as though their presence peels off my layers of attachment and ego to reveal the luminous Core that lies within.

So pay attention to your inner experience when you are in the company of others. Is the energy they radiate predominantly a happy or a depressed one? Restless or peaceful? Bitter or grateful? Self-oriented or attentive to others? People are living museums; their life history and the feelings they stir within you indicate: "If this is the path you choose in life, this is where you will end up."

LEARNING BY IMAGINING

The more experiences you can collect, analyze, and learn from, the wiser you will be. A powerful way to add to your repository of experiences is to conduct thought experiments and then learn from the inner perceptions that accrue. The greatest scientist of modern times, Einstein, arrived at many of his breakthroughs via thought experiments. At the age of sixteen he asked himself, "What if you could ride alongside a beam of light? What would that be like?" It seemed to him that you would perceive a light wave to be stationary since you were traveling at the same speed. He kept deepening his understanding of this concept for the next ten years until it led to his famous theory of relativity.

Thought experiments allow us to mentally craft experiences on demand and then observe what feelings and insights arise within us. They give us an understanding of our true nature without having to go through a real-life event. When I first started to study Mother Teresa, I found myself deeply inspired by her commitment to serving the poorest among the poor. But I also learned that she had consorted at times with people of disrepute, such as a banker convicted of a crime and a dictator. I wondered why she was not more discriminating in whom she engaged with for her cause. Then I constructed a thought experiment. I visualized that I was traveling in a remote country with a loved one. Our car meets with an accident, and my loved one is seriously injured. Her life is in danger as she bleeds by the side of the road. There is no help in sight. One car passes by on the road, and despite our entreaties it does not stop. Nor do the next ten. The twelfth car I try to wave down stops to help us. I am overwhelmed with relief. Then I suddenly notice that the driver of the vehicle is a corrupt dictator I have long been critical of. What would I do in that moment? Would I ask him to leave, because I have judged him to be a bad person? Or would I jump at his offer to help, thank him for doing so, and focus on getting my loved one to the nearest hospital? I realized that this was probably what Mother Teresa had experienced. Her loved ones were the street people that most of the world had abandoned like those eleven cars that I had imagined passing my dying loved one. So whoever offered help, she received it with gratitude and without judgment. Her business was not to investigate their lives or support their agenda; it was to attract love, care, and support for the people on the sidewalks that most of us had chosen to pass by.

On occasion, let your imagination take flight. Construct a thought experiment, and observe the feelings it stirs. Use it to amplify, accelerate, and add to your learnings about your true self and about humanity.

A LEAP OF FAITH

Faith can be a powerful accelerator on our path to knowing, allowing us to benefit from the wisdom of past truth-seekers and people we consider more enlightened than ourselves. But to maximize the possibilities of faith, we must distinguish between faith and *blind* faith. Faith invites us to consider a teaching and use our faculties to discern, analyze, refine, integrate, and absorb the truths of its message into the fabric of our being. *Blind* faith expects us to consider a teaching, suspend our own faculties, and accept its doctrines without critical thinking.

Malcolm X's journey reveals the risk of engaging in blind faith. While in prison, he embraced the teachings of Elijah Muhammad, founder of an organization called the Nation of Islam. Muhammad preached his own version of Islam in which blacks were seen as the original human beings and whites as an evil race that had oppressed black people. Malcolm's acceptance of Elijah's doctrine was absolute. He recounted, "I believed in [Elijah] not only as a leader in the ordinary human sense, but also I believed in him as a divine leader, I believed he had no human weaknesses or faults, and that, therefore, he could make no mistakes and that he could do no wrong."

Some of you may believe that you are following the path of an illuminated prophet or a sacred scripture whose wisdom is beyond question. Yet most prophets and scriptures originated in centuries past; people today receive the teachings in a derivative form based on what has been handed down from the original source through a chain of messengers over the ages. How confident can we be that the interpretation we are receiving is faithful to the original—that no word or idea has been intentionally or unintentionally suppressed, inserted, tweaked, or distorted? When we observe the rivers of blood that have flowed across history in the name of religion, we recognize the perils of blindly following what we are told are a faith's doctrines. Time and time again, imperfect messengers and institutions have sought to amass power by inducing people to take their word as the prophet's word, offering interpretations of scriptures that have suited their ambitions. In describing how both the proslavery and antislavery factions in the United States defended their positions during the Civil War, Abraham Lincoln reflected, in his second inaugural address, "Both read the same Bible, and pray to the same God; and each invokes His aid against the other."

As his civil rights struggle intensified in the 1950s and 1960s, Martin Luther King Jr. encountered criticism from certain preachers who claimed he was acting against Jesus's teachings by sowing unrest in society. King rejected their interpretation of the Bible and gave churchgoers the challenge of questioning their faith and taking on the true practice of religion. While indicting the Christianity of his time, King stayed firmly rooted in the teachings of Christ. His "Letter from Birmingham Jail" beautifully captures his striving to understand the truth in Jesus's teachings: "In deep disappointment I have wept over the laxity of the church [in not supporting the Montgomery bus boycott]. But be assured that my tears have been tears of love. There can be no deep disappointment where there is not deep love. Yes, I love the church. . . . But, oh! How we have blemished and scarred [the church] through social neglect and through fear of being nonconformists."

King was also critical of certain practices in African American churches: "I revolted, too, against the emotionalism of much Negro religion, the shouting and stamping. I didn't understand it, and it embarrassed me. I often say that if we, as a people, had as much religion in our hearts and souls as we have in our legs and feet, we could change the world."

Would King have been true to Jesus if he had passively accepted the forms of Christianity that were being propagated in the churches of his time? Or was he instead true to Jesus by *challenging* the Christians of his time? Like King, we are most true to our faith when we commit to actively analyzing its teachings. If we do not thoughtfully examine the assumptions, agendas, and actors behind the faith sources we lean on—be they preachers, teachers, scriptures, philosophers, parents, or cultures—we may end up living someone else's truth or, worse, someone else's lie: a manufactured "truth" they wanted us to believe.

SCIENCE, MEET SPIRITUALITY

Science and religion are often pitted against each other. The eminent physicist Stephen Hawking said, "There is a fundamental difference between religion, which is based on authority, [and] science, which is based on observation and reason. Science will win because it works." Albert Einstein saw it differently. "All religions, arts and sciences are branches of the same tree," he observed. "All these aspirations are directed toward ennobling man's life, lifting it from the sphere of mere physical existence and leading the individual towards freedom."

The kind of religion Hawking was speaking of is blind faith, while the kind Einstein was speaking of is what we may call spirituality. When we move from blind faith to spirituality, we start to find much synergy with science. In the purest expression of their purpose, science and spirituality concern themselves with the same thing: the discovery of truth. Science gathers data from our outer world and spirituality from our inner world. Although the two disciplines may have opposed each other in the past, they are starting to come together.

Science made great strides in the late seventeenth, the eighteenth, and the nineteenth centuries to uncover nature's secrets, such as through Newton's laws of motion. This progress lulled some scientists into believing it was only a matter of time before science would yield all the practical knowledge needed to master the universe. But the twentieth century shattered this myth. The more scientists advanced their understanding of nature, the more they were astounded with what they were uncovering about nature at micro and macro scales. *Time slows down as you speed up. An electron is both a particle and a wave. One cannot measure both the position and velocity of an object at the same time. It is impossible for a mathematical system to be both complete and consistent. Matter is in fact condensed energy.* Some pioneering scientists who drove these disruptive advancements turned to spiritual wisdom to help them become more at peace with their logic-defying discoveries about the universe. Robert Oppenheimer, the father of the atomic bomb, said, "The general notions about human understanding . . . which are illustrated by discoveries in atomic physics are not in the nature of things wholly unfamiliar, wholly unheard of, or new. Even in our own culture, they have a history, and in Buddhist and Hindu thought a more considerable and central place. What we shall find is an exemplification, an encouragement, and a refinement of old wisdom."

As science has expanded its terrain from studying nature to studying human nature, it is arriving at the place described by Oppenheimer. Scientific findings on cultivating compassion, gratitude, self-discipline, emotional mastery, and habit formation, among other virtues, are "an exemplification, an encouragement, and a refinement of old wisdom." As scientists push forward along the frontiers of human consciousness through their study of meditation and transcendence, the boundaries between science and spirituality are dissolving even more.

Science is at its best when pursued with a spiritual temperament—with great appreciation for the vast intelligence in nature, a sense of awe about all that is yet unknown, a spirit of humble inquiry shorn of one's ego, an opening of one's consciousness to new, uplifting experiences, and a pure-hearted devotion to the discovery of truth. Spirituality, in turn, is at its best when pursued with a scientific temperament; if a spiritual path we are pursuing does not, over time, make us increasingly peaceful, wise, loving, and joyful, well then, scientifically speaking, something isn't right—either the teaching itself, or our understanding of it, or how we are putting it into practice. The rapid growth in the numbers of yoga, mindfulness, and meditation practitioners in recent years beyond those disciplines' Hindu and Buddhist origins has occurred in part because their teachings do not ask for blind faith; rather, they yield, in an observable, tangible, step-by-step way, the promised benefits. "Yoga," Yogananda once said, is "the science of the soul."

WHERE ALL FAITHS CONVERGE

Some of us have come to believe that different world faiths stand in opposition to one another, and so to create a united world we need to put faith aside. After all, there are preachers who claim that theirs is the only path to salvation. But there have always been truth-seekers who have risen above the fray of interfaith divisions. While maintaining a deep devotion to their own prophet and path, they have opened their hearts and minds to find common ground with, and take inspiration from, other faiths. Mother Teresa said, "I love all religions, but I am in love with my own."

While at divinity school, Martin Luther King Jr. struggled to find a practical way to put Christ's teachings into practice. He wrote,

During this period, I had about despaired of the power of love in solving social problems. I thought the only way we could solve our problem of segregation was an armed revolt. . . . Then one Sunday afternoon I traveled to Philadelphia to hear a sermon by Dr. Mordecai Johnson, president of Howard University. . . . Dr. Johnson had just returned from a trip to India, and, to my great interest, he spoke of the life and teachings of Mahatma Gandhi. . . . His message was so profound and electrifying that I left the meeting and bought a half-dozen books on Gandhi's life and works. . . . Prior to reading Gandhi, I had about concluded that the ethics of Jesus were only effective in individual relationships. The "turn the other cheek" philosophy and the "love your enemies" philosophy were only valid, I felt, when individuals were in conflict with other individuals; when racial groups and nations were in conflict a more realistic approach seemed necessary. But after reading Gandhi, I saw how utterly mistaken I was. Gandhi was probably the first person in history to lift the love ethic of Jesus above mere interaction between individuals to a powerful and effective social force on a large scale.

Later, in 1955, when forging the historic Montgomery bus boycott, King reflected, "Christ furnished the spirit and motivation while Gandhi furnished the method."

Gandhi himself was deeply influenced by the Hindu scripture, the Gita. But when considering how Indians could gain freedom from British rule, Gandhi also took guidance from Leo Tolstoy on Jesus's teachings about universal love and how they applied to the nonviolent resistance against oppressive rule. Gandhi began an active correspondence with Tolstoy that lasted until Tolstoy's death, and he called Tolstoy "the greatest apostle of non-violence that the present age has produced." In addition to his deeply held Christian beliefs, Tolstoy himself was influenced by certain practices in Buddhism and Hinduism to which he'd been introduced by the German philosopher Arthur Schopenhauer.

It is not faith but blind faith that is divisive. It is not faith but blind faith that views other faiths as flawed or inferior. It is not faith but blind faith that assumes people who do not follow its path or prophet will fail to ascend to the mountaintop of enlightenment.

FROM EXTRINSIC TO INTRINSIC

Some of us have walked away from a faith that we were introduced to in our family and culture because we have felt uncomfortable with the choices and behaviors it imposed on us. I found myself in this situation in my teens, ready to walk away from my Hindu roots, for I felt stifled by rules and rituals that made no sense to me. But instead of abandoning it, I ventured deeper into it. I sought to investigate Hinduism in terms of its fundamental precepts, and then the breakthroughs came. I realized that Hinduism has an extrinsic form (the outer rituals, the dos and don'ts that are the tradition's visible expressions) and an intrinsic form (the basic beliefs, principles, values, and inner practices that silently guide the practitioners on their spiritual journeys). And over time I realized this is true of other faiths as well. We tend to identify with the extrinsic form—the customs and rituals—and to do less of the inner work that would harmonize us with the intrinsic form. The extrinsic form is situational—what may work today may not work tomorrow, as conditions change—while the intrinsic form is timeless. The extrinsic form makes world faiths look very different, while the intrinsic form makes them look more similar. The extrinsic form can create divisions, while the intrinsic form always unites. When we open up to the intrinsic form of the great religions, we may find ourselves stumbling into our own faith in unexpected places, as I did in Istanbul, Jericho, and Tel Aviv.

Ten years ago, I found myself at the Istanbul airport. With my flight departure still a few hours away, I took a seat in a passenger waiting area and closed my eyes to meditate. I do not know how much time had passed before I felt a tap on my shoulder. I opened my eyes to find a man towering over me in flowing Arab robes, peering down at me with keen interest. He gestured toward the flight departure screen, as though to tell me, "You've been sitting still for a long time. Let's make sure you don't miss your flight." It became clear that neither of us could speak the other's language. He seemed to have been affected in some way by how I had been sitting with my attention withdrawn from the world. "Mussulman?" he asked, using the Turkish word for "Muslim." I shook my head and said, "Hindu." He seemed unaffected. He sat down beside me, took some food from his pouch, and offered half his loaf of bread and a meatball to me. He himself started eating, and I smiled as a way of thanking him and awkwardly started to eat the bread. As a vegetarian, I wasn't quite sure what to do with the meatball. Thankfully, he turned away for a moment, and I used that time to tuck the meatball in my pocket. He opened for me a fresh bottle of Sprite, and after I had taken a few sips, he took the bottle and drank from it himself. A deep, silent bond was formed between us. After this simple meal, I smiled and thanked him, stood up, and walked away. A few minutes later, I looked in his direction. He had placed a mat on the floor and was doing his namaz, the act of prayer performed by Muslims five times a day. I realized that this was the source of our kinship; he had seen me go within and connect with my Core, and now he was doing the same. We were fellow travelers to the same destination even though we were taking different flights.

A few years later, I traveled to the Holy Land of Israel accompanied by my mother, wife, and daughter. We sat in awe and stillness at the Wailing Wall to join our hearts with the devout Jews praying at that site. We visited the holy places associated with Jesus's life in Bethlehem, Nazareth, and Jerusalem. Each time we arrived at one of the sites, I asked our loquacious travel guide to pause his commentary, for we wished to transition from the extrinsic to the intrinsic, to go within, to attune ourselves as best we could to Jesus's spirit, sensing what it must have been like to be in his presence. As the days went by, I privately started to feel disappointed with myself, for I had not been able to calm my mind enough to taste the spiritual nectar I knew was present at these sacred spots we were visiting. It went on that way, from one site to the next. Jesus's birthplace. The site of the crucifixion. The ascension. The Last Supper. The Sermon on the Mount.

And then it happened. We were at the Mount of Temptation, a collection of caves near Jericho, one of the oldest cities in the world. Jesus had gone into seclusion in these caves and fasted for forty days. I sat down yet again to meditate, expecting it to be one more struggle. This time, my mind cleared quickly and became very still. Time and space dissolved, and I felt Jesus's spirit close to me. His peace, his love, his joy were so palpable. All the soul hunger I had brought to Israel was satisfied in that meditation at the final site we visited. It remains one of my most cherished experiences. I could have spent a lifetime there.

A day later, my family and I were having dinner at a restaurant in Tel Aviv. Our conversation turned to the conflicts and crises being witnessed around the globe. I tried to shift the talk in a positive direction, telling myself that we had come to Israel for a spiritual purpose and shouldn't wallow in misery. But the urge to keep scanning humanity for all its defects was just too strong, and we kept going with our lamentations. After the meal, we took a stroll on Rothschild Boulevard, joining the locals and tourists who were soaking in the relaxed energy of that beautiful street at the evening hour. Out of nowhere, an Orthodox Jew—in his flowing beard, big hat, and black attire—walked up to me, looked me in the eye, and exclaimed, "Be like the bee, not like the fly!" I was taken aback. Was he proselytizing, trying to convert me to his faith?

"What do you mean, sir?" I inquired.

"What does the fly do?" he quizzed me, then answered himself. "Even in the presence of beautiful flowers, it buzzes around looking for some dirt to feed on. But the bee, even when it is surrounded by dirt, it looks for the flower to make honey with. There will always be bad things and bad people in the world, but you be like the bee—keep your focus on the goodness all around." His voice had an admonishing but loving tenor to it, like my father's, as though he knew I needed to be shaken up a bit from my spiritual stupor.

I was stunned. I waited a few minutes to see if he would thrust some religious literature in my hand, but he did not. We smiled warmly at each other, I thanked him, and then he was gone. His only intent had been to make me switch perspectives. Later I discovered that my spiritual teacher, Yogananda, had used *the same* fly and bee metaphor to deliver *the same* advice. In that moment, this Orthodox Jew had become, for me, a messenger from my own teacher.

You do not have to visit Istanbul or Jericho or Tel Aviv. You do not have to open yourself up to breaking bread at the airport with a Mussulman or meditating in a historic cave in the mountains or receiving a good-natured scolding from an Orthodox Jew. But as you start to work on your five Core Energies, it is likely that you will find yourself feeling a growing kinship with truth-seekers from across all faiths.

On many occasions, an audience member has come to me and said, "Hitendra, what you spoke about is just what my faith teaches me." Some of them have been Christians, some Muslims, some Hindus, Jews, Buddhists, Taoists, Sikhs, Jains, Parsees, and Baha'is. Even atheists and agnostics. I am always thrilled with the connection they make to their own beliefs, but I am not surprised, because truth is universal.

THE ONE SOURCE YOU CAN RELY ON

Was Elijah Muhammad responsible for deceiving Malcolm X into believing that all white people were evil? Perhaps. But it would also be reasonable to conclude that Malcolm was in part drawn to Elijah Muhammad because he was unconsciously seeking to validate the hatred he felt for white people during that period of his life. He once reflected, "I think that an objective reader may see how when I heard 'The white man is the devil,' when I played back what had been my own experiences, it was inevitable that I would respond positively; then the next twelve years of my life were devoted and dedicated to propagating that phrase among the black people."

The greatest threat to discovering our true nature is not the distortions created by a flawed outer messenger but the distortions we create in our own minds to bend the laws of human nature to our biases. We are unconsciously drawn to teachers and paths that validate our prejudices. But if we work to free ourselves from limiting beliefs, we will be ever prepared to surrender a nontruth or a half-truth as soon as a more accurate, complete, and deeply resonant truth surfaces. Never outsource truth. Tap the sources of faith that you are drawn to, but take full ownership over developing your understanding of human nature—and your own true nature. For as Maya Angelou wrote, "We are only as blind as we want to be."

After a decade with the Nation of Islam, cracks started to appear in Malcolm X's convictions. He distanced himself from Elijah Muhammad's teachings and became like a bird uncaged, ready to fly anew. He made a pilgrimage to Mecca to take part in the holy Muslim ritual of the hajj, where he began to see the world through a different lens: "On this pilgrimage, what I have seen, and experienced, has forced me to re-arrange much of my thought-patterns previously held, and to toss aside some of my previous conclusions."

"[I encountered] thousands of people of different races and colors who treated me as a human being."

"I no longer subscribe to racism. In the past, yes, I have made sweeping indictments of all white people. I never will be guilty of that again."

"A man should not be judged by the color of his skin but rather by his conscious behavior, by his actions."

This transformation was movingly summed up by Alex Haley: "No one who knew him before and after his trip to Mecca could doubt that he had completely abandoned racism, separatism, and hatred."

At the root of Malcolm's outer transformation in developing a kinship with white people was his inner transformation in developing a kinship with his true self. After his journey, he reflected, "There is no greater serenity of mind than when one can shut the hectic noise and pace of the materialistic outside world, and seek inner peace within oneself." He also observed, "In my thirty-nine years on this earth, the Holy City of Mecca had been the first time I had ever stood before the Creator of All and felt like a complete human being."

Less than twelve months after his visit to Mecca, Malcolm was assassinated. If a man is to be judged by the courage he has to live by his beliefs, the capacity he demonstrates to challenge these beliefs, and the journey he makes to arrive closer to his Core, then Malcolm X was a truly great human being.

This brings us to the final pathway to understanding human nature and your own nature, the only pathway you can truly rely on: your inner voice.

When I was in high school, I picked up a book from my father's bookshelf that had a profound impact on me and led, eventually, to the quest that shaped my life: Yogananda's *Man's Eternal Quest*. It featured topics I was deeply curious about, like "Making Religion Scientific," "The Universality of Yoga," "The Soul's Journey to Perfection," "How to Read Character," and "Is God a Father or a Mother?" In reading the book, I never felt it was teaching me anything new; instead, I felt it was awakening me to truths buried deep within that had always been a part of me. Several years later, another compilation of Yogananda's writings, *The Divine Romance*, was published in which he stated, "When those who are receptive hear someone speak truth, it seems so familiar. Their first reaction is 'I thought so!' The mind has simply recognized a truth already known intuitively by the soul."

When you encounter an idea about your Core, enter the calm lake of consciousness that lies beyond your thoughts, feelings, and senses, and check whether the idea rings true to you. This is the path of inner faith: the intuitive awakening to truth from the very essence of your being.

FROM LEARNING TO LIVING

An accomplished scholar of the scriptures met with a nun who was deeply respected for her level of spiritual consciousness. After the meeting, the scholar remarked to a monk who was nearby that the nun's knowledge of certain scriptures didn't impress him. The monk smiled at the scholar and replied, "You see, sir, some of us study and teach the scriptures. But some, like her, are living scriptures."

And that is my wish for you. I hope this book can serve you creditably as a sort of user manual for life. Return to it when you feel drawn to going deeper into one energy or another. Reject any ideas that don't resonate with your Core. But when something does resonate, then seek not just to learn, but to make it your own.

THE JOURNEY

⁓꙼⁓

HIGH UP ON A MOUNTAINTOP, A MONASTERY HOUSED AN abbot and some monks. It had once been a thriving community, but in recent years it had fallen on hard times. Few visitors came, donations were down to a trickle, and young men had stopped joining the order. The garden was unkempt, and cobwebs covered the chapel ceiling. Behind this outer decay lay an inner decay. The monks didn't get along; arguments frequently broke out over petty things, and they blamed one another for their problems. The aging abbot felt greatly demoralized about the future of his beloved monastery but didn't know what to do.

One foggy winter evening there was a knock on the monastery's door. A highly regarded rabbi from the region had come visiting. He stayed for five days. The monks looked after him with great care and respect. It didn't take him long to observe the monastery's challenges. On the final day of the rabbi's visit, the abbot confided in him and sought his counsel. The rabbi nodded, but didn't offer any answers. Later, as he sat with the monks for dinner one last time, he thanked them for their warm hospitality. Then after a pause, he spoke again in a hushed tone. "Brothers, I know these are hard times for all of you. But do not despair. I have seen the Messiah. He is right here, among you. Your monastery has a bright future." Then he bid farewell and left.

The monks were stunned. In the days that followed, they engaged in a flurry of speculation. "If the Messiah is among us, who could it be? Perhaps Brother Patrick? After all, though he is occasionally absent-minded, he is also warm to everyone. Or Brother Nelson? He has a bit of a temper, but it always comes from a place of deep caring for our community. Brother Jacob? He's constantly berating us about how we're not on time with our prayers and our meals. We've started to avoid his company, but sometimes it feels like it is God who is trying to discipline us through him. Then there's Brother James, too. He has such humility and devotion in the way he goes about doing his duties, and he never pushes his own ideas. Could it be . . . *me*? I did join the monastery with a pure purpose, I feel so much peace when I am in the chapel, and two of our monks come to me regularly for guidance on the scriptures."

In small but tangible ways, day upon day, the monks started to change. Now when there was disagreement, they would make an extra effort to respectfully listen to one another. When they passed by a fellow monk, they would nod and smile lovingly. If a monk became irritable, others would give him the space to recover without judgment. They started to discover qualities they much liked in one another. They woke up each day to pray deeply in the chapel, walking out inspired to take on their duties. The monastery became a hive of devotional activity. Residents from neighboring towns started to attend services, seek counseling, and volunteer their time, drawn by the monks' presence and peaceability.

Some spiritually inclined young men applied to join the order.

Occasionally, the abbot's thoughts would turn to the past, and he would silently marvel at the wisdom of the rabbi whose words had triggered this transformation—and at the faith of the monks in trusting that the Messiah was in fact among them, and within them.

Could the "Messiah" the monks searched for in each other and in themselves have been their own Inner Core? What kind of world would we create if we went forth like the trusting monks to awaken this "Messiah" within ourselves, and within all who cross our path?

PART TWO INTRODUCES YOU TO YOUR FIVE CORE ENERgies and how you can activate them. Purpose, Wisdom, Love, and Self-Realization each provide a pathway to your Core; Growth is an enabling energy for the other four.

The chapters titled "Living with _____" introduce each energy and lay out a five-stage path to activating it. Although each stage builds on the previous ones, you do not have to master a stage before progressing to the next.

Each chapter titled "Leading with _____" profiles the journey of an inspiring historical figure toward activating that energy and translating Inner Mastery into Outer Impact.

Chapter 4

LIVING WITH PURPOSE

⤜⤏

It is not enough to be busy. So are the ants. The question is: What are you busy about?

—*Henry David Thoreau*

MY LIFE EQUATION

In 2003, I became aware that my life needed a major reboot. Following a period of much introspection, I met with a mentor (let's call him Brother Arnold) who has been a key force in my life since I was ten. I strode into his office and over the next fifteen minutes proceeded to lay out a fresh blueprint for my future. I had decided, I told him, to walk away from X. Instead, I was going to focus on Y, and start giving time as well to Z. Within two years, I would bring A into focus. Meanwhile, I also wanted to make sure I deepened my commitment to B at home, while not ignoring C along the way. What did he think? Was this a good plan? Was I focusing on the right things, and was I planning them in the right order? I rested my case and took a big breath. Deep down, I was yearning for validation, to be reassured that my choices were right.

Brother Arnold did not respond right away. He gazed at me as though he were looking past my restless thoughts straight into my Core. Then he said, "Hitendra, tell me . . ."

"Yes, Brother," I interjected anxiously. "What more background would be helpful to you?"

"What is the one thing you are seeking in life?"

I was stupefied. One thing, really? Just one? Wouldn't a person with boundless ambition be going for eight or ten things? If I was forced to pick one, what would happen to my other goals? Couldn't he please just tell me what he thought of my carefully constructed plan?

He must have sensed my bewilderment. "You do not have to give me an answer right away. Just promise me that you will think about it." I mumbled incoherently and nodded. He smiled patiently, bending his arms in the shape of a triangle. That left me even more puzzled, but I felt if I inquired about the triangle he would again encourage me to find the answer within. Then he clasped my hands lovingly in his own, signaling an end to our meeting. My life equation with its X, Y, Z and A, B, C was dead on arrival, so I walked out into the sunshine to give it a quiet burial.

I learned a valuable lesson that day. For a life well lived, we cannot simply pursue separate goals across different domains; a good life is not just a bucket list of all the things we wish to do before we die. We need to identify the polestar that will guide the outer expression of our Inner Core, imbue our every move and moment with significance, and steer us gracefully along the sometimes smooth, sometimes jagged landscape of life.

In ancient times, ships sailing the high seas were constantly confronted with the challenge of determining their bearings. With no physical landmarks in the vast expanse of ocean around them, seafarers would look up at the night skies for guidance. Most of the stars could not be trusted—their positions change as the Earth moves around the sun. But one star maintains a steady position relative to Earth: the polestar. Sailors used the polestar to navigate their vessels in rough waters and be guided to safe harbor. We, too, can cultivate an inner polestar, a guiding Purpose that helps us navigate our journey in life and leadership toward the destination we wish to arrive at: a life well lived.

Heroic Purpose is the stuff of legends. Think Abraham Lincoln, Martin Luther King Jr., Mother Teresa, Mahatma Gandhi, Joan of Arc, Nelson Mandela. The great ones take on a mission to create a better world, engage in epic battles, and make supreme sacrifices. And after undertaking an arduous struggle, they bring their followers to the Promised Land.

No wonder many of us live our lives without Purpose. We do not think we can aspire to such heroism. We wish for a life that is not buffeted by struggle and sacrifice. Or if we are willing to dedicate ourselves to a singular mission, we have no idea what it might be. So instead we take a random walk through the garden of life, plucking all the fruits we can while the sun shines but with no clear destination to reach by sunset. Yet deep down, something gnaws at us as we watch the clock of life ticking. When our spirit is stirred by the story of a hero in a book or movie, we wonder, "Why couldn't *my* life be a hero's journey?"

I started to pursue the idea of Purpose after that fateful meeting with Brother Arnold. I studied the science, investigated the great leaders, and sought out my own Purpose. Every time I thought Purpose was within my grasp, it would slip away. I coaxed, implored, and pushed. I moved my inquiry from consultation with outer advisors to listening for my inner voice. Eventually I realized that I needed to abandon my preconceptions and allow Purpose to come to me on its own terms. So let me introduce you to Purpose, the way I have come to know it from up close.

THE ESSENCE OF PURPOSE

I invite you to do a thought experiment.

YOUR IDEAL LIFE

The year is _____, and on a warm spring evening you lie down in bed to sleep through one more night of your eventful life. You are ninety years old today; you have entered the twilight years. Your mind drifts into a life review: a journey across the decades of your life, starting from the day when you first came across this exercise. You have reason to be proud and contented with how you have lived since then. There have been challenges and there have been triumphs, and you weren't always able to stay perfectly directed in your affairs, but the broad course of your life, your strivings and pursuits, has stayed true to your Inner Core. As sleep seeps over your weary form, your face glows with satisfaction and gratitude for your journey.

Put yourself in that moment, when you have just turned ninety, and write down the kind of life you would have led, from today to that day, to allow you to conclude that it has been a life well lived.

Each of the participants who have performed this exercise in my class have a vision that is distinctively their own. But lurking behind the varied visions, we are all seeking the same thing. Can you guess what that is?

Happiness. No one wakes up in the morning exclaiming, "I hope today is the unhappiest day of my life." We pursue goals in life that we believe will bring us happiness. Goals are outer, material things we wish to attain. Education, money, acclaim, love, power, impact, promotion. We become attached to our goals, believing that they, when achieved, will make us happy. But research shows that our happiness in achieving a goal is short-lived. Here's why.

A goal is like a hill we wish to climb. We believe that when we get to the top of the hill, we will be contented. When we do reach the top, we experience a boost in happiness for a few days, weeks, or months, but then our happiness returns to a baseline level as we get used to being on that hill. Because what we were "climbing" all along wasn't a hill—it was a treadmill. The happiness treadmill.

I've been on this treadmill many times, only to see my apparent triumphs dwindle into insignificance and inconsequence. When I learned one historic day that I had been accepted to the doctoral program at MIT, I was ecstatic. A few days later I received a welcome letter from the program director sharing more details about the academic requirements for the degree. I went to my college library to browse the textbooks he'd listed so I might sample the academic adventures that awaited me. The mathematics in those textbooks turned out to be a real terror—a baffling mishmash of Greek symbols, equations, and proofs. I had a sinking feeling that the authorities would instantly discover upon my arrival at MIT that I was a fool, an admissions gaffe, and ship me back to India. My ecstasy was replaced with agony.

The day came when I arrived on the MIT campus, and mercifully my first set of classes was more like a gentle zephyr than a terrifying tornado. But that did not boost my happiness back to its earlier, blissed-out state. I no longer felt ecstatic about being at MIT, because I was at MIT *every day*, and *everyone* around me was at MIT too. I started to harbor new hungers, new goals, because, as Nelson Mandela said, "After climbing a great hill, one only finds that there are many more hills to climb."

Purpose shifts our focus from goals to the values that reside in our Inner Core. Goals are material outcomes that we either achieve or don't—but values have no beginning or end. When we train ourselves to wake up every day committed to putting our values into action, our motivation and happiness start to come from knowing that we have done our best to express them in the conditions that unfolded that day—rather than from whether we got credit for our contributions, or concluded a deal, or launched a product.

There is one problem with moving from goals to values. Goals create ambition, and ambition propels us toward achievement. Without goals, you would just sit around being kind and compassionate, but with no drive to do something to change the world. You would be far removed from your full potential. That's why we cannot afford to abandon goals. Steve Hayes, founder of acceptance and commitment therapy (ACT), has shown how instead of trying to *replace* goals with values, we can *derive* our goals *from* our values. At any point in time, you have certain resources available to you—physical, financial, social, intellectual. Set goals that maximally express your values given those available resources. Your goals can then be the outer markers of your strivings, the milestones that track your progress in the committed pursuit of your values.

A monk who is a dear friend shared this story:

> I was visiting a small town in India when, while walking on the street, I passed by a panhandler. He had lost the lower parts of both his legs, likely due to leprosy. I bought him a cup of tea from a nearby tea stand, and he thanked me for it. As I was turning to leave, I saw him drop some of the tea on the ground. Then he put the cup to his lips and took his first sip, which he was clearly savoring. I returned to him and said, "I couldn't help notice you dropped some tea on the ground. You only had so much tea for yourself. Why did you waste some of it before drinking the rest?"
>
> "None of the tea is wasted, sir," he sought to reassure me. "Come and take a look for yourself." I peered down at that tiny tea puddle. Some ants were now crawling all around it.
>
> "Look!" He smiled. "The ants are enjoying the tea." Then he explained, "Sir, I know you bought the tea for me. But I am not able to consume anything without first sharing it with someone else."

The only resource this man had was a cup of tea. He used it to express, as best he could, the value he held of sharing.

Life invites us to use whatever resources we have to pursue goals that best express our values, given our circumstances. That's what Nelson Mandela had to do when, as a leader of the African National

Congress in its fight against apartheid, he was arrested, tried, and sentenced to prison. "I was now on the sidelines, but I also knew that I would not give up the fight," he wrote. "I was in a different and smaller arena, an arena for whom the only audience was ourselves and our oppressors. We regarded the struggle in prison as a microcosm of the struggle as a whole. We would fight inside as we had fought outside. The racism and repression were the same; I would simply have to ride on different terms."

These weren't just idle words. Some years back, my family and I traveled to Robben Island to visit the prison where Mandela had been incarcerated for most of his twenty-seven years in captivity. During his incarceration, Mandela couldn't tangibly pursue his larger ambitions for dismantling the system of apartheid outside prison, so he used his time there to dismantle the system of apartheid *in the prison*. Black prisoners back then were only allowed to wear shorts, while other prisoners could wear trousers. Blacks were given fewer calories and less sugar than other inmates. Mandela organized protests that made prison authorities reform those practices. Being in prison allowed Mandela to pursue the same values, but through a modified set of goals.

Our external conditions are always changing, and often beyond our control. When we become attached to outer goals, we surrender control over our happiness to the whims of the world. Purpose anchors our motivation in the things we truly stand for, the values we hold deeply at our Core. Purpose liberates us from anxiety about whether our goals will be achieved, giving us the resilience to adapt to whatever headwinds we encounter. Goals can be scaled up, or down, or moved sideways, as our resources change, all in the service of the same Purpose. We are no longer dependent on outer conditions—on the conduct or approval of others, or on the cards that life deals to us on any given day—for our fulfillment. Each time we experience a breakthrough or a setback, we go back to our Core to reaffirm our values and then find the best way to reexpress them as goals, given our new conditions. Our outer game is fluid; our inner game holds steady. This is the essence of Purpose.

THE POWER OF PURPOSE

Think of a time when you strongly pursued a Purpose, even a small one. What did it feel like? How did it influence your behavior? What benefits did it give you?

Research shows that when we are anchored in Purpose, it activates strong motivation from within. We are comfortable making sacrifices to pursue our goals because we connect with the deeper reason behind them. We wake up each day feeling inspired. We happily take on even the most mundane tasks since we see the connection between them and the Purpose we hold at our Core. We are able to make hard choices and trade-offs with greater clarity and equanimity since we are guided by what matters to us deep within. Our strivings and struggles are imbued with meaning, intent, and depth. We feel alive. Our existence has significance.

Purpose makes us put our ego aside so our Inner Core can come shining through. We choose and act in ways inspired by our Purpose instead of being silently influenced by the need to look after our own narrow interests at the cost of the larger good.

In *Altered Traits*, their book reporting on what science has discovered about meditation, Daniel Goleman and Richard J. Davidson describe how after a three-month meditation retreat, practitioners who strengthened a sense of Purpose during the retreat showed an increase in the activity of telomerase, an enzyme associated with protecting cells from aging and death. They write, "It's as though the body's cells were saying, stick around—you've got important work to do."

THE PATH OF PURPOSE

Some of us cruise through life with no interest in Purpose. We walk, talk, eat, work, play, going through the motions with no hunger for anything beyond the enjoyment of our material existence. We allow our life to remain unexamined, focusing on revelry over reflection, and we do not feel any the worse for it.

Others among us have a clear Purpose and know exactly what we want out of life.

And the rest of us wish to pursue a Purpose but have no clue where to find it. We fear that we will bob aimlessly on the ocean of existence with no Purpose in sight. If you're in this third group, then let me tell you one thing. You already have a Purpose. *Your Purpose is to find your Purpose.*

But you cannot expect to simply go to a workshop or read a book or work with a coach and then, voilà, you have Purpose. Life is a maze that involves lots of dead ends and detours, and your true Purpose becomes visible only when you figure out how to find your way out of the maze. There is no formula for acquiring Purpose that will work for us all, for your maze is unique to you, and mine is unique to me. But there are five stages that can guide us through the maze toward the treasure we seek.

Stage 1: Stir

It all starts with a stirring from inside. It may be triggered by an inner awakening or by an external event, like a sudden loss, setback, or other change in life circumstances. Or it may seep in slowly, in a series of little whispers, an increasing feeling of emptiness, a yearning for a richer, more authentic life, the Inner Core crying out for more tangible expression.

Anna Pavlick's Purpose was an awakening from within. When she was in third grade, she got home from school one day and told her mother, "Mom, we learned today about cancer. Cancer cells are smart because they outfox all the normal body cells. I think I am smarter than a cancer cell. I will grow up to be a cancer doctor." Here's what happened next.

While she was in college obtaining a degree in nursing and pre-med biology, her boyfriend, whom she'd planned to marry, was diagnosed with leukemia. She spent two years caring for him before he passed away. She went on to medical school. At one point during her fellowship, on a bet, she went on a blind date—and ended up marrying that person. "I knew the day I met him that it was going to be right," she said in my executive MBA class. "We had an incredible life together." Anna pursued her Purpose of outfoxing the cancer cell: her research has contributed to improving the odds of survival for people with stage 4 melanoma from 5 percent to 65 percent. Then, after twenty years with her husband, cancer came back, this time to claim his life.

As an oncologist, Anna has served patients and their families with the deep-felt empathy she resolved to cultivate years ago when the physician who was treating her ailing boyfriend in college made a rather perfunctory remark that shook her world: "You realize he only has a few weeks to live." Her personal experiences, she says, have "given me the ability to talk to patients' families. They understand that I get it, that this is not a job, this is personal to me; this is why I am there for people from the time they walk into my office and say, 'Here you go, take care of me.' I will be there either until the day that they are cured and become part of my extended family or until they pass away. And if they pass, I will ensure they pass away with dignity, knowing they were loved and cared for."

Katharine Graham was serving as a housewife in 1963 when her stirring came—not as an inner call but as an outer whack. That year, her husband died by suicide, leaving the family business, the *Washington Post*, in her untutored hands. Women almost never took the helm of companies in those days, and most people expected her to sell the newspaper. But she had been stirred. "I cared so much about the paper and about keeping it in the family that, despite my lack of knowledge and feelings of insecurity, I felt I had to make it work." She originally intended to keep a low profile. "I saw my job now as that of a silent partner, watching from the sidelines as I tried to learn about the company to which I had tragically fallen heir. I saw myself as a bridge to my children and viewed my role before they could take over as supporting the strong men."

She later reflected, "I fretted that I wasn't up to it, that all the qualities I was lacking added up to an overwhelming deficiency that might very well work to the detriment of the company." She also noted, "I didn't understand the immensity of what lay before me, how frightened I would be by much of it, how tough it was going to be, and how many anxious hours and days I would spend for a long, long time. Nor did I realize how much I was eventually going to enjoy it all."

Graham's initial impulse may have been to take this on for her family, but events conspired to draw her toward a more selfless and visionary Purpose over time. Early in her tenure, she faced pressure from prominent politicians who were seeking the *Post's* endorsement for electoral office. She politely declined their requests and began to see herself as a watchdog for a free and unbiased press. "I believe very deeply that we in control of news media have a solemn obligation. . . . I believed intuitively—and the feeling grew with experience—that the news columns had to be fair and detached, even while recognizing that there really is no such thing as 'objectivity.'" When the Pentagon Papers were leaked to the press, she made a courageous call to approve their publication despite tremendous pressure from the Nixon White House. She once reflected, "[We] believed the [Pentagon] Papers were so useful to a greater understanding of the way in which America became involved in the Vietnam War that we regarded their publication not as a breach of the national security, as the administration claimed, but, rather, as a contribution to the national interest—indeed, as the obligation of a responsible newspaper."

A few years later, the *Washington Post* was again thrust into the limelight when it exposed the Watergate scandal that ultimately brought down the Nixon presidency. Graham described her role in these events:

> I was a kind of devil's advocate, asking questions all along the way—questions about whether we were being fair, factual, and accurate. . . . What I did primarily was stand behind the editors and reporters, in whom I believed. As time went on, I did this more publicly, defending us in speeches and remarks to groups around the country—indeed, internationally as well. . . .

Watergate was a transforming event in the life of *The Washington Post*—as it was for many of us at the paper and throughout journalism. Anything as big as Watergate changes you, and I believe it changed not only the Post and me but journalism as a whole.

She took principled and bold stands to support the *Post*'s journalism, opening herself up to relentless attacks, litigation, and more: "I was prepared to go to jail if need be."

By then, Graham was well on her way to becoming a legend in the publishing world, one of the most powerful people in Washington, DC, a pioneering woman business leader, and the first female CEO of a Fortune 500 company. What a remarkable journey for a woman who had in her first forty-seven years "adopted the assumption of many of my generation that women were intellectually inferior to men, that we were not capable of governing, leading, managing anything but our homes and our children."

Graham's journey is a beautiful testament to how Purpose can be co-crafted by the push of our outer circumstances and the pull of our inner voice, and how an indomitable spirit within us lies waiting to be stirred by a heroic Purpose so it can flow to us and through us to do our life's noblest work.

If you are thinking, "I have neither an outer push nor an inner pull. How do I get myself stirred?" then let me introduce you to my favorite stirring tool. When I was growing up, my family and I on rare occasions found ourselves driving past the local cremation ground. "Oh, look at the smoke!" I would say. "Someone is being cremated." My mother would glance at me disapprovingly, keen to turn her children's attention toward more pleasant subjects. That protective response from her is what most of us do every day. We shun death, hoping that it in turn will shun us. But the irony is that when we cultivate an active awareness of death, we become more alive—alive to the need to make every moment count, to the imperative of finding our true path and minimizing the detours, to doing the best we can during our limited time on Earth, and to being true to our inner stirrings. Staying ever conscious of how death will someday lay claim to my body and how I will be required to instantly shed all my earthly roles, identities, and attachments has been an invaluable aid for me to staying actively stirred in a world that can otherwise dull our deeper hungers with its distractions and desires.

At age ten, I started to frequent Yogananda's ashram in Ranchi, India. Each time I went there, I experienced a tiny but tangible tug. A feeling of purity swept over my consciousness and illuminated what was truly important. On one such visit, when I was seventeen, I found myself more intensely affected than ever before. Tears of joy flowed down my face after a group meditation. "Let me stay here," I proposed, as my family prepared to return home. "You can go back. I want to figure out what I really want in life." My parents listened patiently. To them, this sudden call from the cosmos was an unnecessary distraction from the practical goal of getting me to graduate from high school. They urged me to return home with the family. In that moment, I had neither the courage nor the discipline to act on my inner stirrings, so I capitulated. Within a few days, I was once again caught in the tangled web of life. It wasn't until I was thirty-four—exactly twice that age—that I finally sought once more to do justice to the stirrings I had experienced so palpably in the ashram on my youthful visit. That was when I flew to Los Angeles to meet with Brother Arnold and discuss the new equation for my life.

Stirrings, the silent whispers of our Inner Core, occur across the span of our life. But too often we ignore them, like I did that fateful day in Ranchi, and they pass us by, leaving us largely untouched. When these stirrings come to you next, will you take heed? Will you go on a search?

Stage 2: Search

The right stirring catches you on fire, ready to question, challenge, and learn. A new vision for yourself and for life starts to emerge. It may not yet yield any change visible from the outside, but within you, much ferment and transformation are underway.

By the time I was thirty-four, I had bounced around from one set of professional goals to another. Mathematics, consulting, entrepreneurship. I finally had to accept that I was deeply lost. I had the drive and the discipline to pursue a Purpose, but not the discernment to define it in a satisfying way. When we have a bias for action, achievement, and ambition, we run the risk of rushing into Purpose only to emerge from our successes disillusioned. I have since had the time to mend my ways. For Alexander, time ran out.

Alexander of Macedon was told by his mother that he had been conceived immaculately when a thunderbolt struck her womb, that he was the son of the Greek god Zeus, and that he was meant to rule the world. This prophecy did come to pass, for in 334 BC, twenty-two-year-old Alexander embarked on a series of conquests that, within eleven years, made him the ruler of an expanse of over two million square miles. After military triumphs across Europe, Africa, and Asia, Alexander marched into India, where he had a remarkable encounter with a yogi. The quotes and narrative below come from the accounts of Megasthenes, a Greek historian who followed Alexander to India, and Palladius, the bishop of Helenopolis in the fourth century. "Upon arriving in Taxila in northern India, Alexander sent an emissary, Onesikritos, to fetch a great yogi of Taxila, Dandamis, from his forest retreat. 'The son of the mighty God Zeus, being Alexander who is the Sovereign Lord of all men, asks you to go to him. If you comply, he will reward you with great gifts; if you refuse, he will cut off your head!'"

The yogi smiled kindly, did not so much as lift up his head from his couch of leaves, and began by claiming that if Alexander was the son of Zeus, then so was he.

I want nothing that is Alexander's, for I am content with what I have. . . . Alexander is no god, since he must taste of death. How can such as he be the world's master, when he has not yet seated himself on a throne of [inner] universal dominion? . . . The gifts Alexander promises are useless to me. The things which I prize and find of real use are these leaves, which are my house, these blooming plants, which supply me with dainty food, and the water, which is my drink. . . . The earth supplies me with everything. . . . Should Alexander cut off my head, he cannot also destroy my soul. . . . I then, becoming Spirit, shall ascend to my God. . . . Let Alexander, then, terrify with these threats those who wish for gold and for wealth, and who dread death.

When Alexander learned what Dandamis had said, he "felt a stronger desire than ever to see Dandamis," saying that "he who had conquered so many peoples had been conquered by one naked old man." He did visit Dandamis and received his wisdom.

India ended up being Alexander's final frontier. Facing the threat of mutiny from soldiers exhausted by their battles and keen to return home, he retreated from his expansionist ambitions. Along his return journey to Greece, he fell sick and died. With no clear successor, his empire rapidly disintegrated.

In his youth, Alexander once wept because "there are so many worlds, and I have not yet conquered even one." He did end up conquering most of the world known to the ancient Greeks, but he left one world unconquered—the world Dandamis had pointed him to, that of inner dominion. What might Alexander's fate have been—and how might he have changed the world—if he had allowed himself to question his mother's claims about who he was and what he was meant to do? Perhaps he could have actively wrestled with the hard questions implicit in Dandamis's statements, like whether it was possible to be the world's master without mastering oneself, and whether all human beings were children of the same God and hence worthy of respect.

Hard questions are the ones about life, ourself, and the world for which there are no easy answers or proofs. They are the silent shapers of our motivations. What is my highest potential? Who am I, at my Core? What will make me lastingly happy? When my physical self dies, will my consciousness die too, or will it live on? What am I meant to manifest in my time on Earth? Is the universe random, or is there a natural order to things? Is there a higher force behind the universe? If yes, what are the qualities of this higher force, and what is my relationship with it? Why do good things happen to bad people sometimes, and bad things happen to good people?

Many of us accept what we learn from our family or culture without doing the deep work to investigate these hard questions for ourselves. Some of us lose interest in the questions because we believe they are largely irrelevant to the practical course of our lives. But as Alexander's story shows, our answers to these inquiries are the bedrocks that shape our choices and our Purpose. The right bedrocks will guide us to a Purpose that makes us feel increasingly connected with our Core; the wrong bedrocks may mean that decades go by, perhaps even a lifetime, without a lasting feeling of fulfillment.

It is said, "There are only two mistakes one can make along the road to truth; not going all the way, and not starting." You may never obtain answers to all the hard questions, but having sought to explore them and to arrive at a set of bedrocks to guide your life choices, you are much more prepared to take on the world. There are practical steps we can take to investigate these matters. Study the lives of people you admire. Read the great books—scriptures, philosophies, epics. Take note of people whose energy you are drawn to, from any walk of life, and hold soul-searching conversations with them about these complex issues. Reflect on the lessons you have learned from life's twists and turns. Look for what inspires you and gives you intrinsic joy. Keep a diary of your reflections. Step away from the madding crowds on occasion to be in nature, so you can listen more clearly to the voice within. Define your identity based not on your demographics, degrees, or duties, but on your steadfast search for truth. You may be a banker from without, but you are a seeker from within.

Dandamis's ideas must have stirred a deeper curiosity in Alexander. We know he respected Dandamis's wisdom too much to have him beheaded. Other Greek historians of Alexander's time tell us that he persuaded another yogi, Kalanos, to join him on his passage back to Greece and to become one of his teachers.* But Alexander must have felt that openly challenging the path he was already pursuing would be too radical. After all, if you were in Alexander's shoes, possessed of legendary power, glory, and territory, gaining victory upon victory in violent battles, and you started to suspect that the real meaning of life lay elsewhere, would you have been able to walk away from it all?

Just nineteen years after Alexander's death, in the same India that he reluctantly abandoned, another conqueror was born, Ashoka, like Alexander, ascended to power as a young man by summarily executing other claimants to the throne. For the next eight years, he engaged in a series of wars to expand his kingdom, ultimately ruling over thirty million people across most of the Indian subcontinent. One day he witnessed the pain and suffering his army had inflicted in the war on Kalinga, in which over a hundred thousand people lost their lives. Deeply shaken, he asked himself, "What is my relationship with humanity? What are the duties of a king? What aspects of life have the most enduring significance?" He changed his ways to focus on serving his people and propagating spiritual and cultural wisdom through his "sermons in stone," edicts carved into rocks, cave walls, and pillars located throughout the nation, some of which still survive. Rock Edict X "declares that a king's true glory depends on the moral progress he aids his people in attaining." Rock Edict XI defines "'the true gift' to be, not goods, but Good—the spreading of truth." On Rock Edict VI, Ashoka "invites his subjects to confer with him on public business 'at any hour of the day or night,' adding that by faithful discharge of his kingly duties he was thus 'obtaining his own release from the debt he owed his fellowmen.'"

---

* Greek historians of that era have reported that Kalanos fell ill during Alexander's return journey. He bid farewell to the Greek soldiers, then made a baffling claim to Alexander—"I will see you in Babylon"—and died. It was a year later, when Alexander, during a visit to Babylon, fell sick and suddenly died, that the soldiers understood what Kalanos had meant.

Alexander represents the relatable human side of us, prone to being seduced by power and praise, hesitant to engage in soul-searching, unwilling to change course, and untethered from our Core. Ashoka represents the divine potential in us, drawn to stepping back from everyday routines and asking hard questions of life, to going on a search, to consciously forming bedrocks, and to pivoting to our true Purpose.

Stage 3: Define

Clarity emerges step-by-step as you start to define your path. You codify the bedrock beliefs that will ground you and the values that will guide you. You begin to recognize a source of joy that you had not tapped into in the past; it doesn't have to do with what you possess or taste or touch or get from others but instead has to do with a sense of growing clarity about what you believe, what you value, and how to approach life anchored in your bedrocks. You may not have established a singular route to take through the jungle of life, but you now have a number of signposts to help you progress in the right direction.

Values and principles are not all-or-nothing entities that you either have or don't; they require continual refinement. One of my treasured values has been nonviolence. Early on, I translated this into the principle "Do not inflict pain on others." This led me to give up meat when I was eleven, because "others" for me included animals. Then when I was fourteen, I read some of Gandhi's writings. Nonviolence, Gandhi stated, is not only about what we do, but also about what we speak and what we think. Whenever we are unnecessarily critical or disrespectful of someone, that is an act of violence. I modified my principle to be "Do not inflict pain on others *in thought, speech, or action.*"

In my twenties, I realized that people could inflict not just physical but emotional pain as well. I recast my commitment to nonviolence as "Do not inflict physical *or emotional* pain on others in thought, speech, or action." At thirty-three, I had to revise it again. In running my startup, I found it necessary on occasion to give employees critical feedback, and even to fire people. I simply could not avoid inflicting emotional pain in those moments, because I had to do what was right for my organization. My principle now became "Do not inflict physical or emotional pain on others in thought, speech, or action, *except when it is necessary to do so in service of your Purpose.*"

When I began studying great leaders from history, I saw how hard they worked in difficult moments to look for a nonviolent solution. And if they did have to take a path that would cause some pain, they tried their best to minimize the pain. They delivered tough messages to people in the most respectful and loving manner. They laid off employees only after they had sought out all reasonable alternatives, and when they did let someone go, they aimed to support them as best they could. They fought their enemies fiercely but also looked for every opportunity to build rapprochement, understanding, and win-win outcomes. I fell in love with this idea. It made the framework of nonviolence more compelling and more complete. I added the following clause to my principle. "*When you do have to inflict pain, do so only as an instrument of last resort, and minimize the pain needed to achieve your Purpose.*"

As much as I love this value, I slip from grace from time to time, being insensitive in my conduct, and then I feel guilty. I once spoke rudely to a server at the concession stand of a movie theater because I'd received poor service. Throughout the entire movie, my heart felt heavy. Thankfully, he was still there when I walked out at the end of the film. I went over to him and apologized. He broke into a smile as we affectionately shook hands. That moment was the true end of the evening for me, not when the film credits rolled. So I have added a final clause to my principle: "*When you fall from grace, do your best to apologize for it and to avoid repeating the same mistake.*"

This principle has many uses for me. It makes me think carefully about how to deliver a hard message, how to be mindful of others' feelings, how to stand my ground, how to advance my ideas, how to say no to someone, how to respond to a disruptor or resistor in an audience, how to share a sensitive truth, how to refrain from criticizing someone who isn't in the room, how to reach out and apologize when I've failed to live up to my standards—and even how to deal with spiders.

Spiders? I do not want to have a spider in the shower with me, and that's my "higher Purpose." Of course, I could always kill any spider I stumble onto. But killing should be the instrument of last resort. If I can, I trap the spider in a container, walk outdoors, and place it in the grass at a safe distance. If I simply do not have a choice and need to kill it, I make sure it is totally squished, so I don't leave it half-dead, half-alive, in pain—and then I send a prayer to the universe for its departed soul. Principles are principles.

So let us not hang our boots too early once we've codified our values and principles; they may benefit from periodic upgrades throughout our life.

⚘

Besides values and principles, some of us may now be ready to define an overall Purpose that will guide us along a noble and uplifting path. We might wish to set an ambitious target to change the lives of thousands, perhaps millions, even billions. But this is a limiting path to take.

When we are captivated by numbers—when we assume bigger is better—we lose an appreciation for how behind every public achievement lie priceless and countless private contributions. Imagine you are Paul, part of an ordinary household in the 1950s, with an ordinary job, living in an ordinary neighborhood. One day you and your spouse, Clara, adopt a baby boy. You raise him as your own, with love and care. Your son's school is quite dysfunctional, with a high crime rate, so in seventh grade, he insists that you put him in a different school. You and Clara spend all your savings and take out a big mortgage on a new home in a more affluent neighborhood so your son can go to a better school. One day you and your son are doing a woodworking project at home, and you notice that he has left things unfinished: the fence he's building isn't painted on the back side. You ask him to make it just as good-looking as the front side, and he asks you why that's necessary, since no one will know. "You will know," you reply, "and that will show that you're dedicated to making something perfect."

As a young man, your son starts to tinker with technology and opens a computer business out of your garage. As the business grows, the engineers show your son a new creation, and he pulls apart the covers of their machine to look inside. "Look at the memory chips," he says. "That's ugly. The lines are too close together." When an engineer reasons that nobody will see those chips, your son responds that the engineers will know, and he asks them to make it "as beautiful as possible, even if it's inside the box," because "a great carpenter isn't going to use lousy wood for the back of a cabinet, even though nobody's going to see it."

The boy you have raised is Steve Jobs. This is in fact what happened.

When a Steve Jobs changes the world, to whom should the credit go? Does it wholly belong to Steve for pursuing the quantitative cause of transforming the world through design and technology, or does some of it also belong to his parents, Paul and Clara, for pursuing the qualitative cause of adopting and raising a child to help bring out his full potential? Humanity would never survive, let alone flourish, if everyone's calling was to pursue a majestic Purpose over a humble Purpose. The infinite universe smiles equally at every finite act of Purpose. One of my students shared, "As a physician, I have traveled to certain poor nations to provide free care for the ailing. I had just performed a surgery for a man who had a cleft palate, and who had walked for days to make it to the medical camp. I must have looked a bit tired and distracted after the surgery. One of my local helpers came over to me and said, 'To the whole world, he is just one person. But to this one person, you are the whole world.'"

You might ask, "There are so many directions my life could take, some more qualitative, some more quantitative. How will I know which is the right Purpose for me?" There is much we can learn from the tales of two individuals whose life journeys began in similar circumstances but whose Purposes took them in opposite directions. András Gróf was born in Budapest, Hungary, and after struggling through World War II and repressive Communist regimes, he left his home and family at the age of twenty as one of two hundred thousand Hungarians who escaped to the West. Eventually, as Andrew Grove, he became the third CEO of Intel and played a transformative role in Silicon Valley, being named *Time* magazine's Man of the Year in 1997.

Milada Horáková was born in Prague, Czechoslovakia, participated in the underground resistance against the German occupation of her country during World War II, was captured and sent to various prisons, and survived to return to Czechoslovakia after the war. She focused her political activities on supporting women's rights and democratic institutions, and when the country fell to Communist rule, she, unlike many of her political associates, chose to stay in Czechoslovakia rather than leave for the West. She was subsequently arrested, accused of a plot to overthrow the government, and sentenced to her death. On the day of her execution, she wrote the following words to her family: "I go with my head held high . . . Don't feel sorry for me! I lived a beautiful life . . . My conscience is clear and I hope and believe and pray that I shall also pass the test of the highest court, of God."

Who between Andrew and Milada is worthy of greater admiration? Does picking one over the other even make sense? Didn't they both lead luminous lives and approach something close to their full potential? The only thing that matters when choosing your Purpose is that you follow your own inner voice—with passion, persistence, and a purity of heart. Life is inviting all eight billion people on Earth, whatever our station, to pursue Purpose. Each of our lives could be equally special if we followed our inner polestar. No one else can judge you but yourself.

Purpose can have a dark side. It can make us ignore our commitments to others, place unhealthy physical or mental strain on us, or usher in a future that brings not just the blessings we sought but also harm we didn't anticipate. That's why it is important that we also pursue what I call UnPurpose: understanding the risks and costs associated with Purpose, and striving to undo them in our pursuit of Purpose. In masterminding the strategy for India's civil disobedience against British rule, Gandhi did something quite peculiar. He developed a struggle-truce-struggle format in which any national program he launched went on for only a year or two before he called it off for several years. Other leaders objected, but Gandhi knew that people needed periods of rest in between their contributions to the movement. He saw the truces as opportunities for people not just to recharge but also to reform. India's outer liberation from British rule was of no use to him if it wasn't accompanied by India's inner liberation from dark-age social practices. During the periods of rest, he challenged Indians to cultivate self-discipline and a spirit of selflessness, and to advance, among other causes, women's rights, education, religious harmony, and the elimination of caste consciousness. It took him twenty-seven years to gain India's freedom, but the years of rest and reform allowed the freedom struggle to stay strong during that period and prepared the country for more successful self-rule in the decades following independence. Among nations that won their freedom after World War II, India is a rare case of a stable democracy—and that, too, as a nation of 1.4 billion people with a variety of languages and religions. This stability has much to do with Gandhi's decision to invest those twenty-seven years in pursuing not just his Purpose but also his UnPurpose. As with Gandhi, to serve our UnPurpose will require us to temper our Purpose, to sacrifice short-term gains in order to secure a more perfect long-term future.

Stage 4: Focus

As your Purpose becomes defined, you are now ready to focus. This is where the real work begins, where you start to give active outer expression to your Purpose. The purity of your inner aspirations starts to clash with the messiness of the world's expectations and with your own deep-seated habits and insecurities. It is time for some hard choices, for you realize you cannot both hold on to the past and create the future.

One way to harmonize with your outer environment is to choose a vocation that aligns with your Purpose. If your Purpose is to heal, be a physician; to spark joy, be a performer; to uplift, be a preacher. But what if your Purpose-driven vocation won't earn you enough money to meet your financial needs? Or what if it requires qualifications you do not possess? Does that mean your work will need to be bereft of Purpose?

Not at all. Because while you wait to find a vocation that fits your Purpose, you can meanwhile mold your Purpose to fit your vocation. In a study of janitors working at hospitals, scientists found that a few of them reported great fulfillment and joy from their work. "How," you might ask, "do these people find janitorial work uplifting?" A typical janitor might describe their work as follows. "I arrive at eight a.m. I clean all the patient rooms, restrooms, and corridors on floors four and five. I take a break between noon and one p.m. I take out the trash sometime in the afternoon. Then I leave at five p.m." But the janitors who reported satisfaction in their work "didn't see themselves as custodial workers at all. One described forming such a bond with patients that she continued to write letters to some of them after they were discharged. Another paid attention to which patients seemed to have few visitors or none at all, and would make sure to double back to spend some time with them. Some, when asked what their jobs were, would say, 'I'm an ambassador for the hospital' or even, in one case, 'I'm a healer. I create sterile spaces in the hospital. My role here is to do everything I can to promote the healing of the patients.'"

One of my executive MBA students told the following story in class: "My mother is a janitor. She always takes a keen interest in people, and over the course of her janitorial career she has often developed a personal connection with executives whose offices she was cleaning. Several of them have turned to her for advice on their relationships at work and at home, because she is great at understanding people and their problems. In fact, I got the opportunity to interview for this great job I am in right now after my mother reached out to an executive she had helped at my company!"

Without being physicians, performers, or preachers, these janitors have found ways to engage in healing, spark joy, and uplift others in the confines of their role. And that's how we, too, can craft our roles: by **reframing** what we do and why we do it, **redesigning** the tasks we take on, and **reorienting** our relationships, all in the service of our Purpose.

The BBC once profiled a Somalian immigrant who had fled tough conditions in his home country and immigrated to London. To make a living, he drove a taxi, though his heart was in journalism. In between rides, when his cab was free of passengers, he watched for police car sirens, and when he encountered one, he chased the vehicle to discover what was going on. Often he encountered newsworthy stories—a bar brawl gone wrong, a robbery, a bomb threat. He would excitedly call the local radio and TV stations to report the event. Over time, he developed a reputation in the local news community, and one of the organizations offered him a job. He crafted his role to beautify his job—and this eventually led him to a beautiful job!

If your work isn't fulfilling today, look for ways to pivot to a more Purpose-aligned vocation. But while you are still in your current role, remember that life's remaining moments are fleeting and finite. Why let a year, a month, a week, or even a day go by without maximizing the fulfillment you experience by using role-crafting? And why not also apply role-crafting to all the roles you play at home, in tending to a child, cooking your dinner, or doing a chore? As Martin Luther King Jr. once said, "No work is insignificant. All labor that uplifts humanity has dignity and importance and should be undertaken with painstaking excellence. If a man is called to be a street sweeper, he should sweep the streets even as Michelangelo painted, or Beethoven composed music, or Shakespeare wrote poetry. He should sweep the streets so well that all the hosts of heaven and earth will pause and say, 'Here lived a great street-sweeper who did his job well.'"

Ah, you might think, that is so poetic, but can we really achieve this kind of grace? After being released from prison, Nelson Mandela wrote, "To survive in prison, one must develop ways to take satisfaction in one's daily life. One can feel fulfilled by washing one's clothes so that they are particularly clean, by sweeping a hallway so that it is empty of dust, by organizing one's cell to conserve as much space as possible. The same pride one takes in more consequential tasks outside of prison one can find in doing small things inside prison."

ᘎᘏ

Focus is not just about *investing* your energy in things that matter but also about *divesting* your energy from things that matter less. To do full justice to your Purpose, you will want to look long and hard at how you spend your time, and take steps to simplify your life. Because when you find yourself pulled by a grand Purpose, the small tugs of daily distractions should be set aside. "It is not a daily increase," Bruce Lee once said in describing a life well lived, "but a daily decrease. Hack away at the inessentials."

Some "decreases" are easy to engineer. You may trim down the number of Netflix shows you watch, the hobbies you engage in, or the parties you attend because you realize some of them just don't resonate with you anymore. Other distractions require more careful recalibration. Should you skip certain family gatherings, pull back from certain relationships, and stop volunteering for certain causes? How will you get others to understand and accept the choices you make, or handle their disappointment or resistance?

Some of us strive to have it all. We want to be the perfect professional, the perfect spouse, the perfect parent, the perfect friend, the perfect homemaker, the perfect son or daughter to our aging parents, and the perfect citizen. It will never happen. There will always be more desires, demands, and duties than we can fulfill in a day or a lifetime. You will not be able to do justice to all your goals all the time. No one can escape the burden of having to make hard choices— sometimes really hard.

In his address to the court at the time of his trial, Mandela said, "It has not been easy for me . . . to say good-bye to the good old days when, at the end of a strenuous day at an office I could look forward to joining my family at the dinner-table, and instead to take up the life of a man hunted continuously by the police. . . . More powerful than my fear of the dreadful conditions to which I might be subjected in prison is my hatred for the dreadful conditions to which my people are subjected outside prison throughout this country."

In 1969, while in prison, he wrote a letter to his young daughters, Zenani and Zindzi, in which he shared how looking at a photograph of them kept his spirits up in his damp eight-by-seven-foot cell. "Zindzi says her heart is sore because I am not at home and wants to know when I will come back," he wrote. "I do not know, my darlings, when I will return . . . the white judge said I should stay in jail for the rest of my life."

Everywhere around us is evidence of heartwarming—and heart-breaking—sacrifices that people have made in the pursuit of Purpose. I think about the families in Europe during World War II who hid their Jewish friends from the Nazis, risking everything. The New York City firefighters who lost their lives after choosing to walk up the Twin Towers on 9/11 to save other people's lives when all the office workers in the buildings were scrambling to get out. The medical and other frontline workers who served people while putting their own health at risk during the COVID pandemic. These are our brothers, wives, sons, mothers, and friends.

These people's life choices, and how we honor them for making such choices, demonstrate a natural law: the higher your Purpose, the more personal imperative and moral legitimacy you have to say no to other worthy duties. Your inner voice is your best assurance for whether you're doing the right thing. Not the perfect thing, not the "success guaranteed" thing, but the right thing.

Stage 5: Fuse

Mahatma Gandhi was once racing to catch a train. Before he had fully boarded, the train started to move and one of his shoes fell onto the tracks. He didn't want to step down to retrieve it for he would have then missed the train. What would you do next if you were in his "shoes"?

Gandhi took off his other shoe and threw it so that it would land as close as possible to the first shoe, so that if some poor person found one shoe, he would also find the other.

Susan B. Anthony's mission in the 1800s was to gain women the right to vote. When she posted her payment for her grocery bills, she stuffed the envelope with leaflets about her cause. On a tourist visit to a monastery in Florence, she signed the visitors' book, "Perfect equality for women, civil, political, religious. Susan B. Anthony, USA."

One of my students, Mala Chapple, was the producer of a TV show that featured Richard Branson, and she tells this story about her encounter with him:

We followed Richard Branson around for a "day in the life" documentary. You can imagine how busy his schedule was—he had just flown in from London and was opening up the new Virgin terminal at O'Hare and went on to do press conferences and interviews and attend a board meeting and an evening launch party. Our crew was carrying handheld cameras all day, walking backward at times. I was amazed at how many times he asked if they were OK. You don't often get people even noticing that shooting is hard work for the crew!

At one point, we were filming him being interviewed by a journalist. After the interview, when the camera was off, I witnessed a remarkable moment unfold between the two. Richard started by asking the journalist about his dreams, his big goals in life, and then turned the conversation toward his lifestyle. Richard encouraged him, in a deeply caring voice, to take care of his health, to focus on his weight, so he could lead a long and healthy life and achieve the dreams he had set for himself. The journalist was visibly moved, and inspired. Richard was able to be so caring with him, and yet so candid, and he had only just met him.

While vacationing in Florida, First Lady Eleanor Roosevelt, wife of US president Franklin Delano Roosevelt, heard about a strike by seven delivery boys who worked at Aunt Martha's Lunch Box Service, a small local business. She inquired about the reasons for the strike and then helped arrange a settlement between management and the workers.

Steve Jobs's sister, Mona, described his actions when he was in the hospital during his last few days. "Intubated, when he couldn't talk, he asked for a notepad. He sketched devices to hold an iPad in a hospital bed. He designed new fluid monitors and x-ray equipment. He redrew that not-quite-special-enough hospital unit."

What is remarkable about these situations is not that Gandhi, Susan, Richard, Eleanor, and Steve were living their values. That's what you'd expect from them. What's remarkable is that they were doing so in the seemingly inconsequential—and in one case, close to final—moments of their lives, vastly distant from the public stage.

When you have fused wholly with your Purpose, your polestar begins to illuminate every moment of your life, small and big, onstage and backstage, professional and personal. Whether you are at work or with friends, doing your chores, tending to your children, taking a walk, or traveling on holiday, you have reframed your role, redefined your tasks, and reoriented your relationships to allow you to give active expression to your Purpose. You will then have achieved what George Bernard Shaw called "the true joy in life, being used for a purpose recognized by yourself as a mighty one."

WHAT MY SEARCH FOR PURPOSE TAUGHT ME

"What is the one thing you want out of life?" It took me three years to answer the question Brother Arnold had posed to me that day in Los Angeles. I learned a lot along the way.

I learned that when Brother bent his arms into the shape of a triangle, he meant to show me that the pursuit of Purpose starts with a broad exploration, then gets progressively focused, and ultimately becomes one-pointed. I learned that the way to create a feeling of unity in my life is to dismantle the walls between its different parts to allow my Inner Core to shine through everything I do. I learned that true fulfillment lies not simply in doing what I like to do or what I am good at doing, but in directing my passions and talents in service of my Purpose. I learned that the more I am on fire with my Purpose, the more precious every moment of life becomes, for there is then no time to waste. And I learned that my true Purpose—the one thing I most want—is to strive for ever-deepening Inner Mastery and ever-expanding Outer Impact, and to help others do the same.

Chapter 5

LEADING WITH PURPOSE

—3⊱—

When you are inspired by some great purpose, some extraordinary project, all your thoughts break their bonds; your mind transcends limitations, your consciousness expands in every direction, and you find yourself in a new, great and wonderful world. Dormant forces, faculties and talents become alive, and you discover yourself to be a greater person by far than you ever dreamed yourself to be.

—*Patanjali, an authority on yoga, circa 200 BC*

HOW LINCOLN RESHAPED THE WORLD
BY LETTING THE WORLD RESHAPE HIS PURPOSE

Abraham Lincoln's path to Purpose is a beautiful and instructive story, not simply because of how steadfastly he pursued it but also because of the struggles, stumbles, and strokes of seeming serendipity he encountered along the way.

When he was thirty-one, Lincoln broke off his engagement to the same person he would eventually marry, Mary Todd. He then spiraled into depression: "I am now the most miserable man living. . . . I must die or be better, it appears to me." He took shelter at the home of his friend Joshua Speed. "Lincoln went crazy," Speed recalled.

"[I] had to remove razors from his room, take away all knives and other such dangerous things and it was terrible." It was in this dark night of the soul that Lincoln discovered a powerful spark within. When Speed warned Lincoln that he would die unless he rallied, Lincoln replied that he could kill himself, that he was not afraid to die, but that he had "done nothing to make any human being remember that he had lived." On another occasion, he remarked, "Oh how hard it is to die and leave one's country no better than if one had never lived." It is when we confront the prospect of death that we arrive at a full understanding of why we want to live.

"I am naturally anti-slavery," Lincoln once reflected. "If slavery is not wrong, nothing is wrong. I cannot remember when I did not so think, and feel." White citizens at the time were divided on slavery. Lincoln's friend Joshua Speed was a slaveholder, and Lincoln's wife came from a slaveholding family. What made Lincoln hate slavery so viscerally? Perhaps it was because, as he once said, "I used to be a slave."

In Lincoln's day, a child was required by law to be in their parents' care and control until the age of twenty-one. Parents could legally require their children to work, and the children's wages were the parents' to keep. A *Newsweek* article reports, "Until he was 21 years old, Lincoln's father had rented him out to neighbors in rural Indiana at a price of 10 to 31 cents a day, to labor as a rail splitter, farmhand, hog butcher and ferry operator. Thomas, his father, collected the son's wages. Lincoln was in effect an indentured servant. He regarded his semi-literate father as domineering and himself without rights." It was common for parents to use corporal punishment—whipping and beating—back then, and Thomas was said to sometimes use it on Abraham if he caught the boy reading when he was supposed to be doing chores, and for other acts of "impropriety." Lincoln walked away from his father at age twenty-one, never to return; when in 1851 he received word that his father was dying, Lincoln wrote to his stepbrother, "Say to him that if we could meet now, it is doubtful whether it would not be more painful than pleasant." His father's behavior must have seared into Lincoln a lifelong hunger to win freedom for others just as he had won his own. Perhaps the life experiences we go through are simply there to silently prepare us for our ultimate Purpose.

Democracy was a young, fragile institution in the mid-nineteenth century. Lincoln realized that democracy was critical to the project of sustaining and strengthening personal freedoms. He also realized where power in a democracy lay. "Public sentiment is everything," he once said, "With public sentiment, nothing can fail; without it nothing can succeed. Consequently, he who molds public sentiment, goes deeper than he who enacts statutes or pronounces decisions." The United States, to Lincoln, was a nation where a grand experiment was underway to advance democracy. The success or failure of that test, he believed, would ripple across the world.

In his twenties, Lincoln witnessed a series of violent events carried out by enraged mobs at a time of rising tensions over slavery and race. The experience awoke in him a deep concern for the preservation of law and order. At twenty-eight, as a newly minted lawyer recently elected to the Illinois state legislature, he gave a speech in Springfield, Illinois, in which he said, "[America's founding fathers] aspired to display before an admiring world, a practical demonstration of the truth of a proposition . . . namely, the capability of a people to govern themselves. . . . Let reverence for the laws . . . become the political religion of the nation; and let the old and the young, the rich and the poor, the grave and the gay of all sexes and tongues and colors and conditions, sacrifice unceasingly upon its altars." This desire to protect the legal and constitutional fabric of the nation became a primal stirring in Lincoln. Having been a railsplitter, boatman, manual laborer, store clerk, soldier, store owner, election clerk, postmaster, and surveyor, he finally settled into a legal career, with some forays into politics.

As a lawyer, Lincoln seems to have partitioned off his feelings about slavery from his fierce ambition to succeed in his profession. He was "not among those who . . . sought out cases involving blacks, or who volunteered to aid the antislavery cause." In 1847, he even agreed to represent a Kentucky slaveholder, Robert Matson. Matson had brought five enslaved people—a mother, Jane Bryant, and her four children—to Illinois, a free state, where they had asserted their independence. Matson contended that they still belonged to him and filed a case in court to win them back, hiring Lincoln as his lawyer. An antislavery activist, Dr. Hiram Rutherford, knowing of Lincoln's critical views on slavery, approached Lincoln to propose that Lincoln represent the Bryants. "He listened attentively," recalled Rutherford of his conversation with Lincoln, "but I noticed that a peculiarly troubled look came over his face now and then. His eyes appeared to be fixed in the distance beyond me and he shook his head several times as if debating with himself some question of grave import." Something deep was likely stirred in Lincoln that day, for he quickly sought to switch sides so he could fight for the Bryants. Upon learning that Lincoln had initially agreed to represent Matson, Rutherford refused his help for the Bryants. Lincoln ultimately represented Matson. Accounts suggest that he put forth an uncharacteristically feeble argument in court and lost. Matson, enraged, left town without paying Lincoln his legal fees.

In the years that followed, Lincoln began seeing a need to be more active in the public arena to contribute to the fight against slavery, worrying that "that spirit which desired the peaceful extinction of slavery has itself become extinct." He contested a US Senate seat in 1854, but voluntarily surrendered his candidacy when he saw the antislavery vote being split between himself and another candidate, Lyman Trumbull, running the risk that the proslavery candidate would win instead. In 1858, he got a second opportunity to contest a Senate seat. Lincoln and his opponent, Stephen Douglas, had known each other since the 1830s, having engaged in nightly conversations around the fire in Joshua Speed's general store back then. In 1856, when Douglas was already a prominent US senator, and Lincoln a largely failed politician, Lincoln had written a note to himself, not intended for others to read: "Twenty-two years ago Judge Douglas and I became acquainted. We were both young then; he a trifle younger than I. Even then, we were both ambitious. . . . With me, the race of ambition has been a failure—a flat failure; with him, it has been a splendid success."

During the 1858 Senate campaign, Douglas argued that America's new territories in the West should be allowed to decide for themselves if they wished to allow slavery; Lincoln wanted to limit slavery to only the states where the Constitution already permitted it. Slavery was a strong institution at that time in the nation, and a source of great wealth. Douglas claimed that America's founding fathers were open to slavery; Lincoln turned to a document older than the Constitution, the Declaration of Independence. He stated, "I think the authors of that notable instrument . . . did not mean to say all men were equal in color, size, intellect, moral development or social capacity. They defined [that men] were equal in certain inalienable rights, among which are life, liberty, and the pursuit of happiness." Calling the Declaration the "immortal emblem of Humanity," he recognized that its promise was unrealized at the moment. "They meant to set up a standard maxim for free society which should be familiar to all: constantly looked to, constantly labored for, and even though never perfectly attained, constantly approximated, and thereby constantly spreading and deepening its influence and augmenting the happiness and value of life to all people, of all colors, everywhere." He saw it as a bold, sweeping vision for the whole world and for generations to come, "a beacon to guide" not only everyone in his time but "their children and their children's children and the countless myriads who should inhabit the earth in other ages." In our own pursuit of Purpose, we can inspire ourselves and others by defining an ideal vision of the future—our polestar—and then framing what we do as steps that move us closer to that standard.

Lincoln lost the race to Douglas, prompting him to write, "I now sink out of view, and shall be forgotten." But the *Evening Post* opined, "No man of this generation has grown more rapidly before the country than Lincoln in this canvass." Even when we do not win outer victories, if we're doing the right things, our Purpose may still quietly advance.

A year after Lincoln's loss, he received an invitation to speak from the Republican Party. Some party leaders feared that their leading candidate for president, William Seward, was too radical to win popular support, having suggested the use of extraconstitutional measures to fight slavery. Lincoln and a few other individuals were being engaged to speak so party officials could explore alternatives to Seward. Lincoln's position was the same as Seward's—that slavery should not be allowed to enter new states—but he wished to deliver a message that would land well on his listeners so he could win popular sentiment. He needed to honor the past while still embracing the future.

His friend and biographer William Herndon later wrote, "No former effort in the line of speech-making had cost Lincoln so much time and thought as this one." For weeks, he spent long hours at the state library to find historical records to help him prove that a majority of the signatories to the US Constitution were *against* slavery. He showed through their comments and voting records that they had accepted slavery to ensure that the colonies would come together to form the new nation, but they had hoped the nation would someday redeem itself of the institution. In his speech, delivered at Cooper Union in New York City, Lincoln proposed that by limiting slavery from spreading to new states, the citizens would therefore be *continuing* on the course set by the founding fathers—to bear with slavery where they couldn't legally abolish it, but not to extend it. One audience member wrote, "When Lincoln rose to speak, I was greatly disappointed. He was . . . so angular and awkward that I had, for an instant, a feeling of pity for so ungainly a man." But then, "his face lighted up as with an inward fire; the whole man was transfigured. I forgot his clothes, his personal appearance, and his individual peculiarities. Presently, forgetting myself, I was on my feet like the rest . . . cheering this wonderful man."

Lincoln ultimately won an upset victory over Seward in the Republican primary, catapulting him into the presidential race. Sometimes opportunity comes and knocks lightly on our door, like it did for Lincoln when he received the invitation to speak in New York.

Will we recognize it and work harder than we've ever worked, so we, too, can seize the moment?

Lincoln's main opponent in the 1860 presidential race was, again, Stephen Douglas. This time, it was Lincoln who won—five years from the time he had considered himself a "flat failure" and Douglas a "splendid success." Remarkably, Lincoln barely spoke in public between his Cooper Union address and his inaugural address as president, though privately he continued influencing and guiding his campaigners and supporters. In an emotionally charged atmosphere, Lincoln recognized that nothing he said would sway the views of his opponents, nor would it matter to his supporters. We, too, may benefit on occasion from putting our public pursuit of Purpose on pause because the conditions are not conducive, even while continuing to invest in it in private.

America's southern states fiercely disagreed with Lincoln's position of not allowing slavery to expand into the nation's western territories. With Lincoln as president, those states felt that they had lost all influence with the federal government, and the Civil War began. Overnight, the rules of the game changed for Lincoln: his Purpose would now hinge on how effective he would be not as a politician or an administrator, but as commander in chief of the military. His assistant secretary of war later recounted, "It was not so at the beginning; but after three or four years of constant practice in the science and art of war, he arrived at this extraordinary knowledge of it. . . . He knew human nature. He knew what chord to strike and was never afraid to strike it when he knew the time had arrived." When we fuse with our Purpose, we acquire the drive to build whatever skills and play whatever roles are necessary to advance it.

Early in the Civil War, a Union army general issued, on his own, a proclamation to free all enslaved people in Missouri who belonged to enslavers who did not swear allegiance to the Union. Lincoln rescinded the general's proclamation, fearing that it may make slave-holding border states like Missouri and Kentucky leave the Union for the Confederacy. Among those who roundly criticized Lincoln for this action was Frederick Douglass, a formerly enslaved man who had escaped to the North, won his freedom, and dedicated himself to the abolition cause. Douglass announced that "the friends of freedom, the Union, and the Constitution, have been most basely betrayed." Two years later, Douglass traveled to the White House to meet with Lincoln and shared certain concerns about the treatment of black soldiers in the war. He later recounted, "Mr. Lincoln listened with earnest attention and with very apparent sympathy, and replied to each point in his own peculiar, forcible way." At the conclusion of their meeting, Douglass felt that "though I was not entirely satisfied with his views, I was so well satisfied with the man . . ." Even when we cannot immediately win over those who challenge our positions, we may find a way to engage with them that can warm their hearts and build mutual trust.

After a bloody battle at Gettysburg, Lincoln arrived at the battle-field to join the citizens gathered to commemorate the soldiers who had died there. His speech that day is remarkable for what it says, but even more so for what it doesn't say. He honored the soldiers who sacrificed their lives to defend the idea that "all men are equal" and that "Government of the people, by the people, and for the people shall not perish from the earth." Remarkably, he made no reference to who won or who lost, nor to the location or date of the battle. His focus lay beyond the horizon, on all people of all nations for all time to come. In our own pursuit of Purpose, we, too, can step back to frame it in terms not simply of what we wish to attain for our audience in the here and now, but of how those attainments could be a blueprint for advancing humanity toward a more ideal future.

Once, as president, Lincoln was considering a promotion for General Ulysses Grant after appreciating his performance in battle. Some advisors approached him to warn that Grant had a reputation for drinking too much. They expected Lincoln to reject Grant, especially since Lincoln himself was a teetotaler. Instead, Lincoln replied, "Ah! You surprise me, gentlemen. But can you tell me where he gets his whiskey? Because, if I can only find out, I will send a barrel of this wonderful whiskey to every soldier in the army." Lincoln was differentiating between the public values he was committed to propagating in the world and the private values he was committed to practicing on his own.

The further Lincoln progressed in his presidency, the fiercer his resolve became to abolish slavery. But the path to abolition was not clear. The only way to do so legally was for Congress to pass a constitutional amendment, for which there wasn't adequate political support. Lincoln initially thought the best way to achieve this goal was the way it had been done by other nations in the Americas where slavery had existed: gradually, over several decades, with financial compensation being paid by the government to slaveholders for giving up their "property." Two years into his term, Lincoln found a legal maneuver to more swiftly advance abolition. The law gave the federal government emergency powers to seize enemy property during war. Since the South after seceding had become an enemy of the nation, Lincoln drafted the Emancipation Proclamation, declaring all enslaved people in rebel states to be free. He made clear to his cabinet that he wasn't going to debate this move; his mind was made up. Members of his cabinet expressed a mixture of joy and concern.

William Seward—whom Lincoln had invited to join his cabinet even after running against him in the Republican primaries—was concerned that it would be a hollow gesture. The South had won all recent battles, so how would the proclamation have any material impact on the lives of enslaved people in the South if northern forces weren't able to support them in their quest to act on their legally mandated freedom? Lincoln accepted Seward's criticism, putting his plans on pause. He announced the proclamation weeks later, after the North had won a major victory in the Battle of Antietam. Like Lincoln, we may sometimes find ourselves pursuing the right action at the wrong time. Listening to dissenting voices and extracting the kernel of truth in their positions—without giving up our own principles—can help us refine and redefine our path to success.

Lincoln knew what he wished for—to create a world where all people had the right to "life, liberty, and the pursuit of happiness"—but he was not always correct about the steps to get there. His initial vision of a post–Civil War country was for formerly enslaved people who had been freed to be settled in a colony abroad, and he directed government officials to make such preparations. Eventually, and after being roundly criticized by some for that plan, he recognized the rights of black people to become equal citizens of the United States. We may have a pure Purpose at our Core, but its outer expression will require continual learning and adapting on our part.

As Lincoln's first presidential term drew to a close, Northerners were tiring of the war. Over six hundred thousand lives had been lost. The opposing Democratic Party promised to bring a rapid end to the war by negotiating peace with the Confederacy—the rebel states of the South. Republican leaders told Lincoln that public opinion had turned sharply against him, that "his re-election was an impossibility," and that he needed urgently to end the war. Lincoln was persuaded to draft a letter to the Confederacy offering a truce, with no conditions attached. But deep within, the idea troubled him. Under such an agreement, the push to end slavery would be stalled, and even the enslaved people who had been freed under the Emancipation Proclamation would have to be returned to the former slaveholders. This would have set the country on an entirely different trajectory. The day after he wrote the letter, he changed his mind and did not send it, allowing the war to go on and accepting that all he could do was try his best to resolve it on the right terms while he was president, leaving the ultimate outcome in the hands of a higher power. He told a Republican party official, "I am a beaten man, unless we can have some great victory." Two days later, the northern forces won a decisive battle in Atlanta. The direction of the Civil War turned sharply in the North's favor, public sentiment moved back toward support for Lincoln, and he won reelection.

With victory in the war appearing imminent, Lincoln wished at this stage to dissuade Northerners from feeling superior or vindictive toward their defeated fellow Americans. So he wielded the pen again to draft a speech for his second inauguration that would lay down the case for all Americans to approach this moment with grace and humility. He observed that both warring parties had claimed God to be on their side, and yet both parties had suffered huge losses. Thus, he argued, both parties must in some way bear responsibility for the injustice of slavery for which the suffering in this war was a sort of "karmic" consequence. He was hinting at how even Northerners were complicit in the institution of slavery, having "promoted, prolonged, and profited" from it for a long time. He ended the speech with a stirring invitation to the American people to come together "with malice toward none, with charity for all," to "bind up the nation's wounds," and "to do all which may achieve a just and lasting peace among ourselves and the rest of the world." Later that day, he welcomed, among others, Frederick Douglass as a guest to the White House and asked what he thought about the speech. Douglass replied, "Mr. President, that was a sacred effort."

Lincoln by now viewed the law not as an end unto itself, as he'd done before, but as a means to an end—an instrument to be used for the greater goal of creating a more just world. He bent the law in carefully calculated ways, suspending the writ of habeas corpus,* recognizing West Virginia as a new state without the constitutionally required permission of the parent state, Virginia, and declaring military rule in Kansas—all actions that the US Supreme Court later declared to be violations of the Constitution. As a Union victory in the Civil War became a near certainty, he made a push to finally bring an end to the institution of slavery, engaging in threats, lies, and bribes to secure votes among undecided members of the House of Representatives to pass a constitutional amendment that abolished slavery throughout the nation.

Frederick Douglass was later to say this about Lincoln: "Viewed from the genuine abolition ground, Mr. Lincoln seemed tardy, cold, dull, and indifferent; but measuring him by the sentiment of his country, a sentiment he was bound as a statesman to consult, he was swift, zealous, radical, and determined."

Like Lincoln, we will sometimes encounter strong headwinds and, at other times, tailwinds. We, too, won't have the ability to control everything. We will benefit from regulating our pace and path by

---

* The right of an arrested person to be brought in front of a judge or court.

stepping back whenever conditions change to ask ourselves, "Should I push, pull, pause, or pivot?"

Eleven weeks after the House passed the historic Thirteenth Amendment, Lincoln was assassinated. When he lay dying from the bullet wound, he must have felt a deep sense of peace knowing that these words he had once written were finally ringing true: "I am proud, in my passing speck of time, to contribute a humble mite to that glorious consummation which my own poor eyes may not last to see."

In his life's final—and finest—chapter, Lincoln acted not as a lawyer, democracy watchdog, or president, but as a follower of his inner voice, committed to helping every human secure something that Lincoln so deeply cherished for himself, "the right to rise." Perhaps the greatest lesson from Lincoln's journey is that to fully manifest our Purpose in an imperfect world, we need to meet people where they are and then move them closer to our desired future, sometimes through small steps and sometimes through big leaps, being guided not by a fixed road map but by an adaptive calculus—a calculus that continually reaffirms our Core Purpose and then reexpresses it in the most suitable goals as conditions change.

Chapter 6

LIVING WITH WISDOM

৯৯

Wisdom is nothing but a preparation of the soul, a
capacity, a secret art of thinking, feeling and breathing thoughts of unity at every moment of life.

—*Hermann Hesse*

SAVING MY BABY

"Rick, help me save my baby!" The year was 2002, and I was devastated. My three-year-old was being wrested out of my loving
hands, and I was fighting against the odds to hold on to it. This baby
was my startup, Paramark.

As its founding CEO, I cared deeply about Paramark. It meant
the world to me. We had raised $10 million in venture capital during
a euphoric period in Silicon Valley, and we were not yet profitable.
With the funds running out, we were seeking our next round of
financing. However, the climate was by then very different. Internet
stocks had crashed, and investors were skittish about supporting
startups. Our lead investor had decided they wanted to merge our
startup with another company in their portfolio. They were asking
my cofounders and me to surrender control and ownership in return
for stock in this other company and the opportunity to keep working
on our vision under the other firm's management. That plan was

111

unacceptable to me since I did not believe in the other company's vision or business prospects.

The fight was on in our board of directors, with our lead investor on one side and me on the other. I flew to New York to arrange alternative sources of financing so I could make a counterbid on Paramark. With a new source of funding in place, I called Rick, an early angel investor and a valued mentor, from a hotel in New York City. I shared with him the strategy and financial plan I had come up with and sought his advice on how to manage the dynamics with Paramark's board and legal counsel to make sure I would win.

I remember Rick's response to this day. He paused, as if he were shifting gears in his mind. "Hitendra," he said, "why do you want to buy Paramark?"

I had put my blood, toil, tears, and sweat into Paramark for three years! It had been my first, my last, my everything! I fumbled to find words to express the mix of conviction and confusion I felt. "Rick, this is my startup. If they acquire it, I am certain it will die. How can I allow them to do that?"

"I understand," Rick replied. "But are you certain that sustaining Paramark is what you want to dedicate your energies to at this stage of life?"

"Of course I am!" I thought. "Does he expect that I will abandon my company?" Instead, I said, "I appreciate your guidance, as always, Rick. Let me reflect on what you've said."

But I didn't. I put Rick's remarks aside and made a counteroffer to purchase Paramark. The investor won the board battle, and I lost control over my company. Two years later, the company that the investor had merged Paramark with shut down. Things had gone just as I had feared. But by then I had long since made peace with losing control, and I was even, much to my surprise, grateful for that outcome. Because over time, I had realized the wisdom in Rick's remarks.

Rick had been probing my underlying motivations and could see that I was operating from a place of blind attachment, a belief that "I must save my baby," a desire to not lose my dream, a sense of anger and betrayal, and an unwillingness to face a moment of public failure—and he could sense that those forces were clouding my judgment. If I had allowed myself to rise above the emotional fray, as he had done, I might have concluded on my own that it was time to move on. The vision for Paramark was strong, but its business model was broken. Had I acquired the company, I would have locked myself in for a years-long struggle to breathe life into a tired entity instead of rebooting my career. I thought my dream had crumbled—but in losing Paramark, I found myself. I moved to New York, started teaching at Columbia, and built a whole new vision for my life and my work.

Truth had come knocking on my door in the form of Rick's advice that day, but I was not yet ready to receive it. As a former math addict, a PhD, a consultant, and a founder and CEO who had raised several million dollars and built a thirty-person team that included PhDs in math, computer science, and engineering from Stanford, Princeton, MIT, and Harvard, I was admittedly not lacking in intelligence. So, what was I lacking?

THE ESSENCE OF WISDOM

By enthroning intelligence as the capstone quality for success, we have been worshipping a false god—or at least an incomplete god. We have designed our educational institutions, awards, assessments, and hiring practices around the premise that the more intelligent you are, the more value you bring to the world and the more successful you will be. I got swept up in this mass cult of intelligence as I was growing up. While other kids were reading comic books, I would complete logic puzzles and IQ tests in hot pursuit of the holy grail of intelligence. Over time, I sought to be part of elite institutions filled with highly intelligent people. But I noticed something troubling: more intelligent people weren't necessarily happier, healthier, or more virtuous than less intelligent people, nor were they more successful in relationships. Science is now corroborating my anecdotal observations.

At that crisis moment in my conversation with Rick about the future of Paramark, I was not open to reviewing the situation with fresh eyes, or to accepting the contrarian counsel of a caring mentor, or to reflecting objectively on my startup's prospects. My intelligence was being hobbled by my intention. Research shows that when we make choices, our intellect does not act independently but in service of our intention: the desire we have for a certain outcome, a certain version of "truth," shaped by our emotions, thoughts, beliefs, and attachments. When we are attached to an idea, our intelligence marches forth to prove that the idea is true and to protect and safeguard it from attack. It scans selectively for facts, arguments, and sources that support the idea, and it attacks the reliability of facts, arguments, and sources that challenge it. The more intelligent we are, the more adept we will be at marshaling arguments in service of our intention. A less intelligent person might, in the face of evidence that contradicts their objective, give up at some point and accept that they are wrong. But a more intelligent person will find inventive ways to challenge any data, argument, or expert that opposes their viewpoint. When we have a flawed intention, our intellect becomes our own worst enemy. Psychologists call this "myside bias."

And it gets worse. Research shows that the higher your IQ, the more likely you are to believe you are not prone to such intelligence malfunctions; you believe that myside bias is for lesser intellects. Your own cleverness becomes a trap: you are less likely to check your assumptions, challenge your thinking, or ask for other people's opinions. You stay stuck in a wrong groove, and your capacity to self-correct and grow your understanding is arrested.

We think we are free to make the best choices for ourselves, seldom realizing the silent but potent ways in which flawed intentions can fog our minds, loosen our grasp on truth, and skew our choices. A well-honed intelligence by itself is insufficient to lift this veil of delusion. To see through an accurate mental lens, our intentions must arise from our Inner Core, not our ego. For this, we need to cultivate a hunger to uncover the truth in all matters, embrace it in whatever form it comes to us, abandon dearly held beliefs if they conflict with truth, and follow whatever trail truth wishes to take us down in the service of our Purpose. That is the essence of Wisdom.

An ancient Indian epic, the Katha Upanishad, provides an apt metaphor for Wisdom. Think of your body as a chariot, of which you—your Inner Core—are the lord. You wish to move your chariot forward toward a meaningful destination. The horses—your emotions, thoughts, beliefs, and desires—are what give you energy to move the chariot forward. But left to themselves, one horse might get lazy and want to sit under a shady tree, while another might go wild and turn in the wrong direction. You need a charioteer to rein in and direct the horses. That charioteer is Wisdom.

THE POWER OF WISDOM

By attuning us to truth, Wisdom ensures that we approach all life's moments and challenges from an illuminated place. And yet it sometimes feels more comfortable to hide from the truth. Then we can buffer ourselves from uncomfortable realizations, bend our perceptions to our preferences, and feel no compulsion to challenge or change our favored emotions or beliefs. But this way of life is a fool's paradise. In the long run, living based on limiting emotions and beliefs, and the behaviors they trigger in us, can damage our health, bedevil our mind, erode our performance, and compromise our relationships. By sidestepping Wisdom, we create the conditions that will one day cause us to wake up and discover that we have been living a lie.

THE PATH OF WISDOM

The path of Wisdom guides us through five layers of our mind, presented here as five stages, culminating in the reward of intuitive perception.

Stage 1: Master Your Emotions

Vincent van Gogh wrote, "Let's not forget that the little emotions are the great captains of our lives and we obey them without realizing it." We typically believe that some emotions are good and others are bad. In actuality, every emotion can be good, and every emotion can be bad.

Anger, for example, is usually seen as a bad emotion, and with good reason. When you are caught in the grip of anger, you think, say, and do things you may later regret. You may strain and sometimes sever relations by engaging in disrespectful speech or behavior. Instead of building bridges, you destroy them. Your judgment is blurred and you make bad choices. Someone who does not have your best interests at heart may take advantage of your short fuse by deliberately riling you so you make the wrong move in an interview, negotiation, or competitive sport. Anger is infectious and mutually reinforcing. When you express it in a conversation, the other person may respond in kind, causing you to react with even more anger. At that point, it may be too late to turn the situation around—what was a spark is now a raging fire. Anger also negatively affects your health. People who have a high propensity for anger are at significantly greater risk of heart disease. And anger can sometimes keep you in its grip for hours and days after the initial trigger, distracting you from being mindfully engaged in your everyday moments; you nod your head politely to someone at work or a friend at dinner, but your mind is actually consumed with angry thoughts about an argument that happened at work that day.

Yet anger can also be a force for good. It makes you wake up and pay attention to what is not right in our world. It gives you the motivation and energy to act. It causes you to lose your fear. It supports you as you rise above constraints and setbacks to keep fighting the good fight. It helps you galvanize people toward collective action on a righteous cause. When people see your anger, it can prompt them to take you seriously. Gandhi said, "As heat conserved is transmuted into energy, even so our anger controlled can be transmuted into a power that can move the world."

Optimism is usually seen as a good emotion. It gives you motivation to work harder at your goal. It keeps you resilient in turbulent times. You are more creative, because you keep looking for new solutions. Optimism has been shown to drive success in education and in many professions. Visionary people have to be optimists, for visionaries are people who can see untapped possibilities where others see only boundaries and constraints. Optimists inspire others with their positive beliefs about the future, infect others with their positivity, and draw others to them. They are happier people and much less likely than pessimists to suffer from depression. Optimists are also physically healthier. Research studies that have tracked people over several decades have showed that optimism adds on average ten years to your life (relative to pessimism).

But optimism can hurt you when it causes you to ignore possible scenarios that could go wrong. When you are optimistic, you may fail to take adequate preventive measures, or to formulate a plan B. To anticipate problem situations, it helps to view things through a pessimistic lens. Optimism can also fool you into making fatal miscalculations about the future, allow you to ignore simmering problems that over time become big and unresolvable, and lull you into underpreparing for high-stakes moments. Moreover, a leader who spouts unambiguously optimistic messages to the team—"We will win!"—at a time when all looks dark and gloomy can come across as unrealistic, even unhinged, and unworthy of the team's trust. Sometimes the downside scenario you have ignored comes true, potentially killing your dream, and even killing you.

What, then, might emotional mastery look like? It certainly should not mean that you disconnect from your emotions, because then they will not be able to guide or motivate you. And it should not mean that you freely identify with and express all emotions, because some of them can take you down a bad path. Mastery is more nuanced.

FOUR STEPS TO EMOTIONAL MASTERY

1. **Be aware, moment by moment, of your emotional state.**
   Without this awareness, you will miss valuable signals or be misled by flawed feelings. An emotion like anxiety can alert you to risks and past learnings that may otherwise be hidden from conscious view, while an emotion like optimism may make you more willing to take risks than you ought to be.

2. **Assess whether your emotional response in any given situation is appropriate by exploring the following possible scenarios:**

   - *The emotion you are experiencing has nothing to do with your present context.* If you arrive at work with your mind in a state of agitation because of a fight you had with your spouse that morning, the right thing to do is to first acknowledge your emotional state to yourself, then calm your emotions down, and then shift your attention to your work interactions. Otherwise, science shows, your behavior and decision-making at work will be influenced, erroneously so, by this emotion that has nothing to do with your work.

   - *The emotion is counterproductive.* I sometimes get riled up when I think a colleague has done something wrong, only to discover that I gave them unclear or wrong directions. Before acting on such an emotion, it's important to first examine and understand the situation to know if the emotion has any value at all.

   - *The emotion is both relevant and useful.* In that case, tune into it to gain the maximum insight and motivation.

   - *You are not experiencing a certain emotion that you could really benefit from.* Perhaps you'd benefit from a little anxiety because you are being too casual about a deadline. Or from a little unhappiness because you are being too passive about disruptive conduct from some teammates.

- *You're experiencing a mix of emotions—even conflicting ones.* Getting an email from a prospective client that says "we decided to go with someone else" may make you sad that your team lost the deal, but it could also trigger relief that you won't have to take on another client at a busy time for the company. Tune into all the emotions, unpack them, then use the earlier options to make the right call about which ones to keep and which ones to dial down (see the next step.)

3. **Dial emotions down or up as needed, based on what you discover in step 2.**

   - *How to dial down an emotion:* Create some distance from the situation that has provoked it by finding a way to hit pause: go for a walk, perform some other form of exercise, take a shower, put on soothing music. Close your eyes and zoom out, visualizing the emotion-triggering event in the larger context of your life. Take several slow, deep breaths. Or sleep on the situation and see how you feel the next day.

   - *How to dial up an emotion:* Act out the emotion in your tone, words, facial expressions, and body language. By mimicking the physical aspects of an emotion, you are more likely to initiate and intensify it. If you'd like to feel more cheerful, act like you are cheerful; if you'd like to feel less angry, act like you are calm. But don't just act it. Believe that the emotion is true to you in that moment so you can let it flow authentically.

4. **Finally, direct your emotion toward a productive end.**

   If you're feeling discouraged about your prospects for success, perhaps that sentiment is telling you that you need to work harder or ask for help from someone. If you're feeling remorseful about something you did or said, perhaps you need to apologize in a heartfelt manner and commit to ceasing that conduct. If you're feeling anxious about a project, perhaps you need to investigate the risks and address them.

When you reach a state where you can stay aware of your emotions, identify which ones are right for the present context, dial them up or down as needed, and direct them toward the desired end, know that you would have made Aristotle proud. He said, "Anybody can become angry, that is easy; but to be angry with the right person, and to the right degree, and at the right time, and for the right purpose, and in the right way, that is not within everybody's power, that is not easy."

Stage 2: Untwist Your Thinking

I once taught a course at Columbia titled "Driving Strategic Impact." One of my students, Maria, was totally disengaged during class, which upset and unnerved me. On some days I would exit the classroom annoyed with myself, thinking, "Maria was so disengaged today. My class must have been quite dull and irrelevant. I'm so incompetent!" On other days I would fume at her: "Maria was disengaged again today. She must be at business school just to land the right job. What a nightmare to have to teach these kinds of students." After class one day, midsemester, Maria approached me and said, "Professor, can I have five minutes of your time?"

I sat down with her in the corner of the classroom. She said, "I have to confess, I have been quite disengaged in class this whole semester."

I thought, "Oh, wow. Finally, she's admitting it. The truth is out." I said to her, "Okay, yes, tell me about it," attempting to sound casual.

"It's all quite painful," Maria continued. "During the summer break, my father passed away. Ever since I've returned to school this fall, I have found it a real struggle to be motivated." She described feeling disconnected from her classmates. She fretted that job-recruiting season was just starting, and that her family had high hopes for her— yet she was still trying to cope with her father's death. "I know you teach a class on personal leadership," she said. "I was wondering if you might have some guidance to give me on how I can make peace with my loss and learn to move on."

Can you imagine what a fool I felt like in that moment? I had been flip-flopping between thinking I was a bad teacher and thinking she was a bad student, while all along it had been about her painful personal loss. All those hours and days I had spent being upset—how wasteful, how unnecessary!

A few decades ago, two pathbreaking psychotherapists, Albert Ellis in New York and Aaron Beck at University of Pennsylvania, quite independently of each other, stumbled into the same insight that the Stoic philosophers in Greece had discovered some twenty-three hundred years earlier: our emotions aren't caused by the things that happen to us, but by the thoughts these events trigger. I've benefited from learning about the beautiful discipline of cognitive behavioral therapy from one of its preeminent exponents, Dr. David Burns of Stanford University; this section is largely based on his work.

My feelings of frustration didn't arise because Maria was disengaged, but because of the thoughts that her disengagement triggered in me: that my class was dull and irrelevant, or that she was academically unmotivated. These are ANTs—automatic negative thoughts. We experience them all the time. "This project is a disaster." "Those people just don't understand." "It's useless talking to him." "She is so uncaring." "I'll never be able to do this right." In situations where we experience ANTs, we depart from fact-based reasoning and fall prey to mental distortions. My favorite distortions are the following:

FIVE COMMON MENTAL DISTORTIONS

Mindreading: When I thought, "My class is dull and irrelevant," I was assuming that Maria was disengaged because she didn't like the class. Mindreading happens when we assume we know what the other person is thinking or feeling. "I haven't heard back from him. He must have not liked my proposal." Mindreading can have a punishing impact on our interactions and relationships. And our digital age has made mindreading even more pervasive. You text someone, and now that it's been twenty seconds and they haven't texted you back, you think, "He doesn't love me." Ten minutes later he responds after coming out of a meeting, and now you are at peace—until your next mindreading crisis.

Mental filtering: Mental filtering makes you pay attention to a small set of observations and ignore all others. In entertaining the thought "My class is dull and irrelevant," I was ignoring how engaged the *other* forty-three students were. You might focus on one critical comment someone made during a meeting, ignoring the positive comments others made, or on a few disappointing actions by someone you know, looking past all their positive contributions.

Labeling: When I called myself "incompetent" or described the situation as a "nightmare," I was labeling—using dismissive words that caricature one's thinking and feelings about situations and people. When your thoughts include words like "moron," "disgusting," "ridiculous," "frustrating," or "craving," you're likely labeling. These words carry a strong emotional punch, trapping us in an extreme view and restricting us from thinking more freely and objectively.

Blame: When I concluded that my class was no good, I was engaging in self-blame. When I concluded that Maria had no academic motivation, I was engaging in other-blame. In this mental distortion, you assign blame to yourself or to others, while the true cause for a problem may lie elsewhere, as it did in this case.

All-or-nothing thinking: In Chapter 2 we encountered the research scientist Babette and her boss, Gordon. When Gordon told Babette that her paper was "rubbish," his comment was motivated by his unhappiness with the quality of writing in the paper, and he was ignoring the strong research it reported on. He had fallen into the trap of all-or-nothing thinking, which causes us to view things in a polarized manner, as wholly good or wholly bad. Someone is either a hero or a zero. A certain choice is either perfect or totally flawed. Either your job is great, or it sucks. Either your subordinate is awesome, or they're awful. In most cases, people and situations are more textured and truth more nuanced.

Distorted thoughts typically have a whiplash effect on our emotions, making us experience an unproductive dose of anger, anxiety, or other emotions. Our aim should be to replace these ill-conceived ANTs with thoughts that are more precise, logical, and fact based. When you find yourself getting consumed by ANTs, challenge your thinking through questions like "Am I mindreading here? Filtering? Blaming? Labeling? Engaging in all-or-nothing thinking?" "Is there good evidence to support the ANT's claim?" "What additional evidence should I collect before reaching a conclusion?" "Could there be another explanation for this?" "Could the opposite of this also be true, and if so, what's a more balanced view?" "Instead of calling it a 'nightmare,' could I call it 'very troubling'?"

I could have challenged myself with questions like these in the class that Maria was enrolled in. That would have helped me replace the ANT that said "My class is dull and irrelevant" with "Other students seem quite engaged, so something must be going on with Maria. I should check in with her to learn how she's doing."

Henry David Thoreau wrote, "As a single footstep will not make a path on the earth, so a single thought will not make a pathway in the mind. To make a deep physical path, we walk again and again. To make a deep mental path, we must think over and over the kind of thoughts we wish to dominate our lives." Once you have a rescripted thought to replace an ANT, repeat the new thought whenever the ANT gets triggered. For it *will* get triggered, again and likely again. But with sufficient repetition, you will one day have a new thought-groove in your brain, and the old ANT-groove will dissolve away.

An executive at one of my workshops, Rohan, described a powerful personal journey. A plant worker, Kamal, was to be given the Employee of the Year award at the annual holiday party of a production facility where Rohan was head of human resources. A few days before the event, which was to be a gala affair in the small town where the company resided, Kamal came to Rohan's office, looking very anxious, asking that he not be made to speak in front of the group on the day of the event. Rohan was in a rush to get to a meeting, and he'd heard this concern before. He told Kamal, "Congratulations for this recognition you are receiving. Don't worry. This happens every year. You are afraid of public speaking, isn't that it? We'll prepare a very short speech for you, and all you need to do is read it. You'll be fine—trust me. Now I must go to meet with some executives on an important matter." And then Rohan moved on.

On the day of the event, Kamal did not show up. His employers later discovered that he had died by suicide that morning. He had been having an affair, and the woman he was involved with had wanted their relationship to become public, but he didn't. When she learned of his impending award, she threatened to blow their cover by walking up to the stage when it was Kamal's time to make a speech. That was the reason for Kamal's anxiety, not a fear of public speaking.

Rohan had thought, "I *know* what's on Kamal's mind. He'll be fine once we give him a script to read. I'm great at managing people issues, and I've got this one. This is a trivial issue." These assumptions had prevented Rohan from pausing, inquiring, and discovering the true cause of Kamal's discomfort. These weren't negative thoughts—they were positive thoughts. And yet the thoughts contained distortions like mindreading, all-or-nothing thinking, and labeling. There is a sobering lesson here for us all. When you feel highly confident, impatient, proud, powerful, or bold, take pause to see if you are engaging in any APTs—automatic positive thoughts—that may be clouding your mental lens. Use the same approach I've described with ANTs to challenge and rescript your APTs.

Ten years ago, I began to experience symptoms of poor health. I consulted with a doctor, then another, and then a third. All of them diagnosed in me the onset of a chronic disease that the National Institutes of Health calls "rare, progressive and irreversible." They could not do anything about it, they said, besides prescribe me immunosuppressant drugs that would regrettably have a harsh effect on my immunity. I refused the medications and accepted my destiny. Every time I experienced ANTs ("This is terrible! This will destroy your life, your dreams, your everything!"), I countered them with more affirming thoughts ("I'm mostly OK. My inflammation will go away in an hour or two. I'm not dying").

But my health slowly grew worse. One day, quite suddenly, I found myself welling up with deep, unresolved feelings. I was forced that day to accept that my ANTs were *true*, not distorted. This *was* quite terrible. It *did* seem to be just a matter of time before the disease would destroy my life, my dreams, my everything.

What does one do when one's ANTs are true?

For a few minutes, I cried. It was the first time I had acknowledged my sense of utter despair about what was happening to my body. Then I rose and paced up and down my apartment. "These thoughts you are having are true, Hitendra. Now what are you going to do about it?" I decided I wanted to find a pathway to healing. If the medical experts weren't going to get me there, I would look elsewhere. I flew to India to visit a monk in the Himalayas whom I had known for thirty years. After hearing me out, he responded, "Hitendra, tell me about your diet."

Much good came out of the monk's counsel, all centered on reforming my food choices. I changed my diet completely. Two years later, my symptoms disappeared, and my body started to repair the damage wrought by the disease. I have never experienced the symptoms again. My physician described the disappearance of the disease as a minor miracle. I owe a lifelong debt to the monk and to that moment when I finally allowed myself to accept that my ANTs were true.

We all go through occasional experiences that are deeply upsetting. They trigger in us negative thoughts that are not distorted, but true. It is natural in such moments to want to wallow a bit in misery, consumed by our ANTs, lamenting our fate. Wisdom invites us to acknowledge the important though uncomfortable truths in our ANTs and then say to ourselves, "Thank you, ANT, for pointing me to an uncomfortable truth. Now what am I going to do about it?" This is how we move from being a victim to being a hero in our life story. We may not be able to change our circumstance, but we can, by taking appropriate action, change our response to it.

On any given day, I, like you, have thousands of thoughts. Some of them I am proud of, some less so, and some are an outright embarrassment. Trying to figure out why unproductive words or thoughts arise will only take me down a rabbit hole. Perhaps a belief became ingrained in me through some childhood experiences. Perhaps I've inherited a certain way of speaking or thinking from my environment. Or perhaps the belief was in my DNA, based on habits of thought I'd acquired in lives past. Does it really matter? The important thing is for me to discern a good thought from a bad one, a fact-based one from a distorted one, an empowering one from a victimizing one. And so, moment by moment, I play the inner game of noting and regulating each thought as it comes. Those I wish to disown I allow to deflect off the surface of my consciousness. Most of these are legacy thoughts, habits of my past, and I do not wish to wallow in them. Those I wish to affirm I make my own, repeating them to myself and holding on to them like a loyal friend. And from those I have mixed feelings about, I extract the part that is true and untwist the part that is distorted, scripting an improved version of the thought that I then welcome into my inner chamber. Every time I resculpt such thoughts I am beautifying myself from within.

Stage 3: Evolve Your Beliefs

Four years after my parents got married, my father was serving in Punjab state as an officer of the Indian Police Service. A skirmish broke out on Punjab's border with Pakistan, and, tragically, some Indian border guards were killed. The chief minister of Punjab* faced great pressure to show that he was being decisive and taking responsibility. So he found a scapegoat in my father and demoted him to a lower rank in the police force. My father was devastated. He had played no role in the mishap and had been turned into a pawn in a larger political game. He was proud of having succeeded at making it into India's elite civil service after much struggle in his early life; this career gave him an opportunity to grow beyond his family's lower-class roots. And it was a primary reason my mother's parents, who came from a much higher rung of the social ladder, had agreed to allow their daughter to marry him. The demotion, he believed, would shatter the family's reputation. During that dark period, he returned home from work one day in a grave mood and announced to my mother, "The time has come. You need to prepare to live independently."

"Why?" my mother asked, bewildered. "Where are you intending to go?"

"I have received word that the chief minister plans to fire me from the police force this week on trumped-up charges because of the way I have protested his earlier action. Once I receive notice that he has let me go, I will ask for a meeting with him. On the appointed day, I will wear my police uniform, walk into his office, take out my revolver, and shoot him. I will be arrested and receive a sentence of life imprisonment or worse. You will have to then raise our daughter on your own." His twenty-two-year-old wife, her firstborn in her arms, was speechless in shock.

---

* This is the equivalent of the governor of an American state: the elected official who runs the state's administration.

Why did my father decide on such a radical course of action? An event from the year 1947, when he was seventeen, may help us understand. That was the year India gained its independence from British rule and was partitioned into two separate nations. Millions of people migrated across the new border, religious tensions flared, and riots broke out. Hindus killed Muslims, Muslims killed Hindus, and over one million people died. My father's family, who were Hindus, lived in a village located in what was going to become the Islamic state of Pakistan. They learned that a large crowd of Muslim rioters was closing in on their community, intent on raping and killing Hindus. To save the young women from the terrible fate they feared awaited them, the elders agreed that the young women should be killed right away. My father's oldest sister was rushed to the rooftop and beheaded by her own uncle's sword, as was his brother's wife. Mercifully, before other women in the family could meet with the same fate, an escape route was forged. The family fled the village, made their way to India, and began life anew.

The family had decided to sacrifice their young women because they believed, as was the custom in their community, that death was preferable to dishonor. When my father resolved to shoot the chief minister and to accept the punishment that would come to him as a result, he was acting on the same belief, and on the belief that an attack on one's honor must be met with a commensurately punitive response to save face. As luck would have it, the chief minister did not fire his would-be assassin. My father's rage died down, and he found a more peaceful path to justice. He filed a legal petition to reverse his demotion on the grounds that he had not abandoned his duty. When the state high court dismissed his request, he appealed the decision to India's supreme court. He could not afford the high fees of a supreme court lawyer, so he decided to learn the law and argue his case in India's highest court by himself. This time, the court ruled in his favor, and he gained his rank and reputation—and with that, his life—back.

Over time, my father mellowed. He encountered many challenges, including threats to his career, reputation, and life, but he never made a wrong move out of a miscalculated need to salvage honor or exact vengeance. That's because his beliefs had changed. In the years I knew him, his deep concern was for justice over public honor. And the weapon he used in his fights for justice was the courts. He earned a law degree, and during his police career and later in retirement, he fought many legal cases to remedy injustices and serve the common good.

When we go beyond our emotions and thoughts to dig deeper in the soil of our consciousness, we eventually hit the hard rocks of our beliefs. Beliefs define the frame through which we perceive the world. They shape our thoughts, motivations, actions, and, ultimately, our lives. Wisdom invites us to choose our beliefs wisely, and to challenge and change those that are holding us back from seeing the fullest possibilities. Yet we seldom if ever consciously rescript our beliefs. We encountered this phenomenon earlier in the chapter: the idea of myside bias. When we hold a certain belief—"My partner is uncaring," "This career is going nowhere," "We need to make this investment"—we perceive the world through the lens of that belief. We pay attention to the facts that support our beliefs, ignore the ones that don't, and take actions guided by the beliefs.

How can you ferret out your limiting beliefs, the ones that are holding you back? After all, some of your most closely held beliefs may be false, but you may never realize it if you don't open yourself up to questioning them.

I believe each of us goes through cycles of birth, life, death, and reincarnation until we evolve our consciousness into realizing our true divine nature. I believe in karma, that our every thought and action sets into motion a force that will return to us in a mathematically precise way in this life or a future life, so that over time and across lives we start to understand the consequences of our conduct and progress toward enlightenment.

Perhaps you believe that people are simply physical beings; that when our body dies, we disappear forever from existence, our consciousness extinguished; that people do what they do, good or bad, without any karmic outcomes; that some human beings are incorrigibly bad, with no divine potential.

If you and I hold two opposing beliefs, then at least one of us is entrapped in a false conviction. Perhaps it is me, perhaps it is you. One way we might attempt to draw out the truth is by engaging in a dialog, listening to each other's points of view, and staying open to revising those beliefs that we discover are incomplete or flawed. But that is not going to happen. You see, I am not open to putting time and effort into questioning my most dearly held convictions. They are my bedrocks. I am very happy and comfortable with them; they give me tremendous clarity, understanding, and grounding; they are my closest friends. Instead of pouring energy in investigating alternative opinions, I would rather devote energy to deepening my understanding of my beliefs and translating them into right action. If I am not open to questioning my cherished views, what gives me the right to encourage you to question yours? Neither you nor I wish to shake up the beliefs that define us at our Core. And yet some of those beliefs may be seriously flawed. Should we simply reconcile with the idea that we'll never discover which were right and which were wrong?

It does not have to be that way. Life has given us a powerful aid to help us unearth our limiting beliefs: adversity. Each of us experiences times when things don't go our way. We struggle to get the results we are looking for, mourn the loss of people or things that are taken from us, or feel beaten up in some other way. What are we to do in such difficult moments?

How Adversity Can Reform Our Beliefs

All cultures have myths—stories that are passed from one generation to the next, that encode the community's basic values. Joseph Campbell studied myths from across the world. He discovered that although cultural myths were quite varied in their outer form, they were very similar in their inner structure. Every myth contains a hero's journey. The hero is enjoying an uneventful life until one day he is struck by adversity. At first, he seeks to tackle his challenges by seeking to change his circumstances, but that does not work. He then discovers, in his moment of greatest despair and often with the guidance of an illuminated mentor, that what he really needs to change is himself. He experiences a big shift in his beliefs. A limiting belief is shattered; a new, empowered one takes root. He starts to think and act with Wisdom. Having accomplished this personal transformation, he is able to take on the challenge and emerge victorious.

You and I have the opportunity to go on this hero's journey every time we encounter adversity. We become true heroes not when we simply accept the adversity, nor when we instinctively fight it, but when we go within our Core and ask ourselves, "What am I meant to learn from this?" The answer may not come immediately, but if we create a space for humble inquiry, it will come, and it will take one of three forms.

First, our inner voice may tell us, "You're not winning because you're approaching this the wrong way. You hold a limiting belief that you need to challenge." This happened to me once when I was at McKinsey. I was working in the Chicago office, expecting to be staffed on a new engagement. A partner in New York offered to have me lead a digital marketing project for his client. I was keen to work on digital, so this was going to be ideal. But my staffing manager in Chicago, Sarah, wanted me to take on a different engagement with a home furnishings company. She pushed, then I pushed, and we paused. We picked up the conversation the next day, and the next, but neither of us was giving in. Then a senior director who had been an erstwhile champion for me took me aside to say, in effect, "Hitendra, fall in line." I was quite shattered. McKinsey had told us when we were hired that we could "Make my own McKinsey." And now I was being told to do Sarah's bidding and give up on my digital dream!

Much later, I recognized that the problem in that case wasn't McKinsey's broken promise; it was my limiting beliefs. I had believed that when two people clash, for one to win the other must lose, and I didn't want to lose. But in fact, there is often a way to allow both people to win. I could have accepted Sarah's request to take on the home furnishings project, and in turn asked for her commitment to find and staff me on a digital project in three months. My digital dream would have been deferred, not destroyed. I believed that the firm owed me something because I was doing so well, rather than believing, more correctly, that there is always give-and-take—you do for the firm, and the firm does for you. In subsequent years, I've approached such situations with better beliefs, and they have helped me obtain better outcomes.

Alternatively, our inner voice may tell us, "You brought this adversity upon yourself without knowing it, because you've got a flawed belief. Change this belief now so you and others may avert such difficulties in the future." That's what I learned from my health challenge. I had assumed I was living a healthy-enough lifestyle; that as long as I *looked* healthy, I *was* healthy; that having a chronic disease must simply come from bad luck, bad genes, or bad karma; that certain food products that promoted themselves as healthy, well, they must be healthy. The monk's guidance, and my experience since, has made me rescript those views. I now believe that certain processed foods can slowly erode your health. I understand that a person may appear healthy from the outside even while certain lifestyle choices could be inflicting slow damage on vital body parts, showing up years later as chronic illness. I now recognize that chronic disease can in many cases be the body's way of saying to us, "I've been doing the best I can for you, but it's becoming increasingly hard, so I'm sending you this appeal. Take better care of me."

A third scenario is that our inner voice may say, "You are suffering because you believe there's nothing redemptive about the experience you are going through. You will be at peace once you accept your situation and translate the pain you're struggling with into a noble, uplifting purpose." By the age of thirty-six, V. R. Ferose was leading a five-thousand-person group at SAP and winning leadership awards. The world was his oyster. Then his eighteen-month-old son, Vivaan, was diagnosed with autism, and his world came crashing down. A mentor told him, "You are fortunate, Ferose. Most people need to find their purpose. In your case, your purpose has found you." It was a turning point. His wife, Deepali, and he decided that for a period of time she would prepare Vivaan for the world, while he would prepare the world for Vivaan. Ferose started an initiative within SAP to hire people with autism, demonstrating that although they may lack social skills, they may be especially talented at certain focused, repetitive, attention-to-detail tasks such as software testing. His success culminated in the company's co-CEO committing to hiring 1 percent of their workforce from among people with autism. Ferose has since launched a number of global initiatives to create opportunities for people with disabilities, including an inclusion summit and an inclusion fellowship. His work continues to inspire many to forge their own path to finding meaning out of disability. Ferose's transformation began with him accepting his situation and then channeling his pain into a cause that had deep meaning for him. As Viktor Frankl, a renowned psychotherapist and Holocaust survivor, wrote, "When we are no longer able to change a situation, we are challenged to change ourselves."

What if there is no apparent purpose to translate one's pain into? During his imprisonment, Nelson Mandela found much solace from a poem titled "Invictus." Its author, William Henley, suffered from tuberculosis, ultimately succumbing to the disease at fifty-three. "Invictus" was his message affirming that even when we are denied an outer victory, we can always earn an inner victory. The last four lines of the poem read,

> *It matters not how strait the gait,*
> *How charged with punishments the scroll,*
> *I am the master of my fate,*
> *I am the captain of my soul.*

I invite you to commit these lines to memory, take them to heart, and recite them with conviction when your spirit feels a bit broken.

"A smooth life," Yogananda noted, "is not a victorious life." When you experience adversity and can't seem to move beyond despair, take aim not at the world, not at yourself, but at the beliefs that may be holding you back—because a belief that is thwarting your progress toward peace and possibilities is one worth shattering.

Getting to Higher Truths by Fusing Opposites

Is there a way to proactively evolve your beliefs and take them closer toward Wisdom without waiting for adversity to strike? This brings me to a story told by Stanley, a US Secret Service officer who participated in one of my leadership workshops:

> My wife, Melanie, and I were sitting on the back porch of our home in Washington, DC, when a man with a gun broke in to our backyard. With the gun pointing at me, he said, "Go back into your home, pick up all the valuables—jewelry, cash—put them in this bag, and bring it back to me."
>
> As a security expert, I was mentally preparing myself for my next move when Melanie said to the armed man with deep concern in her voice, "I can't believe you're doing this. What could ever compel you to take this kind of risk? You must be going through a difficult time." After a pause, she continued, "You know, my husband and I were just having some wine and we were going to have dinner in a few minutes. Why don't you join us? I want to hear about what's happening in your life because I am really worried about you."
>
> My jaw dropped when I heard her. But the next minute this man had put down his gun and was sitting with us, having dinner. After the meal, as he was reaching for his gun, I said, "Sir, you can leave but you cannot take this gun." The personal story he had shared with us at dinner was of course a very sad one, and I didn't want him to run into any more trouble, with others or himself. And so he left without his gun.
>
> The next day there was a knock on the door, and it was him. He said, "Listen, I have not come here for the gun. I just wanted to let you and your wife know that I'm deeply grateful. Thank you for what you did for me last night."

How would you or I have reacted if an armed man had broken into our home? Perhaps you would have believed the intruder to be wholly, irredeemably evil, that you should hate him as much as you believe he hates you, that he should be in prison, that you need to capitulate to his demands since he has a gun, that you need to counterattack with your own gun, that you have no choice about how to react, that nothing good can come from this moment, and so on. These attitudes have an all-or-nothing quality to them, making us see the situation in either-or terms. They would certainly be reasonable given the circumstances. But they would also prevent us from seeing the full potential in the situation—the potential for compassion, understanding, growth, kinship, forgiveness, redemption, reflection in the midst of a crisis, reconciliation, taking the high road, owning the outcome, staying in command of your emotions, stepping out of your comfort zone, and bringing out the best in yourself and in him. Melanie was able to accomplish all of this because her beliefs were nuanced, and she could see many possibilities in the situation. That's because she was a master at one discipline you and I can also learn: fusing opposites.

We have been brought up in the world of binary logic. If something is true, its opposite must be false. Yet scientists in the twentieth century discovered that this was too limiting a framework. Mathematicians developed new forms of logic where statement A and its opposite, not-A, could both be true, and quantum physicists posited that electrons were both waves and particles. In formulating our beliefs, we, too, can benefit from fusing opposing ideas to arrive at higher, more integrative truths. F. Scott Fitzgerald wrote, "The test of a first-rate intelligence is the ability to hold two opposing ideas in the mind at the same time and still retain the ability to function."

When you encounter a belief you oppose, study it and find some truth in it. You don't need to embrace the whole belief, just the part that contains truth. Then merge this part with what is true in your own belief. You now have a revised belief, and you have grown in your understanding of truth. Melanie had fused several such pairs of opposing beliefs. *The intruder is doing an evil act **and** he could be a good person at heart. He needs to feel in control **and** I need to take control. I totally disagree with his actions **and** I empathize with the circumstances that may* *have compelled him to do this. This is a dangerous situation **and** it could be an opportunity to build a warm connection.*

Consider my belief in reincarnation. The opposite belief would be that there is only one life. In my twenties, I ignored this opposite perspective, and I became relaxed and complacent about my own growth. I felt content, recognizing that I had plenty of this-life and future-life opportunities to get serious about serving the world and pursuing Self-Realization. In my early thirties, I finally acknowledged to myself that I was squandering the unique opportunity this life was giving me to maximize my growth and pursue an ennobling purpose. By fusing opposites, I emerged with a new belief: "I will have repeated chances in this and future lives to reach my full potential, *and yet* this life affords me an irreplaceable opportunity, right here, today, in this role I am playing as 'Hitendra,' to grow and to serve, a possibility that will never come back in this form." This new belief has helped me infuse greater significance into each passing day.

What if you believe that we only live once—that there is no reincarnation? How could you fuse your belief with its opposite? The belief in reincarnation may help you to avoid seeing any personal flaw or fumble as permanent, because each life offers a fresh opportunity to die to past transgressions and pains and move closer to your Inner Core. You may find this to be an attractive idea to cultivate even in the confines of a single life—the chance to feel untethered to your failings, to be open to lifelong reinvention in pursuit of your full potential, and to awaken each day as though you have died to yesterday and gained a fresh lease on life, a chance to lead it in the way that will make you proud. By integrating this idea, you may find you have improved on your original belief.

Fusing opposites did not require me to give up my belief, nor does it require you to give up yours. And yet we both benefit in meaningful ways from integrating some of the truth that exists in the opposing belief. Next time you encounter a claim that you are diametrically opposed to, take pause. Resist the urge to argue, ignore, or defend; instead, find a way to fuse opposites.

Now, you might say, "I wish to know and live the truth in all I do, but could there be, perhaps, an even *simpler* way to acquire a clear mental lens than to have to perfect all my emotions, thoughts, and beliefs?" There is in fact a simple path to the altar of truth—the path of nonattachment.

Stage 4: Surrender Your Attachments

Larry Ellison, the founder of Oracle Corporation, has described a conversation he had with Steve Jobs: "My thirty-year friendship with Steve Jobs was made up of a thousand walks. . . . Over the years one particular walk stands out. Back in mid-1995 . . . Steve was finishing up *Toy Story* at Pixar and running NeXT, the computer company he founded after he left Apple."

Apple at that time was in deep financial trouble and its stock price was depressed. Larry suggested that they buy all of Apple's stock and make Steve the company's CEO. Steve demurred. He felt that Apple should be persuaded to buy NeXT Computers. Steve would then join Apple's board of directors. Eventually, he believed, the board would make Steve the CEO. Larry told Steve,

> "Ok, that might work, but Steve if we don't buy Apple how are we going to make any money." Suddenly, Steve stopped walking and turned toward me. We were facing each other when he put his left hand on my right shoulder and his right hand on my left shoulder. Starring [*sic*] unblinking into my eyes, Steve said, "Larry, this is why it's so important that I'm your friend. You don't need any more money." I said, "Yeah, I know, I know." Then I said, "But we don't have to keep it. We could give it all away." I was whining.
>
> Steve just shook his head and said, "I'm not doing this for the money. I don't want to get paid. If I do this, I need to do this standing on the moral high ground."
>
> "The moral high ground," I said. "Well that might just be the most expensive real estate on earth." But I knew I had lost the

argument. Steve had made up his mind, right there and then, at Castle Rock in the summer of 1995, to save Apple his way. . . . I went on the Apple board and then I watched Steve build the most valuable company on earth.

On another occasion, Larry said, "Apple became the most valuable company on earth and it wasn't even one of Steve's goals. He wasn't trying to be rich, he wasn't trying to be famous, he wasn't trying to be powerful. He was obsessed with the creative process and building something that was beautiful."

We live in a material world, a world that expects us to harbor ambition and to channel it into a relentless pursuit of our goals. But essentially all great faiths guide us in the opposite direction, to practice nonattachment. Which is the right path?

Growing up, I saw these two views as irreconcilable. "If you want glamour and glory," I told myself, "then by all means, be attached to your goals as all earthly beings are, but if you wish to gain enlightenment, then live in that state of serene surrender the great scriptures recommend." Later in life, when I started to study people who have experienced outsize success, I found to my surprise that they operated with remarkable nonattachment. How could surrender breed success? Gradually, as I assembled the equation of Inner Mastery and Outer Impact, I started to see how.

Science today is showing what these great ones have always known: that when we are nonattached to the outcome of our actions, we make wiser choices in our pursuit of success. We free our mind to do its best work, undistracted by anxiety about our performance, what the score is, and whether we're going to win or lose. We don't feel the need to keep showing that we're smart by playing to our strengths all the time; instead, we remain willing to open ourselves to new learnings, experimentation, practice, and growth. We focus on refining and improving those actions we can control while making peace with the fact that the outcome may ultimately be influenced by factors beyond our control. When the odds of success are low, which they sometimes are in any heroic pursuit, we do not feel demoralized, nor do we quit, because we're pursuing a noble goal, as Gandhi said, "without fear of failure and without hope for success." We are comfortable taking an unpopular stand, for our nonattachment makes us immune to others' praise and criticism, allowing us to pursue whatever ideas our Wisdom guides us to. We are not limited by a particular definition of success, or a particular path to it, and so as conditions change, we are able to pivot with agility. By surrendering our attachments, we are no longer trapped in a blind, possessive love of our own ideas, habits, or beliefs. We open ourselves to voices that are different from our own, and thus we keep learning and growing.

During the height of the Civil War, Abraham Lincoln faced a terrible trade-off. Should he bring an end to the war and let the South secede from the Union, or should he continue with a war that was killing tens of thousands of his countrymen on both sides? On one occasion, a pious individual sought to give Lincoln solace by assuring him that "God is on our side." The president replied, "My concern is not whether God is on our side; my greatest concern is to be on God's side, for God is always right." In the face of daunting challenges and choices, the leaders we admire in history have all practiced some form of inner surrender like Lincoln's. Their primary concern has been to do not what was their right, but what was right.

You might be thinking, "This may work in some situations, but it surely won't work for me. I operate in a competitive, dog-eat-dog world! If I practice nonattachment, they'll eat me for lunch." Then meet John Wooden. Wooden was UCLA's basketball coach in the 1950s and 1960s. He had a distinctive approach to the sport:

> Many players are surprised to learn that in 27 years at UCLA, I never once talked about winning. Instead I would tell my players before games, "When it's over, I want your head up. And there is only one way your head can be up and that's for you to know that you gave the best effort of which you are capable. If you do that, then the score doesn't really matter, although I have

a feeling that if you do that, the score will be to your liking." I honestly, deeply believe that in not stressing winning as such, we won more than we would have if I had stressed outscoring opponents.

And win they did. Wooden is the most successful US college basketball coach in history, leading UCLA to ten national championships. The second most successful coach has won *only five championships*. If ambition gets you success, nonattachment gets you outsize success.

Nonattachment is powerful not simply as a guide for the larger arc of our career and life, but also as a moment-by-moment discipline. I sometimes get approached by students who are keen to ace a job interview with a highly attractive employer. I give them this counsel: "In any interaction where you find yourself seeking the other party's approval—be it a date, a job interview, or a sale of your product— enter the room with a conviction that you are already whole. Take a deep interest in the other party and in the rich possibilities that exist in what they and you could do together, but also know that they can have a rewarding future with or without you, and you can have a rewarding future with or without them. Be deeply committed to the exploration, but be nonattached to the outcome."

Nonattachment is also highly beneficial in conversations where you need to build alignment, resolve a critical issue, or negotiate a deal. By approaching these interactions with clarity and conviction about your position and yet a curiosity about what you may learn from others, you are better able to observe events as they unfold—a new fact divulged by the other party or a troubled expression on their face—and then adjust your behavior suitably. You are anchored on the inside, but agile on the outside.

The path of nonattachment is a razor's edge. It requires you to have ambition, but to focus it on following your inner voice and doing your best rather than on forcing a particular outcome. Without the striving, you will not go far. And without surrender, you will not be able to free your mind from worries so it can do its best work, to stay open to new understanding, or to act upon the truth as it is revealed to you at different stages. Viktor Frankl wrote, "Don't aim at success—the more you aim at it and make it a target, the more you are going to miss it. . . . Listen to what your conscience commands you to do and go on to carry it out to the best of your knowledge. Then you will live to see that in the long run—in the long run, I say!—success will follow you precisely because you had forgotten to think of it."

You might say, "Dr. Frankl, that may be easy for you to say, but sometimes it's hard to know what my conscience is commanding me to do!" And so I want to introduce you to the final stage in cultivating Wisdom—the awakening of your intuition.

Stage 5: Awaken Your Intuition

In 1992, I took a leave of absence from the doctoral program at MIT to gain some work experience in business analytics. I flew to the Bay Area to interview with two consulting firms, Decision Focus, Inc. (DFI), and Applied Decision Analysis (ADA). I was fortunate to receive job offers from both. The logical choice for me would have been DFI. They were working on more interesting business problems, growing faster, and offering a more attractive salary. But somehow, each time I was about to call DFI to say "I accept," I stopped in my tracks, feeling a pang of regret about having to say no to ADA. After two days of soul-searching, I decided to override my intellect and accept the offer from ADA—because I just couldn't imagine missing out on the opportunity to work there. I never regretted my choice. During the two years I spent at ADA before returning to MIT, I grew to love the work and the people.

Why did I not follow my intellect in making this decision? Because the wisdom I'd acquired over the years was alerting me to a factor that my intellect had ignored. During my visit to ADA, I had experienced a culture that was warm, joyful, and playful. The employees were passionate about their work, but they were also deeply invested in their human connection with each other and their pursuit of happiness at work. I'd never worked at any company before, and so I hadn't realized how much this human dimension would matter to

141

me or how organizations can be quite varied in this regard. My intellect assumed that these were qualities one looked for in friends and family—and that one went to work to work! But intuitively I felt quite drawn to those aspects of a workplace. It was intuition that pushed me toward ADA.

Steve Jobs discovered the power of intuition during a trip to India when he was nineteen: "Coming back to America was, for me, much more of a cultural shock than going to India. . . . Western rational thought is not an innate human characteristic; it is learned and is the great achievement of Western civilization. In the villages of India, they never learned it. They learned something else, which is in some ways just as valuable but in other ways is not. That's the power of intuition and experiential wisdom. . . . Intuition is a very powerful thing, more powerful than intellect, in my opinion."

Intellect takes time and effort, consciously breaking a problem into parts and then attending to each separately. In contrast, intuition looks at a problem in totality, tapping not just our conscious but also our subconscious mind, making unexpected connections, helping us approach things from a new perspective, and drawing from all life experiences—automatically, instantly, and effortlessly. Intuition can alert us to a risk we were ignoring, offer a creative idea, suggest a promising new direction, or reassure us about the rightness of a choice. It often arises more as a feeling than as words. Einstein observed, "Words and language . . . do not seem to play any part in my thought process," and "I believe in intuitions and inspirations. I sometimes feel that I am right. I do not know that I am."

You might say, "But wait. There have been times when I have trusted my gut or followed my heart only to discover later that I went down the wrong path. How do I know if I can trust my intuition?" These moments do not signify a failure of intuition, but a misapplication. What we take to be our intuition can at times be a misguided urge triggered by an emotional attachment, a bias, a limiting belief, or an ill-informed hunch that did not view a situation in totality. Intuition can be an indispensable aid, but only when it arises from a calm mind and partners with an active intellect.

Early in my ADA career, I was frequently dazzled at the speed with which senior partners would sometimes cut to the core of an analytics issue facing the client. "These partners are geniuses," I would think. Later I realized they were mere mortals like me; they had just developed expert intuition, having worked over the years on several similar situations for other clients. Expert intuition works in contexts where we have acquired mastery through learning, reflection, practice, and feedback. Our brain gets programmed with an if-then pattern-recognition system and is able to, rapidly and subconsciously, assess situations and guide us to the most effective responses. Although our responses may appear effortless from the outside, behind them are the years of hard work and learning that went into wiring our brain that way. Expert intuition helps us discover hidden dimensions, factors we may have missed paying conscious attention to that can give us a quick and accurate read of a situation.

Expert intuition can fail us when the conditions we encounter depart from those we have seen in the past—because in new conditions, the pattern-recognition system we have developed is no longer accurate. This is where intellect must step in—to take a mindful look at the new conditions and override our snap judgment.

I was spending some time at my parents' home in November 2009. My mother said to me one morning, "Son, I am so glad you're with us today to celebrate your dad's eightieth birthday. I've invited a large circle of family and friends this evening, and I want you to give a speech in honor of your dad and what he's meant to you." I happily accepted, then spent the whole morning trying to figure out what I would say. My father had been a pivotal influence on my life, I knew that, and I had such love and appreciation for him. But when it came to identifying specifically how he'd shaped me, I was hitting a dead end.

You see, when I was growing up, Dad wanted me to stay in my hometown after graduating from high school; I instead decided to move to New Delhi for college. He wanted me to pursue a career in law and to work for the United Nations; I went in other directions. At each turning point in my life, Dad wanted me to go one way, and I went another. Was that all to the dad-and-son story? I agonized, soul-searched, and came up with nothing. And then something magical happened.

My mother had organized a group meditation at our home in the early afternoon. In that stillness, as I meditated, a veil was lifted from my mind, and a new insight arose: "If you want to uncover your father's true impact on you, focus not on what he preached—focus on what he practiced." Flashes from the past raced through my mind: the grace with which my father managed his grief when his mother passed away; the moral strength with which he, as a police officer, took actions against criminals who sent him death threats; the frugal lifestyle that led to his toothbrush and razor blade becoming worn out with overuse so he could save money and secure his family's financial future; the deep love he had for the creative force in the universe in the form of Divine Mother; the uncompromising discipline with which he performed his daily meditation; the indefatigable spirit with which he helped friends and strangers every day; the fierce resolve with which he took on causes to right certain wrongs.

My conscious mind had processed these incidents simply as "Dad being Dad," but my unconscious mind had cataloged them for later use. Over the years, on various occasions, certain scenes from his life had flashed in my mind to guide my choices and give me inner strength. I realized during that meditation how much of who I had become was a result of the silent inspiration I had gained from the experiences where Dad was just being Dad. This is what I spoke about that evening to celebrate my father's life, and when I saw tears well up in his and my mother's eyes, I knew I had done justice to all that he had quietly practiced, not preached.

Our brain has acquired a vast library of knowledge, everything we've experienced over the course of our life. Some of it we have conscious access to, but much of it lies hidden from view in our subconscious. Our brain compartmentalizes and organizes the material into different sections, and when we are solving a problem we go looking for an answer in the conscious part of our mind, and only from the section we believe the problem belongs to. This kind of rational thinking can be very limiting when we face critical or complex dilemmas because it hides what lies beyond our conscious mind and doesn't make us draw connections across different segments of our internal knowledge-library to uncover the most effective insights. What we need in those moments is to activate creative intuition. This form of intuition makes connections across disparate areas, scanning the full breadth of all we've experienced and learned, even things that may be lost to conscious memory, to allow novel ideas to emerge.

Science is showing that although we cannot predict when intuition will strike us or what flashes of insight it will bring, we can create the conditions to maximize the intuitive sparks we receive, some of which can make all the difference.

USING EXPERT AND CREATIVE INTUITION

Step 1: Activate the right intention. Become calm, and surrender your attachment to any particular decision or outcome. Alert yourself to how emotion and bias can cloud your judgment, and step away from those states. Come to peace with whatever the right decision might turn out to be.

Step 2: Apply your intellect. Maximize your understanding of the situation.

To prepare for expert intuition, spend time understanding the specifics of the problem. Draw in others' perspectives if useful. Ask yourself how similar or different this situation is to what you've encountered in the past. Identify your options, and assess their pros and cons. For each option, simulate possible scenarios so you can eliminate those that aren't feasible. "How could this unfold? What might make this path fail? How would I respond? What would happen next? What outcome would this lead to?"

To prepare for creative intuition, write down your overall goals, objectives, and constraints, making them neither too specific nor overly vague.

Step 3: Awaken your intuition. Release your conscious mind from the problem. Your subconscious mind will of its own accord keep working in the background to find a solution. If you intentionally push for a solution, your rational mind will take over, and intuition will be suppressed. Step away to take a shower, go for a brisk walk, play a sport, meditate, pray, or just sleep. Wait for a flash of insight to arrive in an unprompted, relaxed moment. When it arrives, pay heed. Write it down. Sometimes, a partial understanding will emerge, or guidance on where to look for an answer or whom to consult; at other times, a complete solution may flash in your mind.

If this is a high-stakes issue, give time for the right ideas and insights to bubble up—do not settle too quickly. When I wake up every morning, before getting out of bed, I focus my mind on a critical challenge to which I am seeking a solution, and I wait for ideas to bubble up. I repeat these actions the next few mornings. I am rarely disappointed with the insights and ideas that flow. Science has shown this first-thing-upon-waking-up time to be very helpful for tapping intuition.

Intuition does not always take a linear path. You may get an idea in step 3, then go back to step 2 to assess its costs and benefits. You may find that some part of the idea works and some part of it doesn't, and then return to step 3 to refine it further. You may not always reach a perfect solution in the end, one that meets all your needs, but as you balance intellect with intuition, you will feel an increasing sense of reassurance that the road you are being guided to take is the one that is true to you. Intuition has been, for me, one of life's most precious gifts.

HOW I ROSE FROM THE ASHES

After rejecting Rick's advice and losing the board battle over Paramark, I moved to New York to do digital-marketing consulting for a Wall Street bank and a pharmaceutical company. A year later, I began teaching at Columbia Business School. A growing sense of emptiness and urgency continued to gnaw at me from within; I wanted to slow down and invest more in my inner life. Having followed an on-again/off-again quest for Self-Realization since age ten, I was starting to worry that I simply did not have the motivation or discipline to pursue the inner journey. I flew to India to visit Yogananda's ashram in Ranchi and spent some days searching inside for answers, until one day my inner voice broke its silence:

> You have not made the space and time for daily meditation all these years, not because you are slothful or uncommitted or exceptionally busy, but because you live with a belief. A belief that by giving a few hours to your spiritual practice every day, you will be taking time away from important outer goals, and then you will lose your edge in the world, fall behind in the race to be the best whatever-it-is-you-want-to-be. For twenty years you have had a pathway to Self-Realization but kept it at a convenient distance. If you truly wish to pursue this goal, you first need to be convinced that two hours given to meditation does not imply two hours taken away from your pursuit of success. Surrender your attachment to success, take on your meditation practice with discipline and devotion, and then all that is rightfully yours will come to you, in the right way, to the right degree, at the right time.

That day in Ranchi, I made a pact with myself. All other goals could wait, but my pursuit of Self-Realization could not. I would clear my daily calendar for meditation and simplify my overcommitted life, no matter what outer sacrifices were required.

It was not easy at first. I would receive emails announcing the latest director appointments at McKinsey, featuring some of my Class of '96 buddies, or celebrating the IPO of a friend's company, or sharing a glowing media profile of a former colleague who was going places. In those moments, my belief in nonattachment was shaken. "You're a go-getter too, Hitendra. So why not go and get it?" But then the inner commotion would settle down, and I would remind myself, "You are in a phase of renewal and reinvention. Celebrate your peers' success, but don't covet it. That is not your path; that is their path. Keep pursuing your own. In due course, the right inner and outer rewards will come."

It took me two years to permanently quell those ANT explosions. The rewards, ever since, have been priceless.

Chapter 7

LEADING WITH WISDOM

⟶♎︎⟵

I never lose. I either win or I learn.

—*Nelson Mandela*

HOW MANDELA WON OVER HIS NATION
BY WINNING OVER HIMSELF

As a bitter opponent of the apartheid system in place in South Africa, Nelson Mandela trained in guerilla warfare and assumed leadership of the militant arm of the African National Congress (ANC). He later reflected on how he drove around the country imagining rural landscapes as battlefields and cities as places where soon "the sweet air will smell of gunfire, elegant buildings will crash down and streets will be splashed with blood." He once exploded with rage and told an accomplice, "Wolfie, one day I am telling you, it's going to be an eye for eye and a tooth for a tooth."

This bitter, belligerent Mandela was arrested by the government in 1962 and sentenced to life imprisonment. Incarceration limited him from pursuing outer reform, but it gave him the opportunity to pursue inner reform. The prison cell, he observed, "is an ideal place to learn to know yourself, to search realistically and regularly the process of your own mind and feelings. . . . The cell gives you the opportunity to look daily into your entire conduct, to overcome

149

the bad and develop whatever is good in you. Regular meditation, say about 15 minutes a day before you turn in, can be very fruitful in this regard. You may find it difficult at first to pinpoint the negative features in your life, but the 10th attempt may yield rich rewards."

One such "negative feature" Mandela sought to overcome was his temper. A prison official, Lieutenant Prins, said something offensive about Mandela's wife, Winnie. Enraged, Mandela came close to physically assaulting the man, but just in time he switched instead to a verbal attack. He returned to his cell that day and thought, "Even though I had silenced Prins, he had caused me to violate my self-control and I consider that a defeat at the hands of my opponent."

Archbishop Desmond Tutu observed about Mandela, "When you heard some of his utterances before going to jail on the subject of violence, for instance, you are aware that a transformation happened." And his ghostwriter, Richard Stengel, noted, "The man who walked onto Robben Island in 1964 was emotional, headstrong, easily stung. The man who emerged was balanced and disciplined." Mandela himself said, "I came out mature."

Mandela opened himself up while incarcerated to reexamining his beliefs. The inmates watched a documentary on the Hells Angels, a controversial American motorcycle club accused of criminal activity. After the film, the inmates criticized the Hells Angels for their lawless ways. But a young prisoner, Strini, challenged his fellow inmates and expressed his support for the bikers for rebelling against the authorities. Emotions were roused, and several longer-tenured prisoners denounced Strini. Mandela had quietly been observing the inmates' reactions, and he stepped in. "I considered what Strini said, and while I did not agree with him, I came to his defense. . . . I was not interested in the Hells Angels, but the larger question that concerned me was whether we had . . . been stuck in a mind-set that was no longer revolutionary. We had been in prison for more than fifteen years; the world that we left was long gone. . . . The movie reminded me once again that on the day I did walk out of prison, I did not want to appear to be a political fossil from an age long past." Two Wisdom actions are in display in this story—looking for the truth in your opponent's position even when you disagree with them, and stepping back from small debates to take a metaview.

Mandela said, "I like friends who have independent minds because they tend to make you see problems from all angles." Having diligently sharpened the axe of his thinking and his beliefs, he arrived at a state of Gandhi-like authenticity where what he felt, thought, spoke, and did were the same. A fellow inmate, Neville Alexander, remarked, "He thinks things through very carefully, and then the force and the power of his conviction makes him spontaneous. He is genuine, but it's because it's been thought through very, very carefully." Patti Waldmeir, a *Financial Times* correspondent, described how, when she asked Mandela a question, he would be quiet for a while, then speak "when reason had extinguished passion in his breast. . . . There are no cheap glimpses into Mandela's soul. He is too disciplined for that." This is perhaps the simplest and yet most pivotal of all Wisdom actions: to hit pause, to refrain from speaking or acting until one has clarity over one's thoughts and command over one's impulses.

Over time, Mandela became less bitter and more purposeful about his dealings with the ruling white minority in South Africa, the Afrikaners. "Our emotion said, 'The white minority is an enemy. We must never talk to them.' But our brain said, 'If you don't talk to this man, your country will go up in flames. . . . And for many years to come . . . this country will be engulfed in rivers of blood.' So, we had to reconcile that conflict. And our talking to the enemy was the result of the domination of the brain over emotions." Mac Maharaj, another person incarcerated with Mandela, recounts, "He said to me, Mac . . . if you don't know your opposite, how are you going to get them to respond the way you want? . . . 'What must I do?' I ask. He says, 'Learn the language.' 'OK,' I said, 'I'll learn.' He says, 'No, learn their poetry, understand their culture." And that is what Mandela did, having realized, as he said, that "you don't address their brains. You address their hearts."

His quest for peaceful reconciliation between blacks and Afrikaners began in a quiet manner: by first learning to win over the prison guards. Some of them even started to ask Mandela for help in writing their applications for promotion. One guard, Christo Brand, said that "Mandela became like a father to me."

He also sought to win over prison officers, like Major van Sittert, who was known to be aloof and unaccommodating to political prisoners. Mandela wanted a hot plate on which to heat food in his prison cell after hours, something that required Van Sittert's approval. Mandela peppered prison guards with questions to discover that the major was a "rugby nut." So he learned all he could about the game. When the major came by next, Mandela greeted him with a big smile and started to talk about rugby—which players were doing well and which were performing poorly, and so on. Van Sittert was instantly engaged. After an animated discussion, Mandela explained why he wanted a hot plate and asked the major to arrange one for him because he was sure this was a problem the major would not want another rugby man to endure. Without hesitating, Van Sittert turned to a prison guard and asked him to get Mandela a hot plate. Instead of arming himself with guerilla gear, Mandela was now learning to disarm his opponents with Wisdom.

Benjamin Pogrund, a South African journalist, recalls, "Despite the lack of contact, word was coming out of Robben Island that Mandela was assuming a new stature. Released prisoners reported that he had become the acknowledged leader of all the political prisoners; that not only the ANC, but also Pan Africanist Congress members, the African Resistance Movement and others respected him and accepted his authority. He was the wise man who adjudicated in disputes." This evolution in Mandela did not escape the notice of South Africa's government. The situation in the country was deteriorating fast; protests against apartheid had intensified, the apartheid government had declared a state of emergency, the army and police had been deployed to fight the African National Congress, and violence had escalated. President Botha sent emissaries, including Niël Barnard, the head of the South African National Intelligence Service, to start a dialog with Mandela. John Carlin, in his book *Invictus*, reports on what happened next. Barnard was "seen as a dark and demonic figure [who] had waged a war on Mandela's ANC." But he was charmed by Mandela, later reflecting that he "is one of those strange individuals who captivates you. . . . You find yourself wanting to listen to him." At a time when the oppressed black community's rage was ripping through the nation, Mandela's growing sensitivity and statesmanship made the government see him as their first and last hope for a peaceful future. Barnard recounted, "There was, in our minds . . . never the slightest doubt. This is the man—if you cannot find a settlement with him, any settlement will be out."

A direct meeting between Botha and Mandela was arranged. Botha, nicknamed the Big Crocodile, was known to be an aggressive and uncompromising man. Barnard counseled Mandela to focus his conversation with Botha on easy topics, and warned him that if he asked for the release of Walter Sisulu, a fellow ANC leader who had been in prison for twenty-five years on milder charges, "Mr. Botha will say no. I know him." Mandela prepared for the meeting "like an actor about to go onstage. . . . [He] read over the notes he had been preparing for several days, rehearsed his lines, played himself into the role." Prepare. Practice. Play out the role. These are small actions we can all take before our high-stakes moments.

The defining moment of Mandela's life arrived. He was secretly whisked out of prison after swapping his prison uniform for a specially tailored suit. As the two men waited for Botha outside his office, "Barnard did a remarkable thing. . . . He kneeled before Mandela and tightened the old man's shoelaces."

The door to Botha's office opened and Mandela was ushered in. "In his mind, [Mandela had] rehearsed what he would say and what he would do. He would, if he could, take the initiative. For that very reason, he deliberately strode across the room, greeting Botha with a robust handshake and a wide smile. He disarmed the South African president with his own friendliness and informal manner, something that he had planned and practiced. He put up a front."

Mandela spoke to Botha in Afrikaans and, using the knowledge he had acquired of Afrikaner history while incarcerated, compared black people's struggle with that of the Afrikaners during the Boer War a hundred years before, in which they had fought to win their freedom from British rule. Botha was moved; both his father and grandfather had fought in those battles. Through his actions, Mandela was having a silent *inner* conversation with Botha, helping him rescript his ANTs about Mandela and the black South Africans into thoughts like "Mandela is not my enemy." "He actually likes us Afrikaners." "What the blacks are seeking is just what we Afrikaners sought years ago." Sensing that this was his moment, Mandela let his intuition override Barnard's advice by directly asking Botha to release Sisulu. Botha turned to Barnard and said, "I think it must be done."

This historic meeting catalyzed a series of developments that led, over the next year, to Walter Sisulu's release, then Mandela's release, the legalization of the African National Congress, and the start of negotiations about a democratic future for South Africa. F. W. de Klerk assumed the presidency of South Africa.

Political violence was escalating, and a commission, headed by Richard Goldstone, a Constitutional Court judge, was set up to investigate its causes. In its report, the commission highlighted multiple factors, including colonialism, the apartheid system and its cruel policing, and battles between different black factions. The South African government released the report, claiming only that Goldstone's commission had pointed a finger at black-on-black violence. Mandela had just returned from a foreign visit to face these media headlines on the government's spin. He castigated the report and made critical remarks about Goldstone. Then at three o'clock that day, Goldstone's phone rang. It was Mandela. "I'm calling you for two reasons," he said. "The first is to tell you that I did a terrible thing, I commented and I criticized your report without having read it. I relied on media reports. . . . That's the first reason I'm calling, to apologize. I should have never relied on the media, I should have read your report. I have now read it and agree with most of it." He continued, "The second reason I'm calling is to let you know that I've called a press conference for an hour from now, at four o'clock, and

I'm going to publicly apologize to you. My question to you is, may I say you have accepted my apology?" This is a powerful action we can all take, to offer an unqualified apology, privately and if needed publicly, anytime we say or do something we're not proud of because we got emotionally triggered.

On a later occasion, Goldstone witnessed Mandela's remarkable command over his anger. Mandela's physician was checking his blood pressure one day when he received an urgent call from President de Klerk to discuss the forthcoming elections. Goldstone, who was present to observe this moment, recounts what happened next:

> "Good afternoon Mr. President," Mandela said politely. De Klerk must have then said something or asked him to do something that annoyed him and he said "Now, look here, de Klerk"—no longer Mr. President—"look here de Klerk, I won't have that, I won't do it, I will not agree to it." And this went on for two or three minutes and while Mandela, very annoyed, was talking to de Klerk, the doctor was taking his blood pressure. When the phone was eventually almost banged down by Mandela, I said, "Nthato, what happened to Madiba's blood pressure?" He said, "You won't believe it, it didn't budge." And Mandela, laughing, said, "Of course not, it was a big act."

Mandela had to win over black leaders like Daliwonga, who supported a plan by the South African government to establish Bantu authorities that would give tribal chiefs like him more power. But Mandela did not approve of the scheme. In their meeting, Mandela told the chief that if Mandela had been in his shoes, he would have subordinated his own interests to those of the people. Mandela describes what happened next: "I immediately regretted [this]. . . . I have discovered that in discussions it never helps to take a morally superior tone to one's opponent. I noticed that Daliwonga stiffened when I made this point and I quickly shifted the discussion to more general issues." Keeping an awareness of the emotional energy in the room. Understanding how your demeanor, words, and actions land on people. Pivoting quickly as you learn something new. Small actions such as these can go a long way.

Mandela also had to build bridges with white leaders like General Constand Viljoen, a Boer military commander who was plotting an Afrikaner guerilla war against democratic rule. When their delegations met, Mandela invited Constand to sit with him in the living room prior to the formal meeting between the two teams. Carlin reports,

He offered Constand a cup of tea, and poured it himself. "Do you take milk, General?" The general said he did. "Would you like some sugar?" "Yes, please, Mr. Mandela," said the general. Viljoen stirred his tea in a state of quiet confusion, thrown by Mandela's show of courtly respect. This was not at all what he had expected. Long cemented stereotypes were crumbling. Viljoen and his people were demanding a sovereign territory for Afrikaners within a black-led democratic South Africa—and were threatening military intervention otherwise. "I am not sure if you realize it, Mr. Mandela, but this [transition to democratic rule] can be stopped." Mandela replied gravely, speaking in Viljoen's native language, Afrikaans, "Look, General, I know that the military forces you can muster are powerful and well-armed and well-trained; and that they are far more powerful than mine. Militarily we cannot fight you; we cannot win. If, however, you do go to war, you assuredly will not win either, not in the long run. Because, one, the international community will be totally behind us. And, two, we are too many, and you cannot kill us all. So then, what kind of life will there be for your people in this country? My people will go to the bush, the international pressure on you will be enormous and this country will become a living hell for all of us. Is that what you want? No, General, there can be no winners if we go to war." "This is so," General Viljoen replied. "There can be no winner."

Mandela started with agreement. The blacks would lose. And then he offered his truth—the Afrikaners would lose, too. He was fusing opposites by establishing not a win-win but a lose-lose.

There were many times during his struggle against apartheid when, Mandela later acknowledged, "Of course I was afraid." Courage, for him, had never been the absence of fear, but the ability to overcome it and to act despite the fear. He continued to employ simple, and at times symbolic, actions to dispel limiting thoughts and beliefs among South Africans about the irreparability of their racial divide. As president of South Africa's first democratic government, he actively supported the country's rugby team in the World Cup tournament that took place in South Africa in 1995—even though the sport, which had no black players, had been a strong symbol of apartheid in the past. He developed a solid rapport with the team's captain and attended the final match to cheer his country's team. When they achieved an upset victory, Mandela strode into the stadium wearing the green jersey and cap of the team, a powerful gesture of reconciliation. White hearts melted, and black anger cooled.

In this way, a nation was progressively won over, a civil war avoided, a painful past left behind, and a democracy birthed. All because one man, while serving twenty-seven years as a prisoner of conscience, and stripped of the ability to use physical force to get his way, humbly invested in challenging and changing his emotions, thoughts, and beliefs—and then helped to bring about the same shift in party members, prison officials, government leaders, two presidents, rebel militants, tribal leaders, and, ultimately, the broader citizenry of South Africa.

F. W. de Klerk once claimed, "Mandela is not a saint." Mandela would have concurred, for he, too, once confessed, "I am not a saint." And then, fusing opposites, he added, "unless you think of a saint as a sinner who keeps on trying."

Chapter 8

LIVING WITH GROWTH

≺⋅≻

> There is no saint without a past, no sinner without a future.
>
> —*Saint Augustine*

OUTER GROWTH, INNER GROWTH

He was raised by poor but loving parents who relied on government food assistance. He received a guitar as a gift when he was ten, though he had hoped to get something different, perhaps a rifle or a bicycle. "I learned to play a little bit. But I would never sing in public. I was very shy about it." He was regarded as a loner in school. His music teacher in eighth grade told him he had no aptitude for singing. He received no formal music training and studied and played by ear. In his senior year, he entered a talent show. "It was amazing how popular I became in school after that." From then on, his star kept rising. By twenty-one, he was the most popular entertainer in America, attracting a record 82.6 percent of the TV viewing audience to his performance on *The Ed Sullivan Show*, releasing a top-selling album, and revolutionizing America's youth culture. He remains the best-selling solo music artist of all time. Forty years after his passing, the house where he lived is second only to the White House in the number of visitors it attracts—half a million annually. I am of course talking about none other than the King of Rock 'n' Roll, Elvis Presley.

Across all spheres of human endeavor—athletics, performing arts, science, business, and beyond—we admire people who engage in the dogged pursuit of excellence and scale new heights in their fields. When they arrive at the summit to claim victory, we look back at their roots and are in awe about how much growth they have achieved. And yet this single-minded devotion to the mastery of their discipline has led many legends to very dark places: depression, loneliness, a struggle to be happy. In 1976, a cleaner at a Hilton hotel found notes that Elvis had scribbled to himself. "I feel so alone now. . . . I wish there was someone who I could trust and talk to." In a letter he wrote to a friend in 1977, he said, "I need a long rest. I'm sick and tired of my life. . . . My willpower is almost gone." Seven months later, at age forty-two, Elvis was dead, his body ravaged by a poor diet and an addiction to prescription drugs.

When we focus exclusively on outer success—on winning the outer game but not the inner game, on what we are accomplishing but not who we are becoming—our victory is a hollow victory.

There was a single purpose behind all that Steve Jobs did. "The goal is not to be the richest man in the cemetery," he stated. "In the broadest sense, the goal is to seek enlightenment—however you define it." So Steve made a trip to India when he was nineteen to meet with a saint he was inspired by, only to find that the saint had recently passed away. He absorbed the teachings of Hinduism and Buddhism, visited Buddhist temples in Kyoto, took training from a Zen master, learned to meditate, and adopted a highly disciplined diet. For a brief period, he even contemplated walking away from modern life to become a Hindu ascetic, but then realized that his calling lay in the world. He wanted to "put a dent in the universe" by taking "computers and society, [which were] out on a first date," and making "the romance blossom."

So he cofounded Apple and eventually took the company public through an IPO. And then he stumbled, badly. People have described Jobs during this period as callous, tempestuous, domineering, self-centered, and condescending. He ignored others' ideas, was blind to market realities, pushed people too hard, and held on to grudges. Most egregiously, he refused to accept paternity of his daughter, Lisa, by a former girlfriend. After the success of the Apple II home computer, his next two major product initiatives, the Apple III and the Macintosh, were commercial failures, and he was forced out of Apple by the CEO and the board of directors in 1985. "At 30, I was out," he later recalled. "And very publicly out. What had been the focus of my entire adult life was gone, and it was devastating."

Jobs 1.0 failed spectacularly because he was trying to shine *solely* from within. He did heroic work on the inside to cultivate his vision and feel a connection with the universe, but on the outside, he simply wanted to push that vision through with little patience for other people's imperfections, contrarian views, lesser intellects, or inability to deliver what he wanted.

Some of us are like Jobs 1.0. We create an inner sanctuary from where we derive our purpose and identity. But in striving to be at peace with ourself, we find that self to be at war with the world. People disappoint us, structures and systems frustrate us, and soaring visions come crashing down in a world that does not wish to move at our pace or along our direction. We then struggle to preserve our inner peace—the very prize we were going for—amidst life's inescapable demands, distractions, and disappointments.

Elvis experienced outer victory but inner defeat. Steve experienced inner victory but outer defeat. But perhaps these two worlds, the inner and the outer, weren't meant to be separate, nor to tear each other apart. What might life look like if we strove to pursue both inner and outer Growth?

THE ESSENCE OF GROWTH

Michelangelo described sculpting as follows: "[In] every block of marble I see a statue as plain as though it stood before me, shaped and perfect in attitude and action. I have only to hew away the rough walls that imprison the lovely apparition to reveal it to the other eyes as mine see it."

Within each of us is a "lovely apparition," a pure, beautiful form, our Inner Core. We are invited by life to "hew away the rough walls" that contain it so we can bring that true self into active expression in all our pursuits. Every struggle we go through on the outside becomes a crucible in which our inner life is tested, refined, and perfected. This is the essence of Growth—to grow in tandem on the inside and the outside, inner transformation driving outer transformation, and vice versa. Growth invites you to recognize that behind your outer Purpose lies an inner one: to use your limited time on Earth to deepen your connection with your Inner Core.

Growth does not require that we sacrifice the outer pursuit of excellence. Instead, it invites us to make every outer victory linked to inner victory so that in the process of becoming a great scientist, artist, athlete, doctor, politician, scholar, engineer, entrepreneur, executive, or frontline worker, we also end up becoming a great human being.

While coaching the UCLA basketball team, John Wooden developed a pyramid of values to guide his players. The principles it codified were as much about becoming a better human being as they were about becoming a better basketball player. One of his star players, Kareem Abdul-Jabbar, reflected, "He was almost mystical in his approach, yet that approach only strengthened our confidence. Coach Wooden enjoyed winning, but he did not put winning above everything. He was more concerned that we became successful as human beings, that we earned our degrees, that we learned to make the right choices as adults and as parents. In essence, he was preparing us for life. . . . Coach Wooden had a profound influence on me as an athlete, but even greater influence on me as a human being. He is responsible, in part, for the person I am today."

THE POWER OF GROWTH

Growth guides us to keep evolving in response to life's ever-changing conditions. Setbacks, failures, losses, dry periods, uncertainties, injustices, boredom—each becomes our teacher. We stop judging our experiences as good or bad and instead simply ask of them, "What is life trying to teach me? How can I grow from this?" Embracing such an attitude gives us the courage to keep advancing, to step even into roles for which we may initially have little mastery, for we know we can learn and grow.

When we stumble in our quest to do well, Growth invites us to forgive ourselves and to "keep on keeping on." Growth concerns itself not with the failures of our past but with the possibilities of our future, and it encourages us to make the effort now.

Growth refuses to see us only in terms of who we are today. Instead, it helps us walk away from maladaptive traits and behaviors to sculpt ourselves, freely and consciously, into the kind of person we want to become.

THE PATH OF GROWTH

The path of Growth leads us from our identities as rough stone to the beautiful, pure form within that represents our highest potential.

Stage 1: Take Stock of Your Stone

You may think you're the same person all the time, but if you are like most of us, you move in and out of three states. To take stock of your stone—your current self—you will benefit from a candid look in the mirror as you contemplate each of these states.

OUR THREE STATES

In the **triggered** state, you get caught in the grip of emotional or sensory arousal caused by an outer trigger (an email, a remark, an encounter) or an inner trigger (a thought, a memory, a desire). You may end up feeling angry or hopeless, anxious or euphoric, or perhaps you feel a strong craving to indulge in something. You experience distorted thoughts like "He's terrible!" or "I'll be so unhappy if I don't get this!" and you may say or do things that you later regret. What situations trigger you? What emotions and thoughts do you then experience? How do you behave in such moments? How long does it last?

Your **everyday** state is how you show up in normal, daily life. In some everyday moments, you operate by habit and instinct, while in others, you make more conscious choices. In your everyday moments, are you predominantly calm or restless, focused or distracted, assertive or open, happy or unhappy? Are you aware in such moments of the intentions, emotions, and thoughts that are silently influencing your behavior?

In the **centered** state, you are closest to your Core. You feel pure, calm, happy, open, connected, and inspired. The pull of everyday habits is weakened. You open yourself up to thinking, feeling, and doing what's right, not what's comfortable, expedient, or instinctual. In what moments in life are you centered? What impact does this state have on your feelings, thoughts, and behaviors? How do others respond when you are centered?

You goal in pursuing Growth should be threefold: (1) minimize your triggers, (2) make your everyday state a centered state, and (3) evolve your centered state so it gets closer and closer to your true self—your Core.

Stage 2: Find Your Core Model

"We must have a proper picture of what we want," Gandhi wrote, "before we can have something approaching it."

In 1890, after studying law for three years in London and passing the bar exam, Gandhi sailed for India. His ship arrived in the port of Bombay in the midst of a storm. Gandhi recounted, "The outer storm was to me a symbol of the inner." As a twenty-two-year-old, Gandhi grappled with feelings of inadequacy and fear. His search for his authentic self had begun but was a long way from completion. Shortly after his arrival he was introduced by a friend, Dr. Mehta, to Raychand, a poet and a diamond merchant.

Gandhi noted how much Raychand excelled at business. "[His] commercial transactions covered hundreds of thousands. He was a connoisseur of pearls and diamonds. No knotty business problem was too difficult for him." But even more so, Gandhi was deeply struck by how Raychand exuded serenity amidst whatever circumstance came his way. "I never saw him lose his state of equipoise. . . . There was a strange power in his eyes; they were extremely bright and free from any sign of impatience or anxiety. They bespoke single-minded attention. . . . He looked an embodiment of peace. There was such a sweetness in his voice that one simply wanted to go on listening to him. His face was smiling and cheerful; it shone with the light of inner joy. He had such command of language that I do not remember his ever pausing for a word to express his thoughts." He also wrote, "The thing that . . . cast its spell over me . . . was . . . his burning passion for self-realization. I saw later that this . . . was the only thing for which he lived." Years later Gandhi recalled, "I must say that no one else has ever made on me the impression that [Raychand] did. His words went straight home to me. . . . In my moments of spiritual crisis . . . he was my refuge. . . . It is from [his] life that I have learnt the most. Such was the man who captivated my heart . . . as no other man has till now."

We all need our own Raychands—people whose personal examples offer an inspiring vision of what awaits us when we uncover our Inner Core and express it in all we do. The more tangibly we can see our highest potential, the more we will burn with the fire required to get there. You need not restrict yourself to people you know personally, or people from your community, your profession, or your era. When I was nine, I discovered Buddha, my first Core role model. I added others over time—Yogananda, Jesus, Saint Francis, Vivekananda, Mother Teresa, Gandhi, Lincoln, and certain monks and nuns I've known. I actively draw upon these people's examples—epitomized through their stories, photographs, writings, and, where possible, living presence—to give me a tangible feeling of the form I wish to sculpt myself into.

Stage 3: Visualize the Form Within

It is not enough to simply see your Core reflected in outer role models. To grow, you will need to visualize it within your own self.

From the hills around Florence, a large piece of marble was cut out and brought into the city in 1464. The local government invited leading sculptors to propose their plan for a statue to be sculpted from this stone for the Florence Cathedral. It was a tall, imposing piece of marble, but one sculptor after another refused the commission. They were all concerned about a gash in the stone, an error made by the masons while excavating it. Nothing could be done to repair the damage, so the city waited.

One day, twenty-six-year-old Michelangelo came upon the abandoned stone, envisioned the pure form within, and accepted the commission. Three years later, he had sculpted from it the statue of David, one of the great masterpieces of Renaissance art.

Regardless of how flawed our current self is, we can all strive to look for the perfect form that lies within, and then chip away at the excess stone and its defects until we find it. Some of us may fear that this quest is quixotic. After all, how much can I overcome the limitations of my personality, habits, addictions, and character flaws? How much can I actually grow? Twentieth-century science claimed that we are fixed in our personality, intelligence, and character. But twenty-first-century science, consistent with the timeless wisdom of great faiths, is upending this view in three important ways.

First, the new science shows that you and I are dynamic, ever-unfolding beings. Who we are today is not who we are destined to be tomorrow. In large part, our ability to grow is influenced by our mindset. People with a fixed mindset—those who believe their traits are mostly static—resist stepping out of their comfort zones to learn new skills, focus on seeing other people's weaknesses rather than their strengths, experience feedback or criticism as a judgment on them rather than an opportunity to learn, and see failure as a sign that they don't have any talent in a given area. In contrast, people with a growth mindset—those who believe their traits are malleable—enjoy learning new skills, gain inspiration from others' strengths, actively learn from feedback and criticism, and use failure as a chance to learn, work harder, and up their game. Consequently, people with a growth mindset end up progressing while those with a fixed mindset do not.

Neuroscience is providing a physiological understanding of how we can, with intention and discipline, grow over time. Each thought and behavior pattern you execute repeatedly, and have therefore grown comfortable with, has an associated neural wiring pattern in your brain. For behaviors that are new to you, your brain lacks the corresponding neural wiring. But if you intentionally and repeatedly practice these novel behaviors, then, over time, new pathways will form in your brain, because "neurons that fire together, wire together." Once the pathways are formed, the new thought or behavior pattern will become second nature to you. Scientists call this neuroplasticity. You are truly a sculptor every time you practice a new thought or behavior—a sculptor of the pathways in your brain.

You may be open to the idea that personality, even intelligence, is mostly changeable, but it is hard for some of us to believe that *character* is also changeable. If that's how you feel, allow Jared to share his story with you:

> My father walked away from our family, so I was raised by a single mother. When I was thirteen, she died. I was the oldest among the three children and faced a big struggle in trying to look after my younger brother and sister. I took to selling drugs on

the street. It was the practical way for me to make money. I sold drugs for several years.

I once had a client who was not paying his dues. I went to his home with a gun in a brown bag and knocked on his door. I wanted to make an example of him in the neighborhood—nobody messes with me. His mother opened the door. "Ronnie is not at home today," she told me.

I came so close to killing him that day! Over time, I realized the folly of my ways. I saw how drugs made many of my friends end up in jail or an early grave, and I saw the damage it was doing to my community. I decided to pull myself out from this dark world of crime. I was suddenly poor again.

My wife decided to leave me and take our one-year-old baby with her. I was in such agony that day. But I moved on. I went back to high school to finish my education, and then went on to college. All that time, I supported myself by driving a delivery truck. Sometimes I would deliver food for swanky holiday parties on Park Avenue in New York, and I would tell myself, "One day, I will be at these parties, enjoying this food!" I got promoted to a supervisory role, then later to manager. Then over the years I became an executive. And now, look!

Jared's eyes lit up. He was one of thirty executives taking a workshop with me at Columbia Business School. "Here I am with all of you," he said. "You are from fifteen different countries. You have accomplished so much in your lives. Quietly, these last two days I have been reflecting on my past. For me to be here as part of this program at Columbia University, with the professor and all of you, I keep pinching myself because it seems like such a dream!"

We had all grown very fond of Jared for his humble, quiet, caring presence, having no idea of his backstory. We were stunned by his remarks, yet also deeply moved by the possibilities he revealed about the human spirit's ability to retrench, recover, and redeem itself.

The people we consider heroes have built their character step by step, over time. Gandhi once stole money from his father; later he became a messenger of truth. Mandela once drove around his country hungry for war; later he became a messenger of reconciliation. Early in Lincoln's political career, he mocked his opponents and made slanderous and false claims about them in the media; later he learned to "destroy my enemies [by making] them my friends." The key to transformation is to refuse to let yourself be imprisoned by your past.

Second, the new science challenges the twentieth-century view that you are either one thing or the opposite. We can, for instance, be an ambivert—both an introvert and an extrovert. We can even exhibit opposing qualities in the same moment; science shows that people who simultaneously coactivate positive and negative emotions—experiencing both the good and the bad in a situation—tend to enjoy better resilience, life meaning, health, and motivation. Martin Luther King Jr. once reflected, "In my own life and in the life of a person who is seeking to be strong, you combine in your character antitheses strongly marked. You are both militant and moderate, you are both idealistic and realistic."

In fact, leading voices in psychology are recognizing that each of us is *already* a bundle of opposite qualities. Your personality is different based on whom you are with, and in what situation. You may be patient in one moment, impatient in another; kind with a certain individual, rude with another. If you want to master a quality that is new to you, look for bright spots—moments in your life when you have already felt, thought, and acted in the desired way, even if it was fleeting. Your bright spots will help you see how a given quality is already present within you; all you need to do is nurture and amplify it. And if you can't see it in evidence in your own life, look for it in others. Research reveals that if you recognize and admire a quality in someone else, then the seed of that quality exists within you as well. As more than one writer has noted, "We don't see people as they are. We see people as we are."

And third, the new science shows that you will feel *more true* to yourself when you act in a way consistent with your values, even when those actions are contrary to your personality. For instance, an introverted manager who has organized a party to celebrate her team's successful launch of a product will feel more authentic acting extroverted at the party because it's the quality she wants to express with her staff. Purpose triumphs over personality because Purpose is part of your Core, while personality is simply a brain wiring that can be resculpted.

Patrick told the following story in class:

> I grappled with drug addiction in college. One time, it got so bad I landed at the hospital because of an overdose, on the verge of dying. My mother came to visit me. I had not spoken to her for a long time. I braced myself for an outpouring of her anger and her disappointment in me. She held my hand and said, "My son, you know how much I love you. I do not want you to do anything for me today. But I will ask you one question. The way you have been living in recent times—is this really the person you truly are? Is this your highest potential?"
>
> The question hit me like a bolt from the blue. I reflected on it for many days. I had had all these aspirations for the kind of life I wanted to lead, what I wanted to manifest, and the person I wanted to be. I realized the thing that was stopping me from it all was my drug habit. I went to rehab and walked away from drugs. Now it's been twelve years and I haven't touched them since.

Patrick's mother used a powerful device to light a fire in her son. Rather than tell Patrick he was bad and needed to mend his ways, she simply reminded him of the dreams he possessed at his Core. In essence, she was saying, "My son, drugs made you drift away. Just reclaim your true nature."

This is not simply a story of a mother's undying belief in her son; this is science. When people think of their future self, most experience it as a person quite distinct and distant from them. A different part of their brain gets activated, similar to when they are thinking of other people. So they keep indulging who they are today instead of investing in who they could be tomorrow. But some people think of their future self as *who they are at their Core.* These people are more likely to make choices today that are aligned with their future interests instead of solely focusing on their present hungers.

So once you have a clear vision of your authentic self, make sure you do not simply admire it from a distance. Place this radical, awe-inspiring vision at the very center of your being. Visualize the beautiful form of David, whatever it may be for you, in your stone. Your human self may occasionally get distracted, despondent, or disgruntled, but the pure inner form is always there within you, waiting to be released.

Stage 4: Find Your Mentors, Allies, and Muse

I ended my freshman year at Delhi University ranked the top mathematics student. I smugly shared my hard-won achievement with friends and family and basked in their "oohs" and "aahs." "Hitendra, you are special," they said, and secretly I had to agree. Over the summer, I visited Yogananda's Ranchi ashram and met up with a monk I counted as a friend, eager to share the news with him. His face betrayed no surprise, delight, or admiration. I felt deflated. After ten minutes with me, he turned to greet another ashram visitor, and I couldn't help but notice that he flowed with the same love for this person as he had for me. In that moment, I did not feel special at all.

All through that day, I reflected on the experience. Something wasn't right. Here I was, meeting with someone who had always offered me such love. Why was he denying me my due right to bask innocently in my accomplishments?

Understanding dawned on me that evening after a peace-inducing group meditation. The monk saw me through a different lens from the one my friends and family were seeing me through. His gaze pierced through my outer form to look directly at my Inner Core. He was more interested in knowing how my spiritual study was going, whether I was meditating regularly, what sculpting I was doing of my character, and how I was serving others. He was honoring my spiritual pursuits while the world was honoring my material pursuits. And he was opening me up to the idea that everybody is special, because of the pure, beautiful form we each have within us.

This pattern became an annual ritual through my years at college. I was ranked the top mathematics student each year and would float for a while on the accolades I received. Then I would visit the ashram and receive a healthy bursting of my ego balloon from the monk-friend as he continued to gently nudge me toward inner mastery, not just outer excellence. Once, four years after college, I stumbled badly in life and shared the uncomfortable news with him. He received news of the failure with the same glow of unconditional love with which he had received reports of my prior accomplishments. On that day, I was especially grateful to him for accepting my life's highs and lows with such equanimity. This monk has remained a treasured mentor to me for decades.

We all need mentors to help us on our inner-sculpting journey—people who offer guidance and inspiration while having advanced in some meaningful measure toward their own Core, who only seek our highest good, have no hidden or personal agenda, are comfortable being candid with us, bring balance and objectivity to their perspectives, and honor our right to ultimately choose the pace and path for our journey. It is valuable to cultivate not just outer mentors but also inner mentors—people whose lives we study, whose stories we absorb, and whose guidance we seek within from time to time.

We also need allies, people we can turn to informally, in day-to-day touchpoints, to help us in more tactical ways. Allies see you as a work in progress and can help hold you accountable, challenge your thinking, offer outside-in perspectives, and encourage your growth. "Did I handle this difficult conversation with my colleague right, or could I have done something else to bring out the best in them?" "Am I doing enough to care for my aging parents even though I cannot be with them every day?" "Can you give me a gentle knock on the head if you find me losing my cool?" "Could I try out this speech on you before I deliver it to my team tomorrow?"

Mark, an executive MBA student, told me how he recruited his assistant to be his ally:

> After taking your class, I decided to work on my anger. I had been getting increasingly irritated with people at work. I talked to my assistant and asked her to observe my behavior and report back to me. I committed to apologizing to people I became irritated with. It was my assistant's job to report to me every single incident where I raised my voice or got more irritated than what she felt was optimal or fair. It turned out to be rather challenging to apologize to people in front of her, but it helped me stay mindful about my commitment. My assistant started to notice that I was behaving differently, and we started to smile at each other. The result was unambiguous—and very impressive.

In studying married couples, psychologists have discovered a "Michelangelo phenomenon." If you have an ideal self you wish to become, your chances of getting there are significantly boosted if your partner also sees this ideal self in you and supports you in moving toward it. In situations where your partner disaffirms you "by communicating indifference, pessimism or disapproval, by undermining [your] ideal pursuits, or by affirming qualities that are antithetical to [your] ideal self," you are more likely to fail. This practice offers a powerful way to assess the health of an intimate relationship. Does each partner accept the other for who they are today, and yet see the best in their partner and support them in moving toward their Inner Core?

I struggled for twenty years to discipline myself into getting my meditation practice off the ground. I nursed a fear that told me, "Hitendra, you aren't ready yet. You aren't virtuous enough, self-disciplined enough, prepared enough." Then one day my wife said, "There is an initiation ceremony in a few days for Self-Realization Fellowship members who wish to get the technique of Kriya Yoga. This is what you've been aiming for. This is your moment. Apply for it and take it now."

"But I am not ready yet," I protested. "I will need to take a vow of doing my meditation twice a day. I still need to get my basics in place. I'll do it next year."

"You are ready!" she responded. "I've never seen you so motivated about this. If there's someone who will make the most of it, it is you. This is your moment. Don't let it pass you by."

It was as though she were rousing me from a deep, long, slothful slumber. I got my initiation, took the vow to do my daily practice, and haven't looked back since. In that moment, my wife gave me the nudge of a lifetime.

The pursuit of Growth requires that we not simply *form* our social circle but *reform* it. Research shows that our emotions, values, and behavior are unconsciously influenced by those we spend time with. If you regularly spend time with people whose values are antithetical to your own, you may, without knowing it, slip into their way of thinking and being. One option you have is to respectfully walk away from such relationships. Another is to place boundaries around the kinds of interactions you have with such people—you will engage in certain conversations with them, but not others, and will do certain things together, but not others. And a third is to gracefully limit the time you spend with them. Making such shifts can be hard, particularly if you share deep mutual bonds with the other person. But if you are committed to your Growth, know that your progress may be seriously impeded if you actively and undiscriminatingly associate with people who affirm you for who you have been rather than whom you wish to become.

And finally we need to learn to tune in to the muse within—our inner voice. Enron was a high-flying energy-trading company that collapsed in the wake of an accounting scandal. An Enron trader was later asked why he hadn't stepped back to question the company's highly troubling practices on the trading floor. He remarked that he regretted not asking himself, "Why am I doing this? Is this the right thing to do? Is this the behavior I truly value, or am I just caught up in the moment?" The din of the trading floor had drowned out his inner voice. It can happen to any of us. That is why it is critical to practice solitude to strengthen our relationship with that voice.

Modern life confuses solitude with isolation, as though spending time by yourself will make you lonely. In one way, this is true. Research shows that when solitude is forced upon an individual, or if they choose it out of a fear of, or disenchantment with, their social environment, they can experience poorer mental health. But research also shows that when you intentionally cultivate solitude, you reap rich dividends.

When you are by yourself, you are free from the expectations of others and no longer compelled to coordinate your experience with theirs. This allows you to think and act in ways true to yourself. By pulling you away from your social environment, solitude unshackles you from various forms of identity that the world imposes on you, like the roles you play in life. You are able to pursue deeper self-examination and make more independent choices about your direction. Gandhi aptly said, "In the attitude of silence the soul finds the path in a clearer light, and what is elusive and deceptive resolves itself into crystal clearness." Einstein wrote about how solitude helped him cultivate certain inner mentors and allies: "Although I am a typical loner in my daily life, my awareness of belonging to the invisible community of those who strive for truth, beauty, and justice has prevented me from feelings of isolation."

Keith LaMar understands this well. Convicted for a murder, and later for a prison uprising, he has been in solitary confinement for over twenty years, isolated in a tiny prison cell. "All of a sudden you're confronted with yourself, and find that in a lot of cases you haven't really put anything into yourself to occupy yourself. Everything is outward directed. . . . You have to learn how to deal with yourself." How did Keith learn to cope with his situation? "I've watched quite a few people fall apart, lose their minds," he recounts. "But I went in another direction. So 27 years later I'm still sound in mind and body and spirit. . . . My cell has a bookshelf with three shelves, and there's a table to sit and write. I have a lot of music, books to read.

Not to distract myself from myself, but to take me deeper into myself. I paint, I work out, I do yoga, I meditate." None of us would wish to be in Keith's situation, and yet we can feel a great sense of appreciation for how he has used his time while incarcerated to become a near master at the art of solitude.

With your mentors, allies, and inner muse in place, it is time to begin sculpting.

Stage 5: Chisel Away Every Day

Some time back, I decided to institute a regular practice of fasting. All of us have a special relationship with the food we eat. Even on days when your boss is grouchy, or your spouse scolds you, you're guaranteed to have those three or four moments when there will be something delicious on your palate to please you, just the way you want it. So at first it was hard to keep my fast. I felt hungry and deprived of pleasure. Then I started to notice that the real problem lay with my thoughts, not my behavior. During my fast, certain tempting thoughts would arise: "If you don't eat, you'll be joyless this whole afternoon." "You've worked so hard. Skip your fast just this one time." "C'mon, take a few tiny bites. Then go back to your fast." "Everyone will be so happy if you ate with them." "You've kept a fast the whole day. You've achieved 90 percent of your goal. You're a winner. Now eat something."

I started to challenge these thoughts. I reminded myself how light and energized I felt when I fasted because my body wasn't consuming energy to digest food, and how many other sources of happiness there were to my day. Every time I redirected my thoughts, I found it a breeze to keep my fast. I noticed that on the days I fasted, my mind was more focused during work and more easily interiorized during meditation. Instead of feeling hungry, deprived, indulgent, weak, imprisoned, rebellious, and self-pitiful when doing a fast, I started to feel joyous, light, energized, and free.

And this is the lesson I want to offer you. When you try to change your behavior, some impulses within you will resist the change.

There's a good reason you have been doing things a certain way thus far, and that part of you will not wish to die. You may find yourself relapsing into old behaviors. But if you chisel your stone at a much deeper level, uprooting limiting thoughts and beliefs, the behavior you seek will emerge more naturally. It is only when you start to feel joy in being the "new you," when your thoughts, feelings, and actions are in harmony, that you will finally experience a lasting release from your old ways.

The popular Sufi poet Rumi wrote, "Every moment I shape my destiny with a chisel, I am a carpenter of my own soul." The chisel in our possession is daily introspection. Anne Frank described this practice so beautifully in her diaries, penned when she and her family were hiding from the Nazis in World War II in Amsterdam. "How noble and good everyone could be if, at the end of each day, they were to review their own behavior and weigh up the rights and wrongs. They would automatically try to do better at the start of each new day and, after a while, would certainly accomplish a great deal . . . 'a quiet conscience gives you strength!'"

Daily introspection is hard. If I were to reflect on all my flaws, I fear I would need the whole day, and yet I might unconsciously miss some of my greatest failings. And anyway, what would I do after I laid out all my shortcomings? How much could I aim to change in one day?

One of my MBA students, Daniel Dixon, who is now on his way to being ordained a priest, introduced me to the Examen, a prayerful practice of introspection that dates back to ancient Greek philosophers and the early days of the Christian church. Saint Ignatius evolved the Examen into a beautiful form of daily reflection. My understanding of the Examen was further enriched by Rev. James Martin, a Jesuit priest and author of *Learning to Pray*, in a conversation we had on the transformative possibilities of prayer. The Examen has everything we need to create a practice of daily introspection, so I adapted it for my students' use and now offer it to you.

CORE REVIEW

This is a dialog you will have with your Inner Core, or a Core role model, or God. You are being invited not so much to review your actions as to examine your consciousness. It is less about applying your intellect and more about listening to your feelings and intuition.

Going through the five steps should take ten to fifteen minutes. Perform it sometime in the evening, as your day is coming to a close, or first thing in the morning, before you "seize the day." Ideally, create a space at home that can be your sanctuary for quiet introspection and other contemplative practices.

1. **Invite the presence.** Do a brief practice—for example, prayer, deep breathing, or meditation—to help you get centered. Withdraw your mind from the world and turn it inward. Feel the peace within. Visualize yourself in the presence of your Inner Core, or one of your Core role models, or God, and approach the steps below as a conversation with this uplifting presence you have invited into your inner space.

2. **Flow with gratitude.** Reflect on the day that has just passed, and let gratitude flow into your heart. What special gifts has life brought to you over the course of the day? Revisit those moments. Even if your day has been challenging, there are always things, small or big, that you can be grateful for. Gratitude opens our heart to a feeling that the universe is on our side, that every experience has meaning.

3. **Review the day.** In what moments of the day did you feel centered in your Core? Were there occasions when you got triggered? What impact did your being centered or triggered have on you, and what impact did it have on others? Let calm feelings "interiorly nudge" you to the parts of your day that are the most important to review. Open your heart to receive whatever intuitively stirs from within, even inner or outer experiences that may have seemed inconsequential at the time.

4. **Reflect on your stumbles.** In what moments do you wish you had done more to help others be more committed, calm, curious, connected, or centered?

   Avoid the temptation to blame others or to lament your circumstances. Instead, turn the spotlight on yourself: regardless of the situation, and regardless of what others said or did, did you succeed or fail to live up to your highest ideals—to activate your Core, and to doing your best to activate theirs? If you find you failed, you may feel remorse. Since you are a work in progress, translate this into a motivating force to learn from your mistakes and take the right actions to address them. In some cases, offering a heartfelt apology may be warranted. At the same time, affirm the purity and power of your ideal form that lies within. Make peace with the day that has gone by.

5. **Plan for the day ahead.** Turn your mind to the coming day. How will you stop yourself from being derailed by triggers? How will you stay tuned to your inner voice so it can guide you through the day? If you're focused on cultivating a Core Energy, how will you activate and express it? Visualize important parts of the coming day in your mind, with you playing out your best self regardless of whether good or not-so-good things come your way.

This is how Steve Jobs described his Growth chisel: "For the past 33 years, I have looked in the mirror every morning and asked myself 'If today were the last day of my life, would I want to be doing what I'm doing?' Whenever the answer has been no for too many days in a row, I know I need to change something." Like our daily Core Review, Jobs's approach was centered not on reasoning but on intuition. Though he may have gone against his inner guidance for days, when he finally found it impossible to ignore, in that moment he became ripe for change. This is what you will experience once you start doing the Core Review. You will begin feeling uncomfortable in fending off the whispers of your inner voice and repeating the same mistakes again and again. You will become increasingly vigilant not simply about what you do or say, but also about what you feel, think, and intend. You will become "spontaneously sensitive when important things happen" and begin taking steps to move in the direction of your Inner Core. By invoking its daily presence, you will feel a pull to doing your best and being your best, from within and without, in moments small and large, private and public.

Chiseling is a lifelong quest. About Abraham Lincoln, newspaperman Horace Greeley said, "Lincoln gladly profited by the teaching of events and circumstances, no matter how adverse or unwelcome. . . . There was probably no year of his life that he was not a wiser, cooler, better man than he had been the year preceding."

My father was raised in the simple traditions of a small Indian village. He walked a few miles, often barefoot, to attend school each day. He and his six siblings had no precise knowledge of their birthdays; rural India of the 1930s had no concept of the Gregorian calendar. Perhaps this portrayal of his circumstances will help you understand why my father did not acquire some of the graces of modern-day love, such as the idea that every husband should present his wife with a beautiful gift on her birthday. He didn't do so, and the absence of this gesture would be a lifelong disappointment for my more genteel mother. Then one year, when her birthday came around, he gave her a big hug, wished her happy birthday, and presented her with an unexpected and lavish gift. My mother was in tears, moved by the unprompted metamorphosis in the man she had loved from the day she was his eighteen-year-old bride. It had taken him fifty-six years of marriage to finally acquiesce to expressing love in the language she had always wanted him to. He passed away a week later. It is never too late; a heart can keep growing till its final beat.

THERE'S MORE, MUCH MORE, TO ELVIS AND STEVE

Beneath his outer hungers, Elvis was hiding a beautiful inner hunger. He told First Assembly of God pastor James Hamill in 1958, "I'm the most miserable man you've ever seen. I've just got all the money I'll ever need to spend. I've got millions of fans. I've got friends. But I'm doing what you taught me not to do and not doing the things you taught me to do." His ex-wife, Priscilla, observed, "Elvis had been searching his entire life. . . . He was convinced his purpose went well beyond music and movies. . . . He was absolutely mesmerizing when he read Scripture and acted out the stories." Elvis told his costar Deborah Walley, "I'm not a man. I'm not a woman—I'm a soul, a spirit, a force."

Elvis's inner stirrings led him to the teachings of Yogananda and to his organization, Self-Realization Fellowship. In the top margin of page 277 of Elvis's copy of Yogananda's *Autobiography of a Yogi* are the following words scribbled in Elvis's handwriting: "Everything else can wait but our search for God can't."

Priscilla reminisced, "I have this picture in my mind: It's a clear sunny afternoon in Los Angeles. Elvis and I are on our motorcycles, roaring through Bel Air, down Sunset Boulevard, over the freeway, past Brentwood into Pacific Palisades. We stop at an idyllic retreat called Self-Realization Fellowship Lake Shrine. Elvis takes my hand and leads me through the grounds. . . . For a long time, we sit in the meditation garden and focus our attention on our breath. I've never seen Elvis this calm. 'It's what we all need,' he says. 'A break from the craziness.'"

Elvis became close to Self-Realization Fellowship president Daya Mata, whom he called his "spiritual mother." Born Rachel Faye Wright in Salt Lake City into a Mormon family, she had entered the SRF monastic order at the age of seventeen. She once spoke of her meetings with Elvis:

> When he came to Mother Center to see me, it was evident that he felt the constant pull of his career and was stressed at times because of it. I recall saying to him at the time: "Elvis, relax about your career. Slow down. Take some time and seek out a quiet place where you can just enjoy the company of your family and forget your concerns about your following. You will be remembered long after you have left this world." Those words were spoken not out of any presentiment that he would soon leave this earth but from a conviction that he had already established his place in the world.

Priscilla remarked, "Elvis wanted to devote his life to helping others fulfill themselves through devotional discipline. In fact, he wanted to be a leader of the Self-Realization Fellowship. In this regard, Daya Mata was especially wise. 'This higher level of spirituality,' he'd tell her, 'is what I've been seeking my whole life. Now that I know where it is and how to achieve it, I want to teach it. I want to teach it to all my fans—to the whole world.' 'You must go slow with this process,' she advised him. 'This evolution isn't instantaneous.' But Elvis, always in a hurry, said, 'I want to get there now. I want a crash course. There have to be short cuts.' 'There are no short cuts, Elvis. This takes discipline and commitment. To teach others would require your full-time dedication. You have to live this life.'"

Elvis frequently reached out to Daya Mata for guidance. He met with her after his marriage to Priscilla ended in 1972 and later recounted the meeting to a friend, Larry Geller:

> There's no hiding from her, Lawrence, that's for sure. The minute I walked into her room she knew exactly where I was at. We

just sat together for a while, first not talking at all, and then meditating. She knew I was hurting without my saying a word, and she didn't judge me or ask me questions; just held my hands. It was so beautiful, like she was giving me love and strength with her eyes and her touch. 'Course she didn't let me off scot-free. She said my mind and my spirit would be fine, as I meditate and grow calmer, but she was concerned that I was neglecting my body. I promised her I would work on it but, let's face it, that's one area where I need some serious help.

Elvis is buried in the meditation garden that he was inspired to create at Graceland after a visit with Daya Mata. His stone needed sculpting, and Elvis knew it. In Daya Mata he had a Core role model and mentor.* He couldn't bring himself to follow her guidance. But unbeknownst to his fans, he held a belief that he was born for something far more meaningful and enduring than the sole pursuit of earthly fame and fortune—that within him lay a beautiful Graceland.

§

Steve Jobs received a second chance to put a dent in the universe when he returned to Apple as its CEO in 1997. By then he had started to supplement his inner strivings with outer strivings, taking pains to learn how to get the best out of people, draw ideas and inspirations from others, and develop rewarding personal relationships.

Some of his outer growth came from actions he took in his personal life. He finally acknowledged that he had been wrong about his daughter Lisa and sought to build a relationship with her. His marriage to Laurene and the three children they raised made him "fairer

---

* I am moved to share a personal story. Elvis died in 1977, the same year I was introduced to Yogananda and Self-Realization Fellowship as a ten-year-old in a small town in India. Through her recorded talks and her book *Only Love,* Daya Mata became my greatest living Core role model and remained so until her passing at age ninety-six in 2010. Meeting her at Mother Center in LA in 1994—perhaps in the same room where Elvis might have met her—remains one of my most treasured memories.

and wiser, and his understanding of partnership deepened." After he became a father, "he was a changed man. He had a sweetness to him, a contemplative quality."

Heidi Roizen, who was CEO of a company Jobs was in negotiations with, once received a call from him. Heidi's father had died the night before, but because it was Steve Jobs, she picked up the phone. When he learned about her father's passing, Steve exclaimed, "Then why are you working? You need to go home. I'll be right over." He went to her house and sat on the floor beside her as she cried for two hours. "Yes, I had sofas, but Steve didn't like to sit on sofas. He asked me to talk about my father, what was important about him, what I loved best about him. . . . I will always remember and appreciate what an incredible thing he did for me in helping me grieve."

Ed Catmull worked with Steve for twenty-six years as CEO of the movie animation studio Pixar, which Jobs had acquired. Ed wrote, "Relentless Steve—the boorish, brilliant, but emotionally tone-deaf guy that we first came to know—changed into a different man during the last two decades of his life. All of us who knew Steve well noticed the transformation. . . . He became more sensitive not only to other people's feelings but also to their value as contributors to the creative process. . . . The change in him was real, and it was deep."

Apple CEO Tim Cook has reflected, "The Steve that I met in early '98 was brash and confident and passionate and all of those things. But there was a soft side of him as well, and that soft side became a larger portion of him over the next thirteen years. . . . He had the courage to admit he was wrong, and to change, a quality which many people at that level, who have accomplished that much, lack. . . . He wasn't beholden to anything except a set of core values. Anything else he could walk away from. . . . It was an absolute gift."

There were still times when Jobs would fume over past grievances, be abrasive, or disengage from people he concluded weren't of value to Apple. Cook acknowledged, "He wasn't a saint," but then went on to say, "but it's emphatically untrue that he wasn't a great human being." Business researcher and author Jim Collins has shared, "I don't see [Jobs's career] as a success story, but a growth story. I wish I could have seen Steve Jobs 3.0."

When Jobs's health started to fail him while he was at the height of his professional success, he used that personal struggle to continue his outer growth. Jeff Goodell, a reporter for *Rolling Stone* magazine, shared his observations of Jobs's final months:

> Late last year, Jobs called me out of the blue to ask about doing another magazine story together. I was struck by how different his voice sounded on the phone. It was not just softer and weaker. It was also more curious. For the first time, he asked me about my kids. I have no idea how he even knew that I have kids—we'd never discussed it. Others noticed the same change in his manner. He no longer seemed as arrogant, and had lots of time and compassion for the suffering of others. When [Jobs's friend Larry] Brilliant's 24-year-old son developed what turned out to be a fatal cancer, Jobs became his "cancer buddy," Brilliant says. Jobs made spreadsheets detailing the pros and cons of various doctors to help him decide whom to see. He called every week, talking Brilliant's son through the chemo, saying, "If I can make it through this, so can you." "Whenever he was down, Steve would call and give him a pep talk to buoy his spirits," recalls Brilliant.

Before his passing, Steve "organized the speakers, the attendees and the performers, Bono and Yo-Yo Ma," for his memorial service. The Silicon Valley glitterati who attended the event received a gift on their way out. "Whatever this was, was the last thing he wanted us to all think about," said one of the guests, Marc Benioff, the founder and CEO of Salesforce. The gift was a book Steve had first read in his teens and then reread every year after. It was the only book he had kept on his iPad. It was the book in which, in the top margin on page 277, Elvis had shared his deepest yearning. Yogananda's *Autobiography of a Yogi.*

Chapter 9

LEADING WITH GROWTH

≼⅋≽

Character building begins in our infancy and continues till death. . . . Readjustment is endless. Readjustment is a kind of private revolution. Each time you
learn something new you must readjust the whole
framework of your knowledge. It seems to me that
one is forced to make inner and outer adjustments
all one's life. The process never ends.

—*Eleanor Roosevelt*

THE SCULPTING OF A HERO

Though she was born in privilege—her family was part of New
York's high society—Eleanor's life from the start was anything
but smooth. She received little in the way of affection and love from
her mother, Anne, who would scold her and say, "You have no looks,
so see to it that you have manners." Her aunt Edith wrote to a friend,
"Her mouth and teeth seem to have no future." The one person who
gave her the love and tenderness she yearned for, her father, was
an alcoholic who eventually had to be taken away to a sanitarium.
Eleanor later recounted, "Mine was a very miserable childhood. . . .
I wanted to be loved so badly, and most of all I wanted to be loved by

my father" and "I often felt that I'd like to have the floor open so that I could sink into it."

Eleanor's mother died when she was eight, and one of her two brothers died when she was nine. When she was ten, her father, who had been spending the night at another apartment, one day became delirious, knocked on the neighbors' door to ask for Eleanor, and said, "Will you tell her [that] her father is so sorry not to see her?" An hour later he died.

As a teenager in a boarding school in England, Eleanor developed a close relationship with the seventy-year-old headmistress, Mademoiselle Souvestre. Souvestre, she recalled, was "far and away the most impressive and fascinating person" at her school. Like other girls of her time, Eleanor had been taught to suppress her natural curiosity. But Souvestre encouraged this quality. "You must cultivate curiosity, for only through curiosity can you learn, not only what there is in books, but what lies around you in the world of things and people." Souvestre became a valued mentor for Eleanor, someone she could rely on "as a guide for me—to think of what I could do, rather than about what I could not. . . . Whatever I have become since had its seeds in those three years of contact with a liberal mind and strong personality. . . . All my life I have been grateful for her influence."

One day Souvestre praised her in front of the school assembly, and Eleanor later reflected, "For the first time in all my life all my fears left me." Souvestre described Eleanor in a letter to Eleanor's grandmother: "She is full of sympathy for all those who live with her and shows an intelligent interest in everything she comes in contact with. As a pupil she is very satisfactory, but even that is of small account when you compare it with the perfect quality of her soul."

While in school, Eleanor began to change the negative beliefs about herself that her mother had ingrained in her. She later wrote, "It may seem strange, but no matter how plain a woman may be, if truth and loyalty are stamped upon her face, all will be attracted to her and she will do good to all who come near her and those who know her well will always love her."

Souvestre was a strong influence, but Eleanor's insecurities would nonetheless persist for years to come. As she entered adulthood, "a certain kind of orthodox goodness was my ideal and ambition." At twenty-one, Eleanor got married and focused on one thing: pleasing the people she wished to be loved by. "I left everything to my mother-in-law and my husband. I was growing very dependent on my mother-in-law, requiring her help on almost every subject, and never thought of asking for anything which I felt would not meet with her approval." This was reinforced by the domineering nature of her mother-in-law, who wished to control all aspects of her household. Eleanor's first son recounted being told by his grandmother, "Your mother only bore you, I am more your mother than your mother is." During this period, Eleanor felt that she "had no sense of values whatsoever." Her friend Joseph Lash wrote, "In return for the privilege of loving and being loved she stifled any impulse to assert herself."

This hapless, dependent woman—Eleanor Roosevelt—evolved to become the Most Admired Woman in Gallup's US polls thirteen times in the fourteen-year period from 1948 to 1961, and was ranked ninth among the "most admired" people of the twentieth century in a 1999 Gallup poll. How did someone whose life was full of such pain and deprivation become such a hero?

The secret to Eleanor's transformation was her pursuit of inner and outer Growth. She used every life experience as a catalyst for self-reflection and inner sculpting. The more she evolved, the more strength and understanding she gained to help advance the world she was part of.

Eleanor's first steps toward independence came in 1910, when her husband, Franklin, won a seat in the New York State Senate and the family moved away from her mother-in-law. "For the first time I was going to live on my own," Eleanor recounted. "I think I knew that it was good for me. . . . I was beginning to realize that something within me craved to be an individual." In 1917, when the United States entered World War I, Eleanor actively poured herself into wartime service. "I was learning to have a certain confidence in myself and in my ability to meet emergencies and deal with them." After a visit to St. Elizabeth's Hospital, a psychiatric facility for shell-shocked soldiers, where she observed shoddy treatment and supplies, she pressured the secretary of the interior, Franklin Lane, to appoint a commission to reform the hospital. "I became," she wrote, "more determined to try for certain ultimate objectives. I had gained a certain assurance as to my ability to run things, and the knowledge that there is joy in accomplishing good."

After the death of her third child in infancy, Eleanor was consumed by grief. But the terrible loss proved to be a catalyst for inner change. "Sometimes I think I cannot bear the heartache which one little life has left behind, but then I realize that we have much to be grateful for still, and that it was meant for us to understand and sympathize more deeply with all of life's sorrows."

By the time Eleanor was in her mid-thirties, Franklin was assistant secretary of the navy under Woodrow Wilson, and Eleanor was "running a household with five children and constant guests streaming in and out, [and] had nowhere to seek refuge." She realized that if she couldn't find calm on the outside, she had to cultivate it on the inside. "I learned that the ability to attain this inner calm, regardless of outside turmoil, is a kind of strength," she wrote. "In this oasis of peace you are better able to cope." Her growth during this phase of her life beautifully illustrates a principle she offered in her later writings: "Today, living and learning must go hand in hand."

But her learning didn't all come instantly. When a state referendum gave New York women the right to vote in the 1918 election, Eleanor—who later would become a great champion of women's rights—refused to cast a ballot. "I took it for granted that men were superior creatures and knew more about politics than women did," she wrote.

When she was thirty-four, she discovered that her husband had been having an affair with Lucy Mercer, her social secretary. "The bottom dropped out of my own particular world and I faced myself, my surroundings, my world, honestly for the first time." She suffered depression and struggled to eat. "There are times, I think, in everyone's life," she later wrote, "when the wish to be done with the burdens and even the decisions of this life seems overwhelming." After the initial shock of discovering the infidelity, Eleanor decided to stay in the marriage. She and Franklin committed themselves to supporting each other's endeavors. Eleanor used the experience to become more emotionally self-sufficient and even more dedicated to the pursuit of her own values, pouring her energies into the social causes that mattered most to her. Her son James wrote that his mother had become "filled with a passion for politics through which she saw the chance to right wrongs, to be of use." She reflected later, "Nothing ever happens to us except what happens in our minds. . . . Unhappiness is an inward, not an outward, thing."

As she entered her early forties, she found that she was "drifting far afield from the old influences . . . thinking things out for myself." Her values were becoming the pillars of her life. "To be mature you have to realize what you value most."

In 1933, when Eleanor was nearly fifty, Franklin was elected president of the United States. During her years at the White House she would transform the role of First Lady, becoming "the first (and only) First Lady to hold regular press conferences, write a daily newspaper column, publish books and articles, travel the nation on speaking tours, chair national conferences in the White House, address national conventions of social reform organizations, give a keynote address at her party's presidential convention, represent her nation abroad, travel battlefields, and direct a government agency." She was famous for the notes, analyses, and recommendations she placed on her husband's desk every night, lobbying fiercely for anti-lynching legislation, for a forty-eight-hour workweek, for a minimum wage, for funding childcare centers for working mothers, and for equal pay for women. All this at a time when women of her background, especially First Ladies, were expected to refrain from venturing into the public arena.

In 1938, as First Lady, Eleanor attended a conference on human welfare in Alabama with fifteen hundred delegates. Black and white participants were required to sit in separate sections in compliance with Alabama's segregation laws. When Eleanor first entered, she sat on the black side of the aisle to express her disapproval of segregation, only to be told by the police that she needed to move because she was violating the law. So what did she do next? Eleanor pulled a chair from the white side of the room, placed it in the aisle between the two sections, and sat in it. "Courage is more exhilarating than fear," Eleanor once advised, "and in the long run it is easier. We do not have to become heroes overnight. Just a step at a time, meeting each thing that comes up, seeing it is not as dreadful as it appeared, discovering we have the strength to stare it down." Lacking the ability to bring about instant change in others, Eleanor often looked to start a national conversation by taking a clear stand, to "interest people and bring about discussion."

In 1942, Eleanor made a controversial visit to see American soldiers stationed in the South Pacific during World War II. She was subjected to criticism over the cost of the trip and the usefulness of a First Lady visiting troops. The US commanding officer in the region, Admiral Halsey, was highly displeased by the distraction her visit would cause to his men's objective of fighting a war. But he later wrote,

> When I say that she inspected those hospitals, I don't mean that she shook hands with the chief medical officer, glanced into a sun-parlor, and left. I mean that she went into every ward, stopped at every bed, and spoke to every patient: What was his name? How did he feel? Was there anything he needed? Could she take a message home for him? I marveled at her hardihood, both physical and mental; she walked for miles, and she saw patients who were grievously and gruesomely wounded. But I marveled most at their expressions as she leaned over them. It was a sight I will never forget.

He also said, "I told her that it was impossible for me to express my appreciation of what she had done, and was doing, for my men. I was ashamed of my original surliness."

On that trip, she traveled twenty-six thousand miles over six weeks, saw an estimated four hundred thousand men in different hospitals and camps—and lost thirty pounds. A woman with no knowledge of warfare won over a skeptical admiral and his troops, just by modeling the power of human touch.

Eleanor Roosevelt didn't reserve this touch for her moments in the limelight; it was part of who she was at her Core. "You must be interested in anything that comes your way," she once advised. An insurance salesman in New York recalled being stuck in an elevator with her for ten minutes. "I think that I am the most uninteresting fellow in the world," he recalled, "and yet Mrs. Roosevelt wanted to know everything about me, as if I were equal to her."

Having grown so much in her understanding of herself, Eleanor took rapid strides in increasing her understanding of others. In 1918, she had lamented about having been required to attend a party to honor the financier Bernard Baruch, a Jew: "I'd rather be hung than seen at [the event]. . . . The Jew party was appalling." At that stage, she was expressing the antisemitism that was standard in her social circle. But over time she radically changed her views. Baruch himself became a treasured friend, "one of the wisest and most generous people I have ever known." During World War II, she personally followed up on visas for Jewish refugees fleeing Germany, reunited families, and supported Jewish organizations, however small. When a Jewish woman, Elinor Morgenthau, was denied membership in the Colony Club, which Eleanor had cofounded, she resigned. Jeffrey S. Urbin, an expert on the Roosevelts, has noted that "she was at first a person of her times, who then explored issues and concerns and determined if she thought they were right or wrong, and then was not afraid to allow herself to change and become a better, more accepting, more balanced and informed person. And she then sought to enlighten those around her."

When Franklin died in office, it was time for Eleanor to leave the White House. President Truman called her back into public service by appointing her to the American delegation to the United Nations. There, she quickly gained the respect of fellow international delegates. She was appointed chair of the committee that drafted the seminal Universal Declaration of Human Rights, a touchstone of liberty to this day. She brought to the task her own convictions, for all through her leadership journey she had championed the causes of the mistreated and the marginalized—women, blacks, Jews, children, the poor, Japanese Americans, war veterans, refugees, and more. But she also changed her ideas as the world around her changed. Article 1 of the declaration initially used the word "men." Eleanor's vice chair, Hansa Mehta, India's delegate to the committee, said to her, "Excuse me, Mrs. Roosevelt, if you say 'All men are born free and equal,' around the world, it will be all men—women not included." Eleanor recognized that Hansa was expressing the aspirations of a new generation of women seeking to question the old order, and agreed to substitute "All human beings are born free and equal." A small step for the English language, but a big leap for womankind— and thus, humankind.

For her distinctive contributions at the United Nations, President Truman called Eleanor Roosevelt the "First Lady of the World." From a timid, needy, rudderless individual, she had sculpted her way to becoming someone Martin Luther King Jr. called "perhaps the greatest woman [of] our time." About her remarkable impact, she reflected, "The influence you exert is through your own life and what you become yourself." And if you were to have asked her, "How do I go about shaping what I become?" she would have counseled, as she once wrote, "We all create the person we become by our choices as we go through life," and on another occasion, "It is useless to resent anything in this world; one must learn to look on whatever happens as part of one's education in life and make it serve a good purpose in the formation of character."

Our world is a much nobler place today because Eleanor Roosevelt embraced life as a school, chose character as her course of study, became an accomplished student, and graduated to teach us all.

Chapter 10

LIVING WITH LOVE

⚘

Love is the bridge between you and everything.

—*Rumi*

WHEN TWO HILLS MEET

On August 20, 2013, as the eight hundred students of Ronald E. McNair Discovery Learning Academy, an elementary school near Atlanta, Georgia, settled into their morning classes, a young man named Michael Hill walked into the school's lobby with an AK-47 and five hundred rounds of ammunition. Another mass shooting in an American school was in the making. Thirty minutes later, Michael was in police custody. There were no casualties at the school that day, because Michael had been overpowered and disarmed. Not by a phalanx of security guards, but by Antoinette Tuff, the school's bookkeeper, who had been substituting at the front desk.

Antoinette used no authority, commands, threats, weapons, or force on Michael. At every step of her ordeal, Antoinette offered Michael respect, kinship, kindness, and compassion. She asked for his permission before giving instructions to the 911 emergency operator who was on the phone with her. "You . . . want me to tell them to come on in now?" When he revealed his name, she forged a bond with him by discovering a coincidental connection. "Guess what, my name is Hill too, my mom was a Hill." Once Michael had been persuaded by her to drop his plan for a mass shooting, he started to turn his weapon on himself. Having saved the students' lives and her own life, Antoinette now focused on saving Michael's. "No, you don't want that. . . . You're going to be OK. I thought of the same thing. I thought of committing suicide last year when my husband left me, but look at me now, I am still working and everything is OK." She reassured him when he was finally ready to allow the police to come in and arrest him. "It's going to be OK, Sweetheart. I want you to know that I love you, OK . . . and I am proud of you. That's a good thing you've done that you have given up. And don't worry about it. We all go through something in life, you know. You don't want that. You're going to be OK."

We might suspect that Antoinette was a good actor, hiding her true feelings of fear and hatred. She did in fact later confess, "I was terrified. . . . That was one reason why I said to [the 911 operator] one time, 'Can I run?' I was just shaking so bad." She hid her anxiety, but she did not have to hide her hatred, for there was none. "I saw this 20-year-old man standing in front of me," she said in an interview. "He was the same age as my kids. I saw a young man crying out for help. At that moment he was not crying silently. He was crying out loud. I didn't see the bullets on his back or the AK-47. All I could see was this youth in front of me." On another occasion she reflected, "When he got to telling me that he wasn't on his medicine and everything that was going on with him and all that, I really began to feel sorry for him," and "He's a hurting soul." And finally, "I had tried to commit suicide myself, so I understood his pain. I pray for him every day."

When we fall in love, or have a child, or develop a strong kinship with someone, our sense of self expands to include that other person. Their joy becomes our joy, their success our success. But perhaps those near to us were meant to be only the starting point; perhaps nature has, all along, wished for us to keep expanding our heart so that it can hold more and more of the world in its embrace.

In overpowering a would-be mass killer with love, Antoinette showed us those grander possibilities.

THE ESSENCE OF LOVE

In its essence, Love is universal, selfless, unconditional.

Love Is Universal

Take a blank sheet of paper. This is the ocean of humanity. Place a dot on it close to the center. This is you. Draw a circle around the dot. Place your loved ones within the circle. Who, then, are the people that remain outside? Are they your "unloved" ones?

The love that arises from our Inner Core is universal. Once the flame is lit, its radiance and warmth project to all people who come into your orbit, without distinction. Over time, the whole page, the ocean of humanity, becomes your circle.

One way you can live is by seeing yourself as distinct and separate from others. When we operate this way, we get focused on meeting our own needs and on getting the world to accommodate us. If the world does so, then we feel connected, committed, collaborative. We build relationships and partnerships. We love, for we wish to be loved, and we give, for we wish to receive. But if the world does not accommodate, we start to disengage from those who get in our way, and we invite into our inner circle only those who give us what we are seeking. We feel a bit alone in the universe.

There is another way to live: the way of Love. Love recognizes that all life, all of the universe, is interconnected and interdependent; that it is an illusion to see ourselves as distinct and separate from things around us; that in our most authentic state, when we operate from our Core, we have an integral connection with the universe.

This is how nature works. Biological cells specialize in doing their part and in supporting one another to create intelligent forms of life like plants and animals. These life-forms interact within their species and across species to keep the Earth in ecological balance. Each cell and each life-form strives to attain its full potential, but also gives and receives from other cells and life-forms as part of a larger whole. Interconnection and interdependence occur at every scale of creation. We may think that planet Earth is the one special place in our solar system that supports life. What about other heavenly bodies? If Jupiter hadn't existed, or the moon chose to quit in a huff, would it make any difference, practically, to our lives? It would. Astronomers have established that Jupiter is like a protective shield, absorbing asteroids that would have otherwise crashed into Earth and destroyed life. The moon helps to stabilize the Earth's axis of rotation; without it, the Earth would become wobbly, leading to sudden extreme fluctuations in temperature—severe cold and heat—that would cause humanity to perish.

Some of us operate with the belief that if we get too enmeshed with other people in a web of giving and taking, we will lose our individuality and hurt our own interests. Let's do a thought experiment. What if your brain told other organs in your body, "I'm the genius here! I don't need any of you. I'm declaring my independence." And then your heart said, "Oh, yeah? Let me stop pumping blood over to you, brain, and then you'll see who's in charge." And your lungs responded, "Wait a second! I'm providing all the oxygen here. I'll go on strike for a day. Then you'll know." Wouldn't it be insane for any organ to believe that it can go it alone? Isn't the give-and-take that happens among these organs the very force that allows each organ to thrive and operate to its full potential?

The idea of a self-made woman or man is a myth. We are all enmeshed in an intricate web of relationships across space and time. The Love that arises from your Inner Core invites you to expand your sense of self by dissolving the boundary between you and the ocean of life that lies beyond you; to recognize that the same spirit that flows in you is flowing in all other human beings, in all other life-forms, and, in fact, in every nook of nature; to keep attuning yourself to what notes the grand conductor of nature wants you to strike in the symphony of life—sometimes giving, sometimes receiving, and always loving. When we love this way, we feel at home in the universe.

Love Is Selfless

In my daily visits to a local café, I would put a dollar in the tipping jar after ordering my tea. One day I realized a certain pattern in my behavior: if the barista's back was turned to me, I would pause a few seconds before tipping. I wanted to make sure he noticed, so I could be appreciated for the tip. "I'm doing the right thing," I told myself, "but with the wrong intention." I decided to start doing the opposite, tipping when the barista *wasn't* looking, so I could cultivate a more selfless form of Love.

Our personal hungers silently shape our intentions. We take joy not so much in being kind as in having people appreciate us for being kind. We engage in public acts of altruism to win acclaim in our community and earn a place in heaven. We love, hoping that we will be loved in return. This is not Love—this is ego. The Love that arises from our Inner Core is selfless; it comes with no agenda, no "What's in it for me?" no sense of entitlement; it is mailed from our heart, with no return address. And yet this selfless form of Love fulfills us in a meaningful way.

Abraham Lincoln was traveling in a coach with a US senator, Edward Baker. He had just remarked to Baker that all people are motivated by selfishness. As the coach passed over a marshy area, the men noticed a pig squealing in despair. Her piglets were stuck in the swamp, slowly sinking under. Lincoln asked the coach driver to stop, then stepped down to rescue the piglets, placing each of them on the dry bank in the care of their mother. Senator Baker remarked, as Lincoln ascended the coach, "Now, Abe, where does selfishness come in this little episode?" Lincoln replied, "Why, bless your soul, Ed, that was the very essence of selfishness. I would have had no peace of mind all day had I gone on and left that suffering old sow worrying over those pigs. I did it to get peace of mind, don't you see?" When we love selflessly, what we are seeking in return is simply the peace of mind that comes from knowing that we have done right by other beings.

One of my students, Danny, shared the following story:

My family and I were blessed to be with my grandfather at the time of his passing. In the preceding hours, he spent a few minutes in private conversation with each of us. When it was my turn, I walked into the room and knelt by his bed. He held my hand in his and said, "Danny, before I go, I wanted to tell you a secret about the relationship between me and your grandmother. She and I have been married, happily, for sixty-two years. Do you know what the secret is to our marriage?"

"No, Grandpa, please tell me," I said. I had just started to date someone I was hoping to marry, so his counsel would be of great value to me.

"The secret is that it was never 50-50. It was always 90-10."

I was taken aback. Here he was, close to his death. Was he going to, at this final hour, take all the credit for his relationship with my grandmother? I furrowed my brow, partly in confusion, partly in disapproval. Perhaps this was the way relationships worked in his generation; it wasn't going to work today. His face lit up with love for my grandmother. "You see, Danny, sometimes it was 90 percent her and 10 percent me. And other times it was 90 percent me and 10 percent her. A relationship is never 50-50. It is always 90-10."

With friends and family, we sometimes fall into the trap of wanting our investment in love to give us a suitable return. But relationships wither on the vine of a 50-50 expectation. It is hard to tell when more will be needed from one partner or the other, and for how long.

None of us are strangers to selflessness. We practice it in small ways all the time—when we tend to a loved one who is sick, rush to the aid of a person who has stumbled and fallen on the street, pause to give directions to a tourist, or open the door for someone. The Love that arises from our Inner Core induces us to do whatever is right in the moment, whatever is needed, whatever is the best we can do. We love because we wish to love, not because we wish to be loved.

Love Is Unconditional

Take another blank sheet. This time, draw a line down the middle. On the left, write the behaviors and qualities in people that are endearing to you. On the right, write the behaviors and qualities that make you feel: "I don't even like this person, let alone love them."

What if you were to erase the line and open yourself to loving people without any conditions? Someone may tire us, upset us, betray us, fight us, oppose us, or even leave us, but life still invites us to love them from our Core. They may not deserve our help, cooperation, trust, or time—that is a different calculus—but our true self will never ask the question "Do they deserve my love?" To make our Love unconditional, we must banish all the preconditions we are tempted to set for loving. *If you do not behave well, I will not love you. If you oppose me, if you compete with me, if you are rude, if we have a fight, if we break up, if you criticize me, if you mess up, if you underperform, if I lay you off . . . well, then I will stop loving you.* Unconditional Love is a choice we make to stay in a state of grace even as we take thoughtful actions in service of our Purpose.

My student Matthew Stevenson relates the following events:

> As an Orthodox Jew, I used to host a Friday night Shabbat dinner at college. A student discovered that one of our dormmates, Derek Black, was a white nationalist—the godson of David Duke. Derek was very active in white nationalist circles and was seen as the future leadership of the movement. Students on campus started to treat Derek very poorly. I decided to invite Derek to our Shabbat dinner, thinking it would be good for him to meet people beyond his white nationalist circle. Some of the regular guests were highly offended by my decision and stopped coming. I asked my remaining guests not to use the dinner to attack Derek.
>
> Derek accepted my invitation, and over the next two years he was a regular guest at our Shabbat dinners, spending hours

in conversations with me and the other guests. I became good friends with Derek, and I asked my other guests not to bring up white nationalism in conversations with him. He and I became very close over time, though I didn't know much about his positions. He gradually started to open himself up to a conversation on race. Some of the guests would debate with him the legitimacy of the science and facts that he had learned from the white nationalist community. One of the guests was a statistician, and she showed him how to do the statistics on crime rates and IQ in the right manner.

Derek opened his mind to this thinking. Eventually, he decided to abandon his group's racist beliefs and reject their agenda. Since then, he and I have gone around the country, giving a number of talks about his transformation journey and how the Shabbat dinners and our friendship provided him the foundation to rethink his views.

In reaching out to Derek when he was the most disliked person on campus, in choosing to respect Derek and foster a friendship with him even though he promoted beliefs that were diametrically opposed to Matthew's, in letting Derek evolve his beliefs and become a better version of himself at his own pace, Matthew showed the discipline it takes to practice unconditional Love and the possibilities it offers for transforming people.

The goal of universal, selfless, and unconditional Love is not to lose yourself but to discover yourself—your true self, a self interwoven with the universe. The Love that flows from your Core is beautifully described in 1 Corinthians: "Love is very patient, very kind. Love knows no jealousy; love makes no parade, gives itself no airs, is never rude, never selfish, never irritated, never resentful; love is never glad when others go wrong, love is gladdened by goodness, always slow to expose, always eager to believe the best, always hopeful, always patient. Love never disappears."

THE POWER OF LOVE

Love offers luminous possibilities in our pursuit of inner and outer success. Research shows that people who practice compassion and kindness are happier. Helping others lights up our brain's pleasure and reward centers, as though we were on the receiving end of the kindness, not the giving end. After helping others, people report feeling calmer and less depressed and experiencing higher self-worth. The practice of Love also makes us healthier—lowering cholesterol levels and blood pressure, alleviating stress and anxiety, and even lengthening life spans. And it improves our relationships, creating the conditions under which rewarding relationships can be born and sustained.

Love builds a bouquet of actions that lie at the core of great leadership. Organizational experts have identified leadership behaviors that are critical to making the workplace more human and to building strong cultures: coaching and developing people, listening mindfully, making compassionate choices, sacrificing personal goals in the interest of the group, acting kindly toward all individuals, building bridges with adversaries, letting go of grudges, giving others credit while cushioning them from blame, and causing people to feel a sense of belonging and inclusion. Love is at the root of all these deeds. If you did not take joy in other people's joy or find success in their success, you would engage in these behaviors only grudgingly, with no heart in what you were doing, and people would see through you. On the other hand, if you have Love in your heart, these actions will flow naturally from you because they are what your heart guides you to do.

As an associate at McKinsey, I worked on a project with a highly respected manager, Jevin Eagle. Within a few weeks, I started to suspect I was the smartest person on the team. The project had a marketing analytics focus, and armed with my PhD I was making strong contributions in designing our surveys and analyzing data. I started to tell myself, "I'm clearly more in command of our deliverables than

Jevin and the rest of the team. Jevin is a star at the firm, so I'm likely to become a star too!" Over the next few weeks, I discovered the source of Jevin's success.

At my weekly meeting with Jevin to review my work, I would show him a trove of tables and charts laden with learnings about the client's market. He would take a step back to refocus on the client's core issues, then creatively draw out strategic insights from my analyses that would provide real value to the client. "Jevin's right," I would have to admit to myself. "I was so deep in the data trenches that I lost sight of the problem we're trying to solve and totally missed these insights." Later, in previewing our findings with senior McKinsey partners before taking them to the client, Jevin would say, "Hitendra has identified three really important strategic findings. Hitendra, why don't you present them?" I would be flattered but also flummoxed, because it was *he* who had come up with the findings. In those moments, he was letting me shine.

Jevin was always looking out for our team—keeping our workload in balance and nudging us to maintain a life outside the job. I saw him invest personal time with certain client executives to support their growth and success much beyond our official duties. In earlier times, I would try to get staffed on projects at McKinsey that focused on industries or business problems that interested me. But after this experience with him, I asked our staffing manager, "Could you staff me on whatever project Jevin is leading next?" After McKinsey, Jevin joined the executive team at Staples and then went on to become the CEO of a retail chain. Seven years ago, I received the following email from him: "I'm thrilled to share with you that I will be attending rabbinic school at Hebrew College this Fall. This has been a dream of mine for 25 years and something I've said is 'when,' not 'if.' 'When' is now. . . . My major professional focus will be Torah and the Jewish people. I'm grateful to [my wife and children] for supporting this move and my heart is filled with great joy about the days to come." Jevin has shown me how the candle of Love can stay quietly lit in our hearts as we go about our work, and that much outer success will flow to us when we stay true to our Core.

Love needn't merely connect you to the people you interact with; it can also connect you to a cause, a company, a community. Steve Jobs's practice of Love at work is best understood in this light. "When I hire somebody really senior," he said, "competence is the ante. They have to be really smart. But the real issue for me is, 'Are they going to fall in love with Apple?' Because if they fall in love with Apple, everything else will take care of itself. They'll want to do what's best for Apple, not what's best for them, what's best for Steve, or anybody else."

THE PATH OF LOVE

The path of Love invites us to become a gardener of our inner life so Love can bloom.

Stage 1: Prepare the Soil

The soil of our consciousness must be fertile to prepare it for Love, and that happens when we feel abundantly valued and loved ourselves.

In Chapter 3, "Ways of Knowing," we discussed the journeys of Martin Luther King Jr. and Malcolm X, starting with their divergent upbringing. King reflected, "It is quite easy for me to think of a God of love mainly because I grew up in a family where love was central and where lovely relationships were ever present. It is quite easy for me to think of the universe as basically friendly mainly because of my uplifting hereditary and environmental circumstances. It is quite easy for me to lean more toward optimism than pessimism about human nature mainly because of my childhood experiences." Malcolm X's childhood, in painful contrast, was bereft of an enduring, nurturing love. He held memories of fighting parents who beat the children, a father who died early, and a mother who had to be placed in a mental health facility. Perhaps this was why in college Martin embraced a more universal love for all people, while Malcolm for a long time could not do so.

Research shows that when children receive strong love and support from their parents (or other caregivers) and are able to rely on them, they are more likely to grow up as warm and loving adults, comfortable with intimacy, open to new things, unafraid of failure, good at resolving conflicts, and with a high level of concern for others. Children who lack this kind of love and support are more likely to grow up with an anxious or avoidant profile. An anxious person is less trusting in relationships, feels the need to be constantly reassured and supported, and struggles with handling conflict. An avoidant person stays away from experiencing warmth or intimacy out of fear that they will be disappointed or lose their independence.*

Research also shows that when, as adults, we have people in our inner circle whom we can lean on and who act as our emotional anchors, we are able to turn our attention outward—to engage positively with the world and pursue success. We are more motivated, curious, and creative, knowing there is someone behind us we can rely on, and we experience less distress during life's challenging moments. Scientists call this the dependency paradox: the more people we have in our life whom we feel loved and supported by, the less dependence we have on them.

We do not need to be in someone's physical presence to feel loved by them. Research shows that when you view a photo or simply visualize the presence of a person you feel deeply loved by, regardless of whether they are even alive, you will feel more emotionally centered and ready to take on the world. A student once told me, "My father died when I was very young. We loved each other dearly, and he was my role model. I carry a photo of him with me. I take it out and look at it whenever I am struggling with something. I ask myself, 'What would he tell me to do in this moment?'"

On his transformational journey to Mecca, Malcolm X found something that Martin Luther King Jr. had been blessed with from childhood: a feeling of belonging, a reassurance that he was deeply

---

* For those of us who have an anxious or avoidant profile in relationships, EFT (emotionally focused therapy) provides a scientifically proven approach to growing ourselves into a more secure profile; our upbringing does not have to determine our destiny.

loved. "What I have seen, and experienced," Malcolm recounted, "has forced me to re-arrange much of my thought-patterns previously held. . . . Thousands of people of different races and colors who treated me as a human being. . . . [I have] stood before the Creator of All and felt like a complete human being." Once his own lifelong hunger for love had been quenched, Malcolm was ready to love the whole world, not just a part of it.

You may source your Love from family, friends, role models, teachers, saints, or prophets. You may do so by spending time with them, revisiting fond memories, reading their words, or visualizing their loving presence. You may feel Love flowing to you from nature, spirit, a Heavenly Father, a Divine Mother, or your own Inner Core. What's important is that you tap an inexhaustible fountain of Love that keeps your own cup full. Because otherwise, your conduct will be driven by a thirst to win people's affection and approval, and you will find it hard to flow freely with Love.

Stage 2: Plant the Seeds

Claude Monet, who produced some of the most beautiful works of impressionist art, once reflected, "I must have flowers, always and always," and at another time, "I perhaps owe having become a painter to flowers." Monet's paintings were simply the outpouring of a heart that was full of love for nature. Warren Buffett, in the vastly different domain of finance, once declared that when he went into the office, "I feel like I am on my back, and there's the Sistine Chapel, and I'm painting away."

The great ones do not simply love—they are *in* love. With people, with life, with the world. When such Love wells up within us, it then naturally flows into our actions. There are habits we can cultivate to sow the seeds of Love in our heart.

The First Seed: Gratitude

John, one of my executive students, told the following story:

Once, in my weekly team meeting, everyone walked in at nine a.m. looking particularly tired and drained. Instead of proceeding with the agenda, I started by asking everyone to stand in a circle, close their eyes, and take a few deep breaths. We were silent for about five minutes. I broke the silence by saying a team member's name. I recalled my first interaction with this individual and expressed my gratitude for what I valued about the work he does and the person he is. I continued until I had gone through the whole team. By the end, we all had our eyes open and I even saw some tears from some people who are typically not that expressive. It was a moment of gratitude that we all shared and connected with. We felt a renewed sense of commitment to our work and to each other as the meeting and the day proceeded.

Gratitude is a choice we make about the heart-space from which we want to operate. One way to practice gratitude is by thinking of a person who has been very helpful to you at a certain point in your life, then writing a letter of gratitude to them, or simply feeling the gratitude in your heart. Another is by maintaining a journal in which you write down, every couple of days, two or three things you feel most grateful for from the preceding twenty-four to forty-eight hours. A third is by asking yourself, whenever you feel upset and want to lift yourself out of it, "What are some things that I feel really grateful for right now?" Science shows that these actions will increase your happiness.

You might say, "Well, this makes good sense when things are going well. But there are occasions when there's no time for gratitude, or no reason for it." Jianyu's story, which he shared in my executive MBA class, may offer a lesson:

I am a heart surgeon in Beijing. I routinely have a powerful impact on the lives of my patients, but on one occasion, one of my patients, Li, had a powerful impact on me. He was a small boy—twelve years of age. He had a congenital heart defect and needed surgery. As Li was being wheeled into the surgery room, he opened his eyes and saw me walking alongside his roller bed.

"Are you the doctor who will be doing this operation on me?" "Yes," I responded. I was struggling to find the right words to uplift his spirits. Li's face beamed with a smile. "Doctor, I am so happy to meet you. You must have worked so hard to become a doctor. I, too, want to be a doctor when I grow up."

His surgery turned out to be very complicated. I could not save Li's life, and he passed away the next day. The nurse who had been with him came up to me and handed me a note Li had written after his surgery addressed to me. It read, "Doctor, I am so grateful for all you have done for me today. You remind me of my older brother in the way you have cared for me, and I wanted to thank you for that."

We will never know whether Li had sensed when he wrote the note that he was close to death, but we can say that he possessed a remarkable capacity for gratitude even as he faced the grimmest moment of his life.

The more we cultivate a practice of gratitude for all life gives us, the more Love will flow through us. When we believe we have received abundantly, we will naturally wish to give abundantly.

The Second Seed: Appreciation

On a crisp fall morning in 2008, I stepped into an elevator on my way to the office of a well-known corporate leader. Let us call him Andrew. Andrew and I were meeting to explore a potential business partnership. As the elevator began its ascent, it struck me that my heart was not in the right place: I felt quite critical of Andrew's character. I had had one past interaction with Andrew and had found him rather self-centered—very focused on his own agenda. A friend later told me Andrew had a reputation for being quite brusque. My thoughts were telling me, "Hitendra, life is short. You want to work with people you like. Andrew isn't one of them. You're wasting your time here. So make this meeting brief, and then exit."

But I realized I was passing judgment on Andrew on the basis of very few impressions. I remembered something a student of mine had told me Warren Buffett had shared with him: "I believe that 10 percent of every human being is very inspiring. When I meet someone, my focus is on finding the 10 percent of this individual that is truly inspiring." I told myself, "Andrew must possess a beautiful Inner Core. Your goal today is to discover and connect with it. *You are going to walk out liking Andrew.*" By the time the elevator reached Andrew's floor, my energy had shifted. Instead of being guarded, skeptical, and disengaged, I was friendly, open, and interested. Over the course of our exchange, I discovered that Andrew and I had a shared interest in certain social causes, and that he was taking major chunks of time away from his business pursuits to support those endeavors. I learned that, like me, he was very fond of animals, and had started a shelter for injured animals. Whereas earlier I had found him self-centered, I now recognized that he was focused in a laser-sharp way on causes he believed in. His purported brusqueness now came across to me as refreshing candor as he flagged certain political sensitivities in a C-suite team he and I were dealing with. By the time I left his office, we had established a warm connection. My relationship with Andrew has blossomed over the years. I smile sometimes and wonder what would have happened if on that day in the elevator I had not made the choice to reset my feelings so I could meet him with an open, appreciative heart.

Appreciation invites us to scan our environment moment by moment for ideas, experiences, and qualities that we find uplifting, and then make it a habit to stay in this uplifted state—about people, about life, and about the world. Scientists have found that people who are in happy long-term relationships have a mental habit of scanning for qualities they admire in their partner, while those in unhappy relationships tend to scan for their partner's flaws.

Vincent van Gogh wrote in a letter to his brother, Theo, "Though I am often in the depths of misery, there is still calmness, pure harmony and music inside me. I see paintings or drawings in the poorest cottages, in the dirtiest corners. And my mind is driven towards these things with an irresistible momentum." What a beautiful testament to the capacity we all possess to do our greatest work even in turbulent times by looking for qualities we admire, within and without.

The Third Seed: Empathy

I once befriended two brothers, Tanner and Toby. They were troubled men. During the time I got to know them, they committed a few bank robberies. I dearly wished for them to stop this behavior, but they didn't. Yet I could not help but love them. Their highs were my highs, their lows my lows.

Then the movie ended. I walked out of the theater, my heart still bursting with love for the main characters. The movie is called *Hell or High Water.* I recommend it.

Some of us believe it is natural to feel empathy for near ones and for those who are part of our "flock"—our nation, our community, our race—and to not feel much empathy for people beyond these groups. And yet when we watch a film, we start to empathize with its characters; their joy becomes our joy, their sorrow our sorrow. Why? After all, these are actors—*the characters they're portraying are not even real people.* Perhaps it is because in watching a film we take the time to listen to a person's story, without judgment and with an open heart, and then we start to walk in their shoes. What might happen if we practiced this form of connection with whoever crosses our path in life? Could it make us empathize even with, say, the people we have a fierce dislike for?

On December 30, 2006, an old man woke up very early to prepare for a journey. He greeted the twelve men who had been living in the residence with him and asked if they'd gotten enough sleep. He told them they'd become "more family to him" than any of his own countrymen, thanked them for having treated him so well, and shook their hands in gratitude. Then it was time. He was escorted into a waiting helicopter by these men, and, upon its landing, into an armored bus. When the bus arrived at its destination, the man walked slowly to the front of the vehicle, stopping "to grasp each of the twelve young [men], and in a few cases, to whisper final private words. Some of [the twelve] now had tears in their eyes. . . . He turned to them one last time and said, 'May God be with you.' With that, he bowed slightly and turned toward the door."

A short while later, pandemonium broke loose. The old man had been hanged, and "a feverish crowd began to beat and spit on him." The twelve men "shared a feeling of sadness, followed by outrage." One of them "was so incensed that he launched himself toward the crowd, only to be held back by one of his colleagues."

The man who had just been hanged was Saddam Hussein, and the "Super Twelve," as they were known, were the American military policemen from Fort Campbell, Kentucky, who had been assigned to guard him in the weeks prior to his execution. When they learned of their assignment, some of them were so appalled by what a monster they saw Saddam to be that they wanted to kill him in his bed. Others wanted to transfer to different units. But as they spent time with Saddam, their feelings for him changed in remarkable ways. They developed a deep, empathetic bond with him. When he was hanged, several of the men experienced post-traumatic stress. One of them said, "I know I should hate Saddam, but it's not easy." Another said, "I felt like I let him down. I almost feel like a murderer, like I killed a guy I was close to." A third reflected on how Saddam had told him, as his execution approached, "I forgive you, you're just doing your job." A fourth spoke about how, even though he knew that Saddam had killed many people, he still couldn't help but see him "more like a grandpa." The interpreter who worked with them said, "Will I miss Saddam the brutal dictator? Of course not. But will I miss sitting in the evening with him as a human being? Yes, I will."

When we find ourselves feeling no empathy for an individual or a group, when we feel that we simply cannot understand their conduct, perhaps empathy is simply lying latent at the Core of our being, waiting to be stirred under the right conditions.

The Fourth Seed: Abundance

Early in my tenure at McKinsey, I worked on an engagement with another associate, Roland. I found Roland pesky and overambitious. When I presented my work in internal reviews with senior partners, he would jump in to say, "Hitendra, you should look at X." "There's a hole here in your argument." "Your analysis should include ABC." I found him distracting and disruptive, engaged in a game of one-upmanship with me in front of the partners.

My manager Chris approached me one day. "Hitendra, I notice that when Roland presents his work at our reviews, you tend to tune out. I want to ask you to actively participate, to share your perspective and ideas on his work just like he does when you're presenting your work. We're all one team, and we can all help make each other's work better."

It was as though I had just been awoken to a higher truth. *Hitendra, there's no war going on. It's not you versus Roland. No one needs to look smarter than the other. Just keep doing the best you can in helping the team, in advancing the solution for the client. There's an abundance of opportunity at McKinsey and in the world beyond. You'll make it, and Roland will make it, and so will everyone else who puts in the right effort.* I became less self-focused, more collaborative, and more open to constructive criticism. I also found myself enjoying the project a lot more.

Our hearts become constricted when we see the world as a zero-sum game where your gain is my loss, or as a ladder where everyone takes a spot above or below one another. Love invites us to approach all situations with a feeling of abundance so we don't see other people's pursuit of joy or success as a limiter to our own. Without this feeling of abundance, we get trapped in a "me versus you" mindset that limits our capacity to do for and share with others.

Gratitude, appreciation, empathy, and abundance. These are the seeds that, over time, germinate into the blossoms of Love.

Stage 3: Remove the Weeds

It was April 2020. With her high school commencement around the corner, my daughter was preparing her valedictorian speech. She tested her early ideas with me, but something wasn't quite right. "Mrinalini, it's a tough thing to have to graduate in the midst of a pandemic. You have such wisdom to bring to a moment like this, at a time when your class needs a big lift," I said to her. "But somehow the spirit isn't there. Something is missing." She became quiet.

Later that evening, I found her huddled in a corner of her room. I tiptoed in, afraid I was trespassing on a moment of private reflection. "What are you doing sitting here in the darkness?" I inquired. "Hush," she replied, placing her finger on her lips. We shared silence for a few minutes. Then she spoke again. "I want to do this speech with affection for my whole class, and my whole school. When I was speaking with you earlier, I was excluding a few members of the school community from my heart, because, over the years, I have not always got along with them. I have been uprooting all traces of judgment and resentment for them from my heart so I can include them too. That's what was missing the last time we spoke."

When she ultimately delivered her address, it flowed with warmth for her classmates, for the school community they were leaving behind, and for the world that would be their oyster. The blossoms of Love cannot flourish until the weeds of hatred, grudges, and judgment are purged. Removing these weeds helps our hearts stay pure, and then, as Gandhi wrote, "To a pure heart, all hearts are pure."

The First Weed: Hatred

Some years back I visited the Topography of Terror, a museum in Berlin. It is built on the grounds of what was the Gestapo headquarters during Nazi rule, and through a series of pictures and historical commentaries, it captures the rise and fall of the Third Reich. Walking through that museum was a very powerful experience. What took me most by surprise was not Hitler's relationship with the people he hated—that part has been painfully and painstakingly documented—but his relationship with the people he claimed to love: the Germanic Aryan "Master Race."

Hitler started by hating the Jews and the Slavs and the Romani, but over time he excluded and persecuted many people from segments of the "Master Race" itself—political rivals, people with disabilities, Germans who rejected Nazi ideology, and more. With every portion of the German population that Hitler turned against, his circle of love grew smaller, and his circle of hate grew larger.

And then came the final reckoning. On March 19, 1945, with the Allied armies advancing on Germany, Hitler issued a decree for the destruction of all German infrastructure—transport and communication facilities, industrial establishments, supply depots, and "anything else of value within Reich territory." Historians have aptly called it the Nero Decree. If it had been implemented, postwar Germany would have been reduced to preindustrial-age conditions. Albert Speer, Hitler's minister of armaments and war production, was so shocked by the order that he asked Hitler for exclusive power to implement it. Once granted that authority, Speer turned around and convinced the Nazi generals to ignore the command.

Why did Hitler issue such a harsh decree? It had become clear to him that his game was up; he committed suicide forty-two days later. But on that day in March, he justified his order by telling Speer that the Germans did not deserve to survive: "Only those who are inferior will remain after this struggle, for the good have already been killed." The Führer showed in that moment that his circle of love had shrunk to just himself, while his circle of hate—the people he was happy to inflict pain on—now included all the survivors of the German "Master Race" he had claimed to love.

Hate puts us on a perilous path where we can slip from despising one person to a more generalized capacity to hate. When we loathe an individual or group, we train our brain's neural circuits to judge some people as "bad." Hatred can then slither unnoticed into our consciousness and take hold across a much wider swath of relationship territory—like cancer cells that metastasize. Research

215

shows that the feeling many people experience for their significant others isn't just love but also, at times, hate. When couples who are in an unhappy relationship encounter conflict, they engage in criticism and contempt. In effect, they are in that moment becoming numb to their partners' feelings, even wishing to hurt them. These are symptoms of hate. A person may come out of this state of hatred after some time, returning their partner to their circle of love, but a little damage has been done. Repeated flare-ups can eventually lead to there being, on balance, more animosity than love in the relationship. Sadly, in some cases, the only thing that eventually remains is the hate.

You may feel that you can detest "bad" people from a safe distance. But every time you hate, you train your brain's neural circuitry. By making hate an occasional, long-distance friend, you create the conditions for it to take permanent residence in your heart and to slither into all your relationships without your even being aware of it.

The Second Weed: Grudges

Someone occasionally will act in a way we find unjust, grievously wrong, or even downright evil. It is natural in such moments to hold a grudge against them and perhaps even plot some form of retaliation. When someone hurts us, should we forgive them?

Forgiveness has many benefits. It allows us to rebuild a relationship. No personal relationship could survive in the long run without frequent acts of forgiveness, for there are always going to be mistakes and misunderstandings.

Forgiveness releases us from a mental burden we would otherwise carry—pain, suffering, anger, vindictiveness, regret—so we can pour our energy wholeheartedly into our goals and Purpose. Research shows that when we learn to let go of grudges, we are happier, less stressed, less anxious, and less likely to fall into depression. We experience better health outcomes—lower blood pressure, an improved immune system, less chronic pain. We experience greater self-worth and a deeper connection with those we care for.

Forgiveness is also critical to fostering peace in communities. Without forgiveness, without rapprochement, how would communities exist in harmony with one another? Troubling instances of injustice inflicted by one group on another litter the pages of history. When an entire community forgives a past injustice done to them by another group, civilization can progress. Without forgiveness, we would end up in an endless and possibly escalating cycle of violence and retribution because "the policy of an-eye-for-an-eye for-an-eye-for-an-eye . . , ends in making everybody blind."

But forgiveness can also get us in serious trouble. Can you think of situations where it would not make sense to forgive?

When we forgive too easily, people can take advantage of us. We may continue to naively trust people we should not, placing ourselves in harm's way and paving the way for future transgressions. If instead we strive to right a wrong, to pursue just punishment for the perpetrator of a crime, we create a valuable deterrent not just for the individual who has wronged us but for potential future offenders as well.

Well, then, what is the optimal path: to forgive, or to hold on to the grudge? Some of you may say "forgive!"; others may say "forgive, but don't forget!" and still others "never forgive a serious betrayal of trust!" But the fact is, there's no right answer that works for all conditions. The breakthrough comes when we shift our focus from the outer to the inner. Forgiveness is not a monolithic thing. There is inner forgiveness (what we choose to feel from within), and there is outer forgiveness (what we choose to do from without). Here is a law of human nature: *regardless of what hurt you are carrying, you will always win if you forgive on the inside.*

Inner forgiveness releases you from feelings of hurt and resentment so you can pour your energy into what matters to you. It helps you make peace with the past. You feel more in control precisely because it is you who has made the choice to let go of the grudge.

Inner forgiveness helps us brush off minor irritations—rude behavior, unfair criticism, poor performance, and more—so we don't get caught up in replaying them and stewing over them. It is invaluable in personal relationships. Our near ones sometimes say or do things that hurt us. By letting go of resentment, we are better able to tide over conflicts and disappointments and create the conditions for success in our relationships.

Inner forgiveness has no bearing on what we choose to do on the outside. That will totally depend on the circumstances. In some cases, you may want to engage in outer forgiveness as well, to reconcile with the perpetrator and to forget the episode, because it was a minor transgression or it was not done intentionally or the perpetrator has realized their error and committed to change. In other cases, you may want to forgive but not forget, so you can stay more vigilant going forward. Or you may choose to break ties with the wrongdoer, or even take just action against them, like lodging a formal complaint or suing them in court. These choices aren't easy to make, but I will tell you this: you will only make the right choice on the outside when you have forgiven on the inside, because inner forgiveness will give you the clear mind and pure heart to make the right call.

Anita, an associate at Mentora Institute, once related the following story to me:

> My parents immigrated to America in the 1980s. After getting his PhD, my father took up a teaching position at a university. Recently, there was a retirement party in his department for another professor. I noticed he didn't go, so I asked him why. My father grew quiet, and then said, "Well, Anita, this colleague wasn't exactly a good friend of mine." I was quite shocked, because I rarely meet anyone who isn't friends with my dad. I asked him what had happened between them. He hesitated, and then said, "Ever since I joined, this professor has been saying racist things about me. He's gone out of his way to make fun of my accent, talk about how I was too young to be there, and point out my shortcomings to the other professors in the department."
>
> I was deeply pained. I nodded and said, "It makes sense that you would skip his retirement party."

He replied, "Yes, and two days ago, I went and bought the nicest bottle of wine I could. Then I sat down and wrote him a thank-you card. I walked into his office with the wine and the card and told him, 'I know that there are very personal reasons you don't like me and you probably never will. But I want to let you know that for the past twenty-five years, you, more than anyone else in the department, have challenged me to go above and beyond to bring my best self to work, each and every single day, and to work my absolute hardest, knowing that I would probably never be able to overcome your prejudices, but also knowing that I was going to try my very, very best.' Then I shook his hand, left the wine and the card on his desk, and walked out."

Anita's father could only have taken these remarkable outer actions if he'd done the inner work to forgive. The behavior of his retired colleague will no doubt replay in his mind for years. Through this action, he was making the choice to cast himself as a hero and not a victim in his story. And that's the gift you give yourself when you forgive from within.

The Third Weed: Judgment

Lisa, a student of mine, told this story in class:

I grew up disliking my mom and younger sister. I felt my mom was playing favorites. She had been very strict with me over the years, but when it came to my sister, she let her get away with anything, never scolding or punishing her. I saw my sister as a spoiled brat.

When I turned fifteen, my mother took me aside and said, "There is something I want to share with you today, now that you are old enough. Once when your sister was a baby, she fell out of my arms and her head hit the floor. We rushed her to the hospital. The physician told us she had a brain injury. She would survive, but it was critical that she not go through any emotional stress for several years while her brain healed. That's why I have been so careful about never letting her get upset. I had to treat her differently, to protect her health."

I was stunned to hear this. I realized how unfounded my perceptions had been. What a waste of energy, all the judgments I had held on to for so many years! My feelings for my mother and sister changed instantly. I am now very careful not to judge people when they behave badly, because I just don't know their backstory.

We can empathize with Lisa, because we all fall into this trap from time to time. We observe a disappointing behavior from a relative, friend, colleague, or stranger, and we impulsively make an unflattering judgment about their intentions and character. We zero in on one aspect of who that individual is or what they're doing, viewing them in an unflattering and monolithic manner rather than seeing them more fully for their talents, contributions, struggles, achievements, and potentialities.

As with hatred, when we judge others, we train our brain to distinguish between those who are "good" and those who are "bad." Once we reach an unfavorable conclusion about an individual, we begin to feel they are unworthy of our love. We may then become bitter, contemptuous, impatient, rude, or withdrawn in our dealings with them. When they experience those attitudes from us, it makes them withdraw their own warmth and support for us. The prospect for a positive relationship declines.

We stop judging people when we recognize that everyone has a backstory we don't fully know, and everyone has the potential for growth and redemption. We believe that a beautiful Core exists within them just as it exists within us, and we constantly seek to remind ourselves of their higher nature. One of Nelson Mandela's archenemies while he was in prison was Colonel Piet Badenhorst, under whose command inmates were verbally abused, made to stand naked in bitterly cold conditions, and sent to solitary confinement for even petty offenses. On Mandela's final day before being transferred from the prison, Badenhorst told him, "I just want to wish you people good luck." Mandela "was amazed," as he wrote later.

> He spoke these words like a human being and revealed a side of him we had never seen before. . . . I thought about this moment for a long time afterwards. Badenhorst had perhaps been the most callous and barbaric commanding officer we had had on Robben Island. But that day, he had revealed that there was another side to his nature, a side that had been obscured but still existed. It was a useful reminder that all men, even the most seemingly cold-blooded, have a core of decency, and that if their hearts are touched, they are capable of changing.

Mandela also reflected, "Man's goodness is a flame that can be hidden but never extinguished."

When we allow hate, resentment, and judgment to take root within us, we start to see the world as a dark place, and love, like a frightened dove, flies out of our heart. And so, as Rumi wrote, "Your task is not to seek for love, but merely to seek and find all the barriers within yourself that you have built against it."

Stage 4: Prune the Branches

In a psychological study, people were told of a ten-year-old girl, Sheri Sommers, who had a fatal disease and had been placed low on a waiting list for a treatment that would relieve her pain. To evoke these people's empathy, they were asked to feel what she must have felt. Then they were given the option of moving her to the front of the waiting list. Most people said they would do it. They were open to favoring this girl over other children who were ahead of her on the list without knowing the other children's circumstances. One would expect that the hospital had a certain medical rationale by which they assigned children to the waiting list, perhaps based on the seriousness and urgency of the child's need. People's empathy for Sheri had made them want to do something for her that wasn't fair to the other children.

When we love, our feelings get intertwined with those of others. This can be a good thing, for it makes us caring and empathetic. But research also shows that it can be a bad thing when it makes our love flow unchecked. Our judgments may get distorted: in seeking to please the person in front of us today, we may compromise the larger good of a community, or the longer-term good of the very person in front of us. We may get so emotional that we are rendered incapable of lifting up the other person's spirits or calming them down. We may become so stirred by the grievances of the person we're wanting to support that we do not seek to understand the other side's perspective before taking action. We may end up giving so generously of ourselves that our own needs are sacrificed, leaving us worn out. Someone may take advantage of us by depending on us instead of taking greater personal ownership. We may avoid expressing our concerns because we don't want to make people uncomfortable. Or we may refrain from making tough decisions—like terminating a project or letting an individual go—because we don't have the heart to inflict pain on others.

Research shows that when people in a marital relationship report that they experience no conflicts with each other, one or both are conflict-phobic: so keen to keep pleasing the other that they simply refuse to recognize and raise sensitive issues. In the short run this leads to superficial harmony as the partner suppresses their voice. But in the long run it leads to simmering resentments or even a breakdown in the relationship. Research also shows that people who are kind and helpful to others at work can significantly compromise their career because they become consumed with helping others without being able to draw boundaries to protect their own interests, make hard calls, and create the space for tough conversations. It is no wonder that love gets a bad rap in many workplaces, where it is seen as a sign of weakness. "If I show warmth," the love-skeptic thinks, "I will be seen as soft and pliable, and people will trample all over me."

It does not have to be that way, as Sung-Ho's story, shared in my MBA class, shows:

Last summer, I interned at an investment bank. I dearly wanted to work for them, so this was a dream come true. But it soon became a huge disappointment. My supervisor, a senior partner at the firm, kept piling work on me. There were several summer socials at the bank for us interns, and I wanted to attend them so I could hang out with fellow interns from Columbia and other business schools and meet the bank's associates and partners. My supervisor disapproved of my attending these events, so I never went. Other interns were having a much better experience with their supervisors!

In my final week, I was preparing my internship presentation for a senior executive team. This is a big deal for all summer interns, and it influences whether the bank makes you a full-time offer. My supervisor came over to my desk and asked me to do a dry run with her. She listened to me with full engagement and gave me some great feedback, and then asked me to schedule one hour with her each day in the week ahead to do more practice. I was amazed that a busy person like her was giving me so much time and coaching. It was so valuable. My final presentation went well, in large part because of her coaching. After that, she called me into her office and said, "Congratulations. You've done very well. Earlier this summer, you weren't ready. You had a lot of investment-banking basics to learn. People are quick to form impressions at this company. I didn't want you to bungle your full-time prospects. So I was shielding you from the senior people at those social events. Now that you are ready, I am going to reach out to four senior partners who I think you should meet. I'll ask for time from each of them for you. That should further boost your prospects of a full-time offer."

I was astonished! Here I was, thinking she was uncaring and uninterested in my experience, whereas all that time she had been preparing the ground for me to secure a full-time offer and strengthen my relationships at the bank. I feel so grateful that she didn't simply indulge my desire for social experiences at this formative stage but instead ensured that I made a strong first impression. And rather than socializing with me, she dedicated all this time, day upon day, to coach me for my big event. I learned a lot from her, and I'm grateful to say I was one of the few interns at the bank who recently got that coveted full-time offer. Now when I'm back there, I'll have all the time and opportunity to attend the socials!

Sung-Ho's story shows how Love becomes stronger once we prune it of certain extraneous branches of empathy. We can do this by using the discerning shears of the other four Core Energies. Purpose guides us to weigh what someone wants from us today against what may be best for them tomorrow, and to balance the needs of a person or group with the needs of other stakeholders or the community. It is Purpose that was guiding Sung-Ho's supervisor's expression of Love. Wisdom can be a helpful shear in making sure our emotions don't get ahead of us. It guides us to actively practice *cognitive* empathy, in which we seek to understand how others are feeling, but to only selectively practice *emotional* empathy, in which other people's feelings become our feelings. In this way, we can buffer ourselves from others' emotions and keep our thinking undistorted. Growth guides us to go beyond empathizing with and validating people's pain or anger to also inspiring them to draw on their inner reserves to act upon those feelings constructively, or to overcome them. And Self-Realization helps us build an impregnable castle of peace and joy within so that as we go about our day, empathizing and loving, we do so from a centered place.

Maria, an executive participant at one of my workshops, recounted this story:

I grew up in Rome. When I was quite young, my mother was diagnosed with cancer. After some months, we could see that her condition was not getting any better. She said goodbye to me and my sisters, and then she and my father went away for a while to help her on her healing journey. We were told they were moving to Jerusalem. We never saw her again, because a few months later, she died while in Jerusalem. For many years, I was deeply confused about her decision to leave us. Why did she not spend her last few months with us? What kind of advanced medical care was she getting in Jerusalem that she could not get in Rome? When my sisters and I grew up, my father once took us on a visit to Israel. In Jerusalem, we visited a monastery. The nuns we met there spoke lovingly of my mother. I realized this is where she had come in her last few months—these kind nuns had looked after her. I also then learned the two reasons why she had decided to leave us and leave Rome. She knew at that time that she was dying. She wanted to protect us children from the experiences that lay ahead. She did not want our feelings about Rome to be scarred by memories of her getting sick and dying in the city. And she wanted our last impressions of her to be of a happy, physically healthy mother; she did not want us to see her body ravaged by cancer. It must have been so heart-rending for her to say her last goodbye to her children and move on to Jerusalem, and yet this was also her final, thoughtful act of love for us.

A love that is ruled by attachments, impulsive choices, or tempestuous emotions is limiting and occasionally destructive. But when we prune love's branches with the shears of Purpose, Wisdom, Growth, and Self-Realization, we get to the Love that can take us and those we love on a hero's journey.

Stage 5: Make Love Bloom

Putting a universal, selfless, and unconditional form of Love into practice can be intimidating. There is so much to do, for so many people. And you are still unlikely to make a big difference, for you are just a drop in the ocean. What would be the point? Even on a smaller, more personal scale, finding meaningful ways to express Love can sometimes be hard. How can you offer Love to someone who is suffering, to an estranged member of your family, or to someone who doesn't like you?

Put Your Love into Action

Rama, a spine surgeon, once told me,

Early in my career, I was abrasive and proud. I would get angry if nurses and other hospital staff weren't doing exactly what I expected from them, and I sometimes threw surgical equipment on the floor to express my frustration. One day, I had to perform surgery on a fifteen-year-old girl. Her case was both critical and complicated. I tried my best, but the surgery did not go well, and by the end of it the girl was in a coma. I was devastated.

I went to my mentor and asked him what I should do. He told me, "Go to her hospital room every day and spend thirty minutes with her parents. Ask them about her, give them support, and listen to them with deep care. Make sure to not unmindfully repeat the same questions or statements from one day to the next."

I did as he suggested. It was not easy to face her parents and to think of new questions to ask and things to say each day, but I did it. After six weeks, the girl died. I was in shock, and I went back to my mentor to ask for more guidance. "Go to her funeral to honor her life," he counseled. "Some people there may not like you, and may even accuse you of taking her life. You may feel the urge to walk away. But be present throughout the service." So that is what I did.

At the end of the service, her parents approached me and requested that I come up to the casket to bless their daughter. I was deeply moved by their gesture. I asked them some days later why they had not sued me for the botched surgery. The girl's father replied, "We have enough money to give us food and give us a home. What would we gain by trying to win more money from you or the hospital? It would not bring our daughter back. We know you cared for her and did your best to save her life.

That is all we could have hoped for from you, and for that we are grateful." This was a deeply humbling experience for me. It made me totally change my attitude toward work, my colleagues, and myself.

When his patient went into a coma, and then later when she died, Rama was devastated, but he had no structure, no blueprint, no language to express his feelings to her parents. His mentor translated Rama's feelings into simple actions that he could take.

We are seldom able to give people everything they seek, but through simple actions we can always offer our selfless, thoughtful Love. Science shows that when we make a habit of translating Love into tangible action, even if it seems small or inconsequential, we will be happier and more at peace.

Samuel, an MBA student, shared this story:

My friend Hugh and I used to serve in the US Navy SEALs. He was part of the elite team that flew into Abbottabad, Pakistan, and took out Osama bin Laden. Several months later, Hugh presented me with a gift. I opened the box to find the Presidential Medal of Honor he'd been awarded at the White House for his role in that operation.

I was stunned. "Hugh, this is an amazing gift, but I can't take it. This must mean so much to you!"

"That's why I want you to have it," he replied.

"What do you mean?" I said.

He said, "Every New Year, I like to take a possession that is most precious to me and gift it to someone who I know will value it."

I realized from this story how we often give away money or possessions that don't require any real sacrifice from us. The act of Love is even more ennobled when in the act of *giving* we are *giving up* something meaningful.

Put Love into Your *Every* Action

Eleanor Roosevelt once talked of her aunt Bye, who was confined to a chair, stricken by arthritis, and had been losing her hearing. And yet "all the young people in the family sought her out to confide their problems and seek her wise counsel" because of her remarkable capacity to listen and her curiosity and interest in new experiences. Eleanor reflected, "We all know the frustrating experience of trying to talk out a problem and discovering that our chosen confidant is giving us only divided attention, or frankly thinking of something else, or waiting to get in a word about some problem of his or her own." This brings me to the story of Henry.

Several years ago, I spent two weeks at TrueNorth Health Center, in Santa Rosa, California, doing a water-only fast to support my healing. While there, I met a photographer, Henry Grossman. Henry took a keen interest in me, and we spoke at length about my life journey and my passions. He made me feel much at home when I first arrived at TrueNorth. I soon discovered that Henry had been a legend in the photography world, having shot for leading magazines like *Time* and *Life* some of the most iconic twentieth-century photos of prominent women and men, including Eleanor Roosevelt, John F. Kennedy, Jacqueline Kennedy Onassis, Robert Kennedy, Lyndon Johnson, Elizabeth Taylor, Barbra Streisand, the Beatles, Luciano Pavarotti, and Nelson Mandela. I marveled at his photos and over the fact that he'd rubbed shoulders with all these luminaries, but I especially was in awe of his association with the Beatles, because I love the Beatles. He had captured them in relaxed, playful moments that hinted at a special intimacy he had forged with his four subjects. There's even a photo of John Lennon combing young Henry's hair.

"Henry, how did you manage to get so close to the Beatles?" I asked. "After all, when they landed in the United States, they were superstars. There must have been a swarm of paparazzi clamoring for their attention!" Henry paused as his mind replayed those epic moments with the legendary band. He said,

I was nobody special. I had nothing to offer them. All I had was a keen interest in them. I didn't want anything from them. I just liked them, and enjoyed them. Other photographers may have been there because they dearly wanted a photo of the celebrities. I was there because I was drawn to these four young men. Who were they? What was their world? What were their dreams? After a while, they started to feel comfortable with my presence, and they started to share more with me about their experience in America and what they missed about home. Soon, I was being invited to their homes and to travel with them. I took photographs along the way, but it was all a celebration of who they were and the magic of their spirits.

In that moment, the source of Henry's charisma came into sharp relief for me: *what Henry did with the Beatles fifty years ago is the exact same thing he is doing with me at TrueNorth today.* He takes a keen interest in his subject, in discovering their inner spark and celebrating their virtues. He puts aside his own agenda to be there for them. He finds a way to weave in his own ideas, but always in service of his subject. I have observed him do this with everyone he meets, even now, when he's in his mid-eighties. Henry's photography, his reminiscences of famous people, his friendships with Pavarotti and the Beatles, his performances as an actor on Broadway and as a principal tenor with the Metropolitan Opera, his interview on the TV show *60 Minutes*—this is the stuff legends are made of. And yet it is not the peaks he has climbed but the Love he has put into his every action that has left the most indelible mark in people's hearts.

In our daily dash, we often race through our motions with the sole aim of getting to the finish line. What possibilities could life hold if, like Henry, we made it our intention to put Love into every action? Love comes into full bloom when we stop playing hide-and-seek with our heart and bring it into active expression in each moment—through a pause to honor someone's presence, a giving of our undivided attention, a warm smile, a caring remark, a genuine interest in how they are feeling, or a keen attunement to their needs. Perhaps the most important person in our life isn't our boss, our spouse, our child, or our best friend: it is the person in front of us at that moment. "Wherever you stand," wrote Rumi, "be the soul of that place."

HOW ANTOINETTE LEARNED TO BE A HERO, EVERY SUNDAY AND WEDNESDAY

In Antoinette Tuff's dramatic exchange with Michael Hill when he walked into her school near Atlanta intent on committing a mass shooting, we see powerful yet simple ways in which she put Love into action. An absence of hatred or judgment. Complete forgiveness, once she'd disarmed him ("I pray for him"). Appreciation ("I'm proud of you. That's a good thing you've done that you've given up"). Empathy ("I really began to feel sorry for him. . . . He's a hurting soul. . . . I understood his pain"). Love merged with Purpose (she called the authorities to have him arrested). Creating a connection with him by sharing that she, too, was a Hill and that she, too, had thought of committing suicide. Simply telling him, "I want you to know that I love you."

How could Antoinette act with such masterly Love in what must have been the most terrifying moment of her life? After the event, she said,

> Well, to be honest with you, I didn't [know what the right things were to say to him]. While I was there and [the 911 operator] was talking to me and he was saying things to me, I was just praying . . . in the inside of myself and saying "God, what do I say now, what do I do now?" . . . I owe that all to my pastor. He has actually trained us. We've had classes and he sits down and teaches us, you know, how to deal with people and how to deal in, you know, desperate situations and how to pray. And we practice that at church. So really, in all reality, all I was doing was carrying out what I'm taught every Sunday and Wednesday.

Suddenly, Antoinette's heroic capacity to love seems so much more within our own reach.

Chapter 11

LEADING WITH LOVE

⋎

It is not how much we do, but how much love we put
in the doing.

—*Mother Teresa*

HOW MOTHER TERESA SWEPT
THE FLOORS—AND SWEPT THE WORLD

Father Leo Maasburg has shared the following story: "I witnessed a rather scary 'armor cracking' incident with Mother Teresa in Nicaragua, which at that time was ruled by a Marxist-inspired authoritarian regime under the Sandinista leader Daniel Ortega." Mother Teresa wished to meet Ortega to get permission to open a new house for her Sisters. She, another Sister, and Fr. Maasburg were ushered into a windowless room where Ortega was sitting between four masked men with big machine guns. Ortega proceeded to give them

a fiery, thirty-minute speech about the legitimacy of his guerilla war and the demonic character of his opponents. When he finally ended, trembling with rage, there was an embarrassed silence. Mother Teresa broke it with a single sentence. "Yes, yes, works of love are works of peace."

The tension mounted. The official translator obviously did not want to translate this sentence, which had been spoken in English, into Spanish for the president. Finally, the other Sister took on this manifestly thankless task, though in a trembling voice. Not only was the room stifling, there was also a dangerous tension in the air.

Suddenly, and without waiting for the dictator's reaction to her remark, Mother Teresa stood up. . . . Rummaging in her bag, she asked the dictator, "Do you have children?"

Clearly not understanding the implication of her question, he replied, "Yes."

"How many?"

"Seven."

Mother Teresa brought seven Miraculous Medals out of her bag, one after the other, kissed each one, and held it up as high as she could toward the platform. . . . Ortega took them—one by one—leaning far across the desk each time so as to reach Mother Teresa's hand.

"Do you have a wife?"

"Yes."

Another medal was found in the bag, which was kissed and held out. "And here's one for you. . . . You need it! But you must wear it round your neck, like this."

With one stroke, she had completely changed the mood.

But now came the masterstroke. "Then she offered the dictator another present—five of her Sisters to care for the poorest of the poor in the slums of Managua! . . . Permission was granted the very next day for the founding of the Sisters' first house."

This story reveals three beautiful qualities in Mother Teresa. First, she loved the "poorest of the poor." Her purpose was to get to them and serve them, and she left it to others to address the world's other problems. Ortega may have wanted to engage her on Nicaragua's politics, but she stuck to her purpose. Second, she steadfastly refused to judge others, including fierce dictators. Instead, she found a way to honor the goodness in all people and to uncover their Inner Core even when it lay hidden behind machine guns and masked men. Third, often when someone entered her presence and experienced her love, their heart would melt, and her purpose would become their purpose.

Years ago, my friend Jan Petrie, her sister Ann, and Richard Attenborough made a documentary film about Mother Teresa. I've asked Jan to show the film to our students at Columbia Business School a few times over the last decade. You might wonder how a nun deeply steeped in faith and committed to serving the world's poor would be of any interest to go-getter MBAs. During the film, my students are riveted. Her life offers a lesson on Love like no other.

Mother Teresa grew up in Skopje, Yugoslavia (now Macedonia). Agnes, as she was then called, received an abundance of love from her mother, Drana, who often invited poor people to join their family meals. Agnes's brother once asked their mother who these people were that they were sharing meals with. "Some of them are our relations," Drana replied, "but all of them are our people." Agnes accompanied Drana on her weekly visits to an old woman, File, who had been abandoned by her family, to take her food and clean her house. In later years, Mother Teresa recalled that File "was covered in sores, but what caused her far more suffering was the knowledge that she was all alone in the world. We did what we could for her." At home in Skopje, whenever the children complained about a teacher, Drana would turn the electricity off and tell them, "I'm not going to pay for electricity for children who [speak badly of] people."

Drana was active in the local Sacred Heart Catholic Church. Agnes participated regularly in its services and sang in its choir. At times her mother took her for private moments of prayer to the chapel of the Madonna of Letnice, on the slopes of Skopje's Black Mountain. Agnes's father had died when she was eight. "Home," Mother Teresa would later say, "is where the mother is."

Agnes left home at eighteen to become a nun, never to see her mother and sister again. (Her brother had departed home to attend military school when she was fourteen; she met him again after thirty years.) A year into her monastic life, she moved to a convent in India operated by the Sisters of Loreto, where she was deeply troubled by the poverty she saw in Calcutta. Twenty years after arriving in India she followed her inner call, leaving the convent to lay the foundation for a new missionary order to serve the "poorest of the poor."

The early months of her newly chosen life were difficult. She wrote in her diary, "Today I learned a good lesson. The poverty of the poor must be so hard for them. While looking for a home I walked and walked till my arms and legs ached. I thought how much they must ache in body and soul, looking for a home, food and health." Her mind often returned to the comfort and security she had enjoyed at the Loreto convent, and a tempting voice within her said, "You have only to say the word and all that will be yours again." But she persisted in her efforts to serve the poor, and eventually she was offered a permanent space for her work in the home of a family named Gomes. Even there, at times she had no food. She wrote notes to her host: "Mr. Gomes, I have nothing to eat. Please give me something to eat."

Gradually, the nuns came, the donations came, and world recognition came as well. Her organization, Missionaries of Charity, spread to 130 countries and grew to include over forty-five hundred nuns. She was awarded the Nobel Peace Prize, and in a 1999 Gallup poll she was recognized by Americans as the most admired person of the twentieth century. Wherever she went, people of all social strata, ages, and faiths received her as a global celebrity. And yet Mother Teresa had none of the trappings of a celebrity. Most people when meeting her for the first time were surprised by her diminutive form. She wore a white sari with a blue border and lived a very frugal life. She spoke plainly, in simple English. She performed the most humble tasks in taking care of the poor—washing them, feeding them, cleaning their toilets, sweeping the floor. The secret to her mystique was not outer charisma but an inner charisma founded on her unconditional Love for every human being and her commitment to put that Love into action.

Many good-hearted individuals and organizations have sought to serve the material needs of those less privileged, but Mother Teresa recognized that there was a much deeper hunger in the world. This was File's hunger, the hunger for love. In Mother Teresa's service to the diseased, the destitute, the dying, and the down-and-out, she focused on feeding this spiritual hunger as much as she did people's bodily hunger. When she spoke to a more materially privileged audience, she offered a call to service that spoke to that audience's hearts. Delivering a commencement address to Harvard graduates in 1982, Mother Teresa said, "You will, I am sure, ask me: Where is that hunger in our country? Where is the nakedness in our country? Where is the homelessness in our country? Yes, there is hunger. Maybe not the hunger for a piece of bread, but there is a terrible hunger for love. We all experience that in our life. The pain, the loneliness." She may have been the nun, and they the Ivy League graduates, but she was forging common ground with them and transcending their differences. Next, she mobilized them for a mission. "You must have the courage to recognize the poor you may have right in your own family. Find them, love them. Put your love for them in living action." In this way, she conveyed a simple call to action after she'd prepared their hearts to receive. The Harvard newspaper reported that she received a long standing ovation at the end of her speech.

Mother Teresa always looked to awaken people to the role of Love—or rather, to the rule of Love. On one occasion, when Prime Minister Margaret Thatcher sought to reassure her that Britain had a fine welfare system, she responded, "But do you have love?"

A two-room facility to serve the poor was set up by Mother Teresa's organization right next to a prominent Hindu place of worship, the Kali temple. One day some protestors gathered outside, concerned about the intentions of Christian nuns tending to the poor and the dying so close to the temple. The group's leader walked into the facility and was struck by "the care with which the suffering, emaciated bodies of the poor were tended." He went back out to tell his fellow protestors that he would be happy to evict the Sisters—on the condition that the protestors persuade their mothers and sisters to come and serve their community's poor in the same way. The crowd dispersed.

The seeds of appreciation and gratitude constantly germinated in Mother Teresa's heart. A priest who knew her observed, "We often encountered very seriously handicapped children. . . . Often, I was horrified and would have preferred to turn away. Mother Teresa only said, 'What a wonderful child!' And very often added, 'See how tenderly it is holding my finger.'" To her, the human side of every individual was ennobling in itself.

Mother Teresa noted and celebrated small acts of heroism in those she served. An old lady who had been abandoned in the streets was picked up by the nuns and taken to the convent. She was nearing the point of death. Mother Teresa said, "She took my hand and a beautiful smile appeared on her face. She only said, 'Thank you,' and died." She continued, "I assure you, she gave me much more than I have given her. She offered me her grateful love. I looked at her face for a few moments, asking myself, In her situation, what would I have done? And I answered with honesty, Surely I would have done all I could to draw attention to myself. I would have shouted, 'I'm hungry! I'm dying of thirst. I'm dying!' She, on the other hand, was so grateful, so unselfish. She was so generous!"

The following incident took place upon her return from Stockholm, where she'd gone to receive the Nobel Peace Prize. "It was late in the day (around ten at night) when the doorbell rang. I opened the door and found a man shivering from the cold. 'Mother Teresa, I heard that you just received an important prize. When I heard this I decided to offer you something too. Here you have it: this is what I collected today.'"

This was a homeless man, and he handed over to Mother Teresa the few pennies he'd collected from passersby on the street that day. "It was little," she said, "but in his case it was everything. I was moved more than by the Nobel Prize."

Mother Teresa once offered a simple, step-by-step guide to world peace:

One year I wanted to do something special for our sisters. I sent out a newsletter to each one of them, to each community, suggesting that each one write down what she thought was beautiful in her sisters and her community. I asked that each sister send her answer to me. A thousand letters arrived. Just imagine! I had to sit down and read each one, making a list of each community and all the sisters. Later I returned the letters to the communities. The sisters were surprised that someone would notice such beautiful things in them—that there was someone who was able to see them. All of this fostered a beautiful spirit of love, understanding, and sharing. I feel that we too often focus on the negative aspects of life, on what is bad. If we were more willing to see the good and the beautiful things that surround us, we would be able to transform our families. From there, we would change our next-door neighbors and then others who live in our neighborhood or city. We would be able to bring peace and love to our world, which hungers so much for these things.

This story has inspired us at Mentora. In our leadership development workshops for client organizations, we sometimes invite participants to perform a similar appreciation exercise with one another. The Love that flows in the room is palpable.

Mother Teresa was often piercing through people's outer garb to see beyond who they were to who they could become. Father Maasburg describes how on a visit to Spain Mother Teresa and her group were driven around by a travel guide, Pascual. When it was over, Pascual asked her to autograph a book for him. When he later opened the book, he was surprised to see that she had begun her dedication, mistakenly, he thought, with "Dear Father Pascual." Ten years later, while sorting through his books, he stumbled onto this one and opened it to read her words again. Over these ten years, his purpose had evolved in a way he had never imagined—he was now a priest.

"If you judge someone," she would say, "you have no time to love them." As the AIDS epidemic grew around the world, Missionaries of Charity opened hospices where nuns could care for AIDS patients who were in the last stages of the disease. When asked, "Mother Teresa, is the AIDS epidemic the result of sin?" she replied, "I, Mother Teresa, am a sinner. We are all sinners. And we all need God's mercy." On another occasion, she was asked, "Some people feel that you're almost like a living saint. How do you feel about that?" She replied, "You have to be holy in your position, as you are, and I have to be holy in the position that God has put me. So it is nothing extraordinary to be holy. Holiness is not the luxury of the few. Holiness is a simple duty for you and for me. We have been created for that." In these ways, when people around her diminished others, she reminded them that she and they, too, were human, and when they exalted her, she reminded them that they, too, possessed a divine spark.

From where did Mother Teresa gain her boundless capacity to love? "You cannot give," she said, "what you do not have." In describing the source from which she quenched her own inner thirst for love, she once said, "My secret is quite simple. I pray." She joined the nuns in performing sixty minutes of prayer and meditation at five a.m. every day. A nun once remarked, "When we see her praying, we feel like praying."

When one thinks of great lovers, one imagines them performing stirring, heroic acts—serenading us from the street, building us a palace, taking us on a rousing tour of the world. In contrast, Mother Teresa's acts of Love were very simple and yet very moving. "The smaller the thing," she said, "the greater must be our love." One such small act she encouraged was smiling at others. "Every time you smile at someone," she said, "it is an action of love, a gift to that person, a beautiful thing." What could be a simpler action than giving someone a smile? And yet doing it genuinely requires us to cultivate joy within, and warmth for the recipient. As Mother Teresa said, "Let no one ever come to you without leaving better and happier. Be the living expression of God's kindness: kindness in your face, kindness in your eyes, kindness in your smile."

A priest who spent time with her at the Missionaries of Charity observed, "The amazing thing about her was that when you were in her presence, you felt that you were the most important person in the world. She was fully focused on you, and although she said very little, she was so undistracted that her personal power engaged you." Father Maasburg has reflected, "She radiated an inner joy toward everyone that usually toppled any prejudices or resentments that may have been present. . . . Some of these people even wanted absolutely nothing to do with the Church. Nevertheless . . . everything that was cold in them melted and they emerged from the conversation, sometimes after only ten minutes, completely changed."

After accepting the Nobel Peace Prize, Mother Teresa stopped in Rome on her way back to India from Stockholm. A reporter challenged her about the seeming futility of her efforts. "Mother, you are seventy now," the reporter said. "When you die, the world will be as it was before. What has changed after so much effort?" Mother Teresa responded with a smile. "You know, I never wanted to change the world. I have only tried to be a drop of pure water in which God's love can be reflected. Does that seem like a small thing to you?" The reporter fell silent. Mother Teresa continued, "Why don't you try, too, to become a drop of pure water? Then there will be two of us already. Are you married?" "Yes, Mother Teresa." "Tell your wife about it, too, and then we are already three. Do you have children?" "Three children, Mother." "Then tell your children also and then we are already six."

This anecdote sums up the essence of Mother Teresa's life, philosophy, and success. Her intention wasn't to do great things, but to "do small things with great love"; it was not to "change the world, but to cast a stone across the water to create many ripples." By connecting with her heart, that drop of pure water, she inspired everyone who crossed her path to connect with their own, and a new revolution fueled by Love was born.

Chapter 12

LIVING WITH
SELF-REALIZATION

꿈

To the mind that is still, the whole universe surrenders.

—*Lao Tzu*

THE SEARCH OF A LIFETIME

In 1930, Paul Brunton, a British journalist and bookstore owner, journeyed to India because, as he later wrote, "One heard much of certain so-called holy men who possessed repute of having acquired deep wisdom and strange powers; so one traveled through scorching days and sleepless nights to find them."

After months of futile searching, Brunton finally found what he had been yearning for. "[As] someone who relies on hard facts and cold reason . . . [my] faith was restored in the only way a sceptic could have it restored, not by argument, but by the witness of an overwhelming experience." He described the experience in his book, *A Search in Secret India*: "The waves of thought naturally begin to diminish. . . . Finally it happens. Thought is extinguished like a snuffed candle. . . . I remain perfectly calm and fully aware. . . . Some deeper, diviner being rises into consciousness and becomes me. With it arrives an amazing new sense of absolute freedom, for thought is like a [shuttle] which is always going to and fro, and to be freed from its tyrannical motion is to step out of prison into the open air."

The experience Brunton had was that of Self-Realization, the last of our five Core Energies.

THE ESSENCE OF SELF-REALIZATION

On the surface of the Earth we find deserts, mountains, oceans, and more. Below the Earth's mantle lies hot molten lava. You might believe that's all there is to the planet, that as you go deeper, there's just more lava. But in 1936, Danish seismologist Inge Lehmann offered a surprising hypothesis—that at the very center of the Earth is a solid sphere of pure metal. It was only in the 1970s that her claim was finally confirmed by other scientists. Today, geologists call this solid sphere the Earth's inner core.

Think of your own self as a sphere of consciousness. On the surface are the five senses through which you experience the outer world. Just below the surface lies the "hot molten lava" of your thoughts and emotions. You may believe that's all there is. But as certain truth-seekers have discovered through the ages, and as modern science is now validating, beyond your senses, thoughts, and emotions lies a solid sphere of pure consciousness, your own Inner Core.

Most of the time, our attention flits from one sensory experience, thought, or emotion to another. Self-Realization invites us to reverse the flow of our energies—to go from the outer world toward the center of our being. When we repeatedly take dives within, going deeper with every expedition, we start to recognize our Inner Core as our true nature. We become more anchored in the peace, love, and joy that reside there and less attached to the outer world. This does not make us disengage from the world. Quite the opposite. We now pursue our outer activities from a place of tranquility, ever mindful of our Purpose, connected with life, open to new understanding, and attuned to the whispers of our inner voice.

Have you, in certain moments, experienced a feeling of well-being, peace, love, or joy bubble up from within, even when it had no connection with your external reality? These experiences, fleeting though they may be, provide hints of the untapped treasure that lies at our Core. And yet it is hard to, at will, gain access to such experiences and sustain them.

Truth-seekers of all eras have sought to develop ways to get to their Core using contemplative practices like meditation, chanting, prayer, and more. Hindu scriptures written by nameless authors from several thousand years ago discuss the intricate practice of meditation, and three-thousand-year-old seals have been excavated from the Indus Valley around India that show figures seated in meditative postures. Kabbalah practices of contemplation in Judaism go back to 1000 BC or earlier. Evidence of Taoist meditation practices exist in China from at least the fourth century BC. Two thousand years ago, Buddha made meditation a centerpiece of his path. The desert mothers and fathers in early Christianity actively pursued inner silence and continual prayer, and the writings of later Christian saints, notably Saint Teresa of Avila, are infused with descriptions of meditative prayer. Sufism evolved as a contemplative movement within Islam to which Rumi belonged. There is no single right approach to reaching one's Inner Core; in seeking out the same mountaintop, you and I may choose different paths.

The contemplative practice that has gained the greatest interest in recent times by scientific investigators is meditation, and so I will focus this chapter on it, while recognizing and valuing other practices that can also contribute to our Self-Realization journey. A pioneering step in bringing meditation to the modern age was taken by Yogananda upon arriving at Boston Harbor in 1920. Yogananda brought the advanced meditation teaching of Kriya Yoga from India's renunciants to truth-seekers worldwide. Today, many different meditation paths and teachers have gained strong followings.

THE POWER OF SELF-REALIZATION

Yogananda called meditation "the most practical science in the world." He wrote, "Most people would want to meditate if they understood its value and experienced its beneficial effects." An explosion of recent scientific research is demonstrating how meditation advances its practitioners' Self-Realization. And yet this modern science is very young, for researchers have only begun to gain a formal understanding of this vast and ancient discipline. As the instruments of science become more capable of measuring subtle energy flows and changes in the brain, more evidence will emerge about meditation's benefits, the systems of the body and brain that mediate these benefits, and how different meditation paths compare.

Physical and Mental Well-Being

Meditation has an all-around positive impact on your health and well-being. It decreases stress levels, heightens stress resistance, improves sleep, lowers blood pressure, reduces inflammation, and strengthens the immune system. Meditation also gives you greater tolerance to pain, by changing the physical and emotional experience of pain.

Meditation slows down the aging process. The strands of DNA in our cells are protected from aging by the telomere caps at their ends. Telomeres shorten over time, and stress can accelerate the shortening process. When that happens, our cells are more susceptible to dying, and we are more vulnerable to disease—poorer immune system function, cardiovascular disease, and degenerative conditions like osteoporosis and Alzheimer's disease. Meditation increases telomere length.

Meditators' brains age more slowly than those of nonmeditators. Normally, the brain starts to lose gray matter (the part of the brain where the capacity for learning, memory, and decision-making resides) from the time we are in our early thirties. But the volume of gray matter of meditators in their fifties has been shown to equal that of people in their twenties and thirties.

Meditation trains our mind to pull away from emotional triggers and distorted thoughts. Meditation also weakens the pull that unhealthy addictions and attachments can have on us by reducing the gray matter in a part of the brain called the nucleus accumbens.

For some of us, our self-esteem fluctuates based on outer circumstances. When we are praised, we feel high self-esteem; when we are criticized, it comes crashing down. This fragile form of self-worth can severely limit us in life and work. Meditation strengthens and stabilizes our feeling of self-worth. Then, rather than unconsciously focusing on protecting our self-esteem, our energies can flow to more productive and creative ends.

Improved Actions, Reactions, and Interactions

As you are headed into a long-planned gathering of your team to celebrate a successful product launch, the phone rings, and you learn that someone you dearly love is very unwell. Your heart is heavy. But you do not wish to carry your gloom into the celebration, because these people have worked hard and deserve to enjoy their moment. Yet wouldn't you be inauthentic if you disguised your feelings and pretended to be happy? What should you do?

When you see yourself as a sphere of consciousness, you start to recognize that while part of you is grieving the bad news about your loved one, another part of you, in the very same moment, is in a celebratory mood because of your team's success. These are both authentic parts of you. Life is not monolithically a happy or sad experience—it is both, and our frame of mind depends on what we focus on. Research shows that with meditation, you learn to honor both states and to move from one region of your sphere of consciousness to another as needed. In celebrating with your team, you are being true to the part of yourself that is proud and happy about what they have accomplished, and later in the day you will turn your attention to the ailing loved one and be true to that concern. This capacity to swiftly and authentically move in and out of different emotions and experiences is critical as you advance in your role as a leader.

Meditation helps you operate with intention rather than instinct. You start to gain a moment-by-moment awareness of your impulses and how they trigger certain speech and behavior. Meditation helps you create psychological distance between trigger and response, giving you more freedom to override an impulse if you see it taking you down a wrong path.

We are often in situations where we would benefit from devoting 100 percent of our attention to a task, be it a meeting with key stakeholders, a complex problem we need to solve, or a report we need to analyze. Meditation builds such concentration. As Daniel Goleman and Richard J. Davidson report in *Altered Traits*, "For most people, concentration takes mental effort; not so for yogis. Once their attention locks onto a target stimulus, their neural circuits for effortful attention go quiet while their attention stays perfectly focused."

Phil Jackson, the most successful basketball coach in NBA history, has described a short visualization he taught the Chicago Bulls:

> During time-outs, the players are often so revved up, they can't concentrate on what I'm saying. To help them cool down mentally and physically, I've developed a quickie visualization exercise I call the "safe spot." During the 15 or 30 seconds they have to grab a drink and towel off, I encourage them to picture themselves someplace where they feel secure. It's a way for them to take a short mental vacation before addressing the problem at hand. This exercise helps players reduce their anxiety and focus their attention on what they need to do when they return to the court.

Meditation has been shown to increase our awareness of others' feelings and reactions and to enhance our compassion for people. The more we are able to tune in to others' feelings, the more effective we will be in creating meaningful connections, handling sensitive moments and conflict, and inspiring others.

Eleanor Roosevelt reflected, "One of the secrets of using your time well is to gain a certain ability to maintain peace within yourself so that much can go on around you and you can stay calm inside." To succeed in a messy, ever-changing world, we need to split our attention in two: one part staying focused on the outer environment, on acting, reacting, and interacting: and the other part staying anchored in our Core, observing the big picture, providing the right direction, regulating our thoughts, emotions, and behavior, and keeping us peaceful, loving, and joyful. Meditation prepares us to operate with this two-part consciousness.

Creative Insight

Meditation creates an open space of possibilities where different parts of your brain—the conscious and the subconscious—are integrated to yield the most effective solution to your problem, like we encountered in our discussion on intuition, the fifth stage on the path to developing Wisdom. Creative insight comes when the brain can break free of what scientists call cognitive inhibition—our tendency to limit our thinking to fewer facts and ideas than we have available to us. Meditation allows you to pull away from confining attachments and beliefs so you can open your mind to free, integrative thinking and access your highest creative potential.

Steve Jobs described meditation as a process in which "your mind just slows down, and you see a tremendous expanse in the moment. You see so much more than you could see before." Ray Dalio, one of the most successful investors on Wall Street, has said, "I've been [practicing meditation] for 44 years, twice a day for 20 minutes. It's such a great investment . . . more than any other factor in my success. It opens up the two sides of the brain, brings a creativity and open-mindedness. It allows you to clear your head and bring an equanimity to everything."

Unconditional Joy

Jacques Lusseyran was imprisoned in the Buchenwald concentration camp during World War II. Later, he wrote a book, "Against the Pollution of the I," in which he dedicates one chapter to Jeremy, an old man who was with him at Buchenwald. "One went to Jeremy as toward a spring. One didn't ask oneself why. One didn't think about it. In this ocean of rage and suffering there was this little island: a man who didn't shout, who asked no one for help, who was sufficient unto himself . . . Jeremy found joy . . . during moments of the day where we found only fear. And he found it in such great abundance that when he was present we felt it rise in us. Inexplicable sensation, incredible even, there where we were: joy was going to fill us. The joy of discovering that joy exists, that it is in us, just exactly as life is, without conditions and which no condition, even the worst, can kill . . ."

We are made to believe that joy comes from outer possessions, experiences, and achievements. But what if joy is simply our natural state? Scientific evidence shows that meditation helps us cultivate inner joy. The left prefrontal cortex, an area of the brain that is associated with states of joy, shows increased activity in those who meditate regularly.

You might say, "This is all fine. But there are so many people in need, so many people in pain. It seems selfish to not serve them, and instead focus on getting more joy for yourself." I respect that. And yet I offer to you, the more we wish to serve others, the more crucial it is for us to cultivate inner joy. When we lack joy on the inside, we will seek it on the outside. Then our actions will be tainted by our own silent need for joy, and we will be unable to give selflessly of ourselves. Moreover, when we are in joy, then whatever we do and whomever we interact with, we bring to that moment and that person the gift of joy.

What do you think would be the most important quality to look for in women who wish to join the nun order at Mother Teresa's Missionaries of Charity? In the documentary film *Mother Teresa*, one of these nuns describes this quality as follows: "First of all, the girls must have the spirit of joy and cheerfulness in the work to be able to lift the people up out of their sufferings." Mother Teresa said it this way: "The people we serve do not need to see your sullen face. Their life is already enough of a struggle."

This goal of cultivating inner joy is a common quest among contemplative traditions. Mother Teresa said, "Joy is not simply a matter of temperament; it is always hard to remain joyful. Which is all the more reason why we should try to acquire it and make it grow in our hearts." What most drew me to meditation early in my life was this promise of discovering the "portable paradise" of joy within. These words by Yogananda were a powerful draw: "Seek the unconditioned, indestructible pure Bliss within yourself," and "This joy is not an abstract quality of mind; it is the conscious, self-born, self-expressing quality of Spirit. Meditation, long and deep, is the way to attain true joy." Across my twenty years of Kriya Yoga practice, I have been blessed to bear inner witness to this statement.

A Self Without Borders

If I were to ask you, "Who are you, really?" how would you respond? Meghan, an executive MBA student at Columbia, shared this story:

> When I turned thirty, I took a DNA test and used Ancestry.com to learn more about my genealogy. When I reached the final page of the report, my blood drained from my face as I saw the names of my parents. I discovered that my father, who had died two years before, had not been my biological father. After I overcame the initial shock, this discovery had a surprisingly positive impact on me. Realizing that I didn't have the genes of the person I all along had taken to be my father, I felt a sense of freedom, possibility, and self-determination about who I wanted to be, rather than seeing myself simply as a collection of good and bad qualities based on my parents. I was able to shed many conscious and subconscious preconceived constraints I had imposed on myself throughout my life regarding my personality and my academic abilities. I now truly believe that you can be whoever and whatever you want.

Most people associate their identity with their family tree, race, gender, sexual orientation, role, title, or the like. Society may associate certain stereotypes with some of these identities, claiming that people from a certain group are a certain way, and can do more of this and less of that. Not only do such stereotypes color other people's perceptions of you, but subconsciously they may affect your *own* self-perception in ways that limit your behavior and performance. Researchers call it the stereotype threat.

You may think, "I don't limit myself this way. My identity comes from my personality." But watch out. You will then place yourself in the prison cell of that personality and may find yourself unable to act in ways that conflict with this personality when a situation calls for you to do so. Research shows that executives overuse their strengths at work, staying stuck with those strengths-based behaviors even in scenarios where a different behavior would be more effective. An individual who is very good at advocating their position, for instance, may actively use this strength to seek to win other people over, even in situations where they would benefit instead from being a good listener and a good integrator of other people's ideas.

Perhaps you think, "At my Core, I am my character." I respect that. But let me offer you a word of caution. If you define your identity based on your character, then, subconsciously, you are identifying not just with your character *strengths* but also with your character *flaws*. Do those flaws represent your true nature, your full potential?

Perhaps it is best to say "I am human" so you can identify with all that humanity is known to be capable of. Would that allow you to reach the peak of your potential? No. You would still be limited by the popular beliefs of your time about what human beings are capable of. For instance, could a human being live for three hundred years? Have an IQ of 300? These numbers seem outlandish to us today. But just in the past two centuries, life expectancy in the developed world has increased from less than thirty to seventy-five years. And every subsequent generation is demonstrating a higher average IQ than the previous generation. What might life expectancy and IQ scores be in five hundred years? My purpose is not to speculate on the arc of humanity's progress but to point out that our present-day beliefs about what human beings are capable of are highly likely, based on past evidence, to be proven wrong on some future date.

The way to release yourself from your identity prison is to focus on what human beings have the *potential* to accomplish rather than simply on what human beings *have* accomplished. Einstein said, "The difference between what the most and the least learned people know is inexpressibly trivial in relation to what is unknown." Einstein wasn't trying to be the "most learned person" of his time; he was reaching for the stars, to access insights about nature way beyond the grasp of contemporary science. This is what meditation can do for you. By stripping away, day upon day, identification with your outer, physical form, you free yourself from limiting conceptions of who you are to see much vaster possibilities. Meditation is a pathway to realizing your true nature—the borderless and boundless spirit that lies within.

A Friend Within

In January 2017, British prime minister Theresa May appointed a minister for loneliness. "For far too many people, loneliness is the sad reality of modern life," she announced. Science shows that loneliness is a disease that can hurt our physical and mental health. The typical societal response to address loneliness is to offer a lonely person avenues to build social ties. But science is showing that loneliness isn't an outer affliction—it is an inner affliction. An individual can have many relationships and still experience strong feelings of loneliness. If you have felt lonely at times in the middle of a dinner with family or friends, then you know what I mean. Conversely, if you have gone on a quiet retreat, taken a long walk in nature, or spent a day by yourself absorbed in a book, without finding yourself yearning for others' company, then you know what it's like being in rich company even without the presence of another soul.

Meditation helps you connect with the love and understanding that reside in your very Core. You might say, "But I get all the love and companionship I need from my friends, my family, my colleagues, my spouse, and my admirers!" If that is your situation in life, I am happy for you. Now visualize yourself at the age of ninety. What if you have outlived your family and friends? Perhaps you'll have loving grandchildren, or not. Perhaps you'll still have companions, or not. The one thing you will certainly have, if you have cultivated it, is the ever-bubbling joy and kinship of your Inner Core. The more you invest over the years in building this relationship, the more it will be there for you in times when no one else is available to give you company. I noticed this with my mother during COVID-imposed periods of isolation—her decades of meditation helped her maintain a rich inner life while she was cloistered in her home for endless months. "Divine joy outlasts everything," Yogananda once said. "It is enduring. When all else melts away, that joy remains."

Kinship with your Core will advance your human relationships, too. As your desire for understanding, love, and connection is met increasingly from within, you will become more able to give love and support to others, rather than to use them to fill the emptiness you feel inside.

⊰⊱

As Self-Realization changes us from within, we start to change from the outside as well. It is as though we are waking up from a dream. We start to look at our thoughts, speech, and actions with greater discernment. What is in alignment with our bedrock beliefs, values, and purpose becomes more central to us. Our true nature gradually starts to take over, and anything that isn't in harmony with it falls away. We realize how fleeting life is, and we feel a heightened desire to make every moment count.

THE PATH OF SELF-REALIZATION

Contemplative practices like meditation help us approach Self-Realization by taking us to progressively deeper levels of mind mastery in five stages.

Stage 1: Tempered Mind

The tempered mind invites you, in your everyday moments, to take over the reins of your mind, to still the agitations that distract you from your highest nature and cause you to resist going within.

Temperance is a moment-by-moment discipline of paying attention to where your mind is, what it does, and how it reacts, and then regulating it. Mastering the energies of Purpose, Wisdom, Growth, and Love will help get you to the tempered mind.

The tempered mind offers an opportunity to approach your whole life with a new vitality, to master your impulses, addictions, habits, thoughts, and emotions. When you sit down to engage in a contemplative practice, your path to your Inner Core will be smooth or rough depending on how tempered your mind has been in your everyday hours. Contemplation isn't a plug-and-play tool that you simply inject into your life for, say, twenty minutes, only to go back to living your life just the way you had been before. This is why in all great faiths, the guidance to pray, chant, and meditate has been placed within the larger frame of how to live consciously and conscientiously. Judaism and Christianity have their Ten Commandments, Buddhism has its Eightfold Path, and yoga has its Yama and Niyama.

Herb Jeffries was a Hollywood actor in the 1930s who took a keen interest in Yogananda's teaching. He later recounted, as shown in the 2014 documentary film *Awake: The Life of Yogananda*,

> I'd been there [with Yogananda and his students] about six or seven weeks, and I said [to Yogananda]: "All my life, I heard thou canst not, thou shalt not, thou must not. These are the rules of the religious teachings that I've heard around my relatives. What I want to know from you is, what canst thou?"
>
> He said, "Well, do you smoke?" And I said, "Yes." He said, "You may continue."
>
> "Do you drink alcohol?" I said, "Yes." He said, "You may continue."
>
> "Do you enjoy the opposite sex promiscuously?" "Yes." "Well, you may continue."
>
> I said, "Wait a minute. You mean that I can come up on this hill, in this good place, with all of these wonderful people, your disciples and the devotees and the brothers up here, and study

these teachings, and I can go back down there and do all these things?"

"Absolutely. But I will not promise you that as you continue to study these teachings, the desire to do these things will not fall away from you."

You need not wait to gain a perfectly tempered mind before dedicating yourself to the pursuit of Self-Realization. It is a virtuous cycle: the more you keep your mind in a tempered state in everyday moments, the more ease and success you will enjoy in your meditations; the more you meditate, the weaker the tugs of intemperate habits and attachments will be.

Stage 2: Interiorized Mind

The interiorized mind invites you to sit in stillness and withdraw your mind from worldly engagement, positioning it for an inward journey. In effect, you are temporarily renouncing the world. I do not mean renunciation in the outer sense, where you give up your material possessions and join a monastic order. I mean renunciation in the inner sense, where you put aside your ambitions, worries, desires, attachments, urgencies, irritations, and other mental burdens. You may return to them afterward, but while you are engaged in your contemplation practice strive to free yourself of such encumbrances.

The interiorized mind invites you to take a spiritual bath—to wash away the debris of all burdens and attachments from your consciousness so that you can dive into the unchanging, pure, tranquil spirit within. Once you have trained yourself to perform this daily act of inner renunciation, you will find it a source of rejuvenation and reassurance in taking on your everyday battles. Different contemplation practices provide different techniques for interiorizing your mind. What's common to most is the discipline of sitting still in a relaxed posture, with eyes closed, withdrawn from thoughts of the world. More advanced meditation techniques, such as Kriya Yoga, teach you to take mental control over the subtle flow of prana, or life energy, in your body so you can withdraw it from your senses and concentrate it in certain centers, or chakras, in your spine and brain—essentially drawing the shades over your sensory windows to allow you to focus within while putting aside all distractions. Learning to interiorize the mind, using the right approach, is a crucial prerequisite to advancing your Self-Realization goals.

Stage 3. Focused Mind

In this third stage, your mind concentrates on some aspect of your Inner Core, such as peace, love, joy, or wisdom. You may not yet be in your Core, but you are approaching its doorway. Contemplative practices offer different techniques to focus the mind, from anchoring it in a mantra—a phrase with an uplifting meaning and sound that you repeat over and over—to engaging in a visualization, doing chanting, focusing on your breath, or concentrating on a pure feeling of loving-kindness, joyfulness, compassion, or the like.

The human mind, like an untamed dog, often runs away excitedly in pursuit of a thought, a feeling, or a sensory distraction. Your goal should be to train this dog to do your bidding—to keep returning to your chosen subject of concentration. This requires you to practice a raw honesty with yourself about where your mind is, rather than giving yourself a pat on the back for simply going through the motions of a prayer or meditation. And it requires you to develop the tenacity to keep bringing the dog back to where it needs to focus each time it drifts away, until it learns. Some contemplative traditions, including my own, invite you in this stage to cultivate devotion, a yearning to go beyond the physical and mental experience of life so you can dissolve into your Inner Core. The right visualization, affirmation, or especially chanting, can help you open your heart to a devotional pursuit of Self-Realization. You are more likely to induce your Core to respond to your human call for connection if this call is serene, focused, and heartfelt.

Stage 4: Tranquil Mind

The tranquil mind throws open the door to the promised land so you can claim the ultimate prize—your Inner Core. It is a highly subtle state. A blanket of outer and inner silence falls over your being. You feel a tremendous sense of well-being arise from within. Your consciousness, unencumbered by the restless waves of senses, thoughts, and feelings, is now dissolved in your Core. You may experience tranquility for only a brief moment before a thought or twitch arises, and then you are restless again. But over time, with more practice, your ability to access the tranquil mind for ever longer periods of time increases.

To make the big leap from the focused mind to the tranquil mind, you have to be open to moving beyond your senses, emotions, and thoughts. Think of your consciousness as a lake, your Inner Core as the moon, and your thoughts, feelings, and senses as waves or ripples on the surface of the lake. As long as the waves are present, moonlight reflecting on the lake's surface gets scattered. But when the waves have stilled, the lake's surface reveals the perfect image of the moon. Steve Jobs said, "If you just sit and observe, you will see how restless your mind is. If you try to calm it, it only makes it worse, but over time it does calm, and when it does, there's room to hear more subtle things—that's when your intuition starts to blossom and you start to see things more clearly and be in the present more."

You may wonder, "How can I withdraw from all my senses, and from my thoughts and feelings as well? What else is there to me?" This experience is not as alien to us as it sounds, for we go into a space of pure consciousness every night when we enter deep sleep. Your senses when you are in deep sleep are turned off; you do not register the conversations people have in your physical proximity, and you are not actively engaged in thought. Yogananda would sometimes describe the deep meditation state as "conscious sleep."

In its deepest and most immersive form, prayer is like meditation—a nonphysical, nonmental act of inner communion that can take us to the tranquil mind. Mother Teresa said, "We too are called to withdraw at certain intervals into deeper silence and aloneness with God . . . not with our books, thoughts, and memories but completely stripped of everything—to dwell lovingly in [God's] presence, silent, empty, expectant, and motionless. . . . In silence we will find new energy and true unity. Silence gives us a new outlook on everything."

Given the bounties of the tranquil mind, how could there be an even more advanced stage of Self-Realization to ascend to? Let me tell you a story. A prince once lived in a palace with his sister. As their father—the king—grew older, the prince involved himself in the affairs of the kingdom, while his sister, the princess, pursued seclusion, taking walks in the palace gardens and practicing long periods of meditation.

The prince noticed the change this brought about in her. "Sister! I am inspired by the tranquility I see you radiate more and more with every passing day. I want to have that same treasure that you have acquired. Can you teach me to meditate?" And she did. As the prince started to experience inner peace and joy, he lost all interest in managing the kingdom. He asked the princess if she would take over the burden of administering the kingdom so he could focus on his meditation, and she agreed.

One day, as the prince was meditating joyously in the palace gardens, he opened his eyes to see his sister walking on the path with her ministers, absorbed in a discussion about the affairs of the kingdom. He broke his silence: "Dear sister, I do pity you! You have to deal with the messy affairs of governance, while I sit here and savor the fruits of meditation."

The princess paused, turned toward him, and smiled. "Dear prince, do not pity me; it is I who pity you. You see, in your case, you have to come here to the garden and sit still, and only then you get to taste that fruit of inner joy. In my case, I have reached a stage where inner joy is always with me, in whatever I do. It never leaves me."

This brings us to the fifth stage of Self-Realization.

Stage 5: Unshakable Mind

The unshakable mind takes you from having moments of mastery to having mastery of your moments. This is the endgame we are all seeking. When we arrive here, our consciousness stays rooted in our Core. We are, like the princess, "in the world, but not of the world," fully invested in our life and our duties while anchored in our authentic self. "A Self-realized master," said Yogananda, "has already left behind the stepping-stone of meditation. 'The flower falls when the fruit appears.'"

The more years we put into our meditation practice, and the deeper and longer we meditate each time, the more our brain gets rewired, and the more deeply rooted we get in peace, love, and joy from within. What used to be a state—the tranquil mind—becomes a trait. As Davidson and Goleman put it, "Our mental stages fluctuate between the healthy states—even-mindedness, composure, mindfulness, realistic confidence—and the unhealthy states—desires, self-centeredness, sluggishness, agitation. . . . The healthy states inhibit the unhealthy states and vice versa. The mark of progress is whether our reactions in daily life signal a shift toward healthy states. The goal is to establish healthy states as predominant, lasting traits." They also write, "Science today is showing that advanced meditators show a brain pattern *while merely resting* that resembles that of a meditative state . . . while beginners do not" (italics are mine).

FORGING YOUR PATH

I was ten when both my parents started a regular meditation practice. I woke up some mornings to the sight of my mother meditating, her face aglow with joy, tears of love rolling down her cheeks. "What is she experiencing? Where has she been transported to?" I wondered. "Wherever she is, that's where I want to go."

During my teens and twenties, I periodically sought out a meditation retreat, the company of monks, or an audience with a saint. I had a fairy-tale notion that some person, place, or immersive experience out there would, in a flash, transform my consciousness. One sitting, one session, one retreat. These encounters often provided me with a spiritual high, but nothing fundamentally changed. Because that's not how Self-Realization works.

You may slam a battering ram against the door of your Inner Core, and you may then loosen the hinges and get a peek at the riches that lie within, but your everyday mental habits—your false friends— will make a quick comeback to repair the door once you're done, and you will again be locked out of the sacred space within. You have to instead gently prod the door open, inch by inch, day by day, by pursuing a more deliberate path to claim permanent residence in your Core. That is how your brain gets rewired—through small, daily effort, not heroic, episodic bursts.

By the time I was in my mid-thirties, the game was up. The same life that was so rich for me on the outside seemed increasingly impoverished on the inside. That is when I took initiation in Kriya Yoga from Self-Realization Fellowship and began my regular practice of meditation. It has been my greatest friend since. After several years of practice, I once wrote to a friend about how I'd figured out why people take drugs, because meditation is after all the perfect drug— legal, safe at any dosage, free of charge, abundant in supply, devoid of side effects, available on demand, more effective (not less) with every use, 100 percent reliable in the joy it brings, and eventually getting us to a sustained high throughout the day.

Some of us take meditation for a test run, and when it doesn't deliver any notable transformation, we start to believe, "I can't be still," or "I can't control my mind," or "It doesn't do it for me." Oh, really? Let me ask you this: Would you ever conclude after a few piano lessons that you aren't meant for playing the piano, that it is not worth your energy because you still can't play Beethoven's *Moonlight Sonata*? Of course you wouldn't. We all recognize that it takes time and effort to learn a musical instrument, or a sport, or a new language, and that our early experience may not be that fluid or fun. We continue to stay committed to our learning journey because we value the rewards that will ultimately ensue. Why then should we expect meditation to work overnight wonders for us?

We have spent years operating with an outward, restless consciousness, and now we are trying to learn a new language of an inward, tranquil consciousness. As Goleman and Davidson report, researchers have found that "when people new to meditation practiced daily for ten weeks, they reported the practice progressively got easier and more enjoyable, whether they were focusing on their breath, generating loving-kindness, or just observing the flow of their thoughts."

In my first year, I struggled while meditating to keep my spine straight. This posture is critical for the smooth flow of prana. In near desperation, I started placing a book on my head to make sure my spine didn't bend. It wasn't much fun to meditate while having to replace the book each time it fell, but mercifully, in a few weeks, the bending of my spine went away. A second struggle I faced was with directing my gaze to the space between my eyebrows, a crucial part of Kriya Yoga meditation. After two years of struggle, I decided over the holidays to make this gaze-fixing my *one goal* for the new year. Within a few months of this single-minded pursuit, I finally succeeded. Sometimes, I do an experiment by letting my back slouch, or letting my gaze drop. Then I straighten my spine, or return my gaze to the right spot. Within a few minutes, I can feel a deepening in the level of interiorization that then leads to tranquility or joy, brought about by these seemingly minor adjustments. I have learned how critical it is to not fall into the wrong habits, not even those that seem innocuous. Meditation is an exacting discipline, but it also rewards our loyalty generously.

While there is an abundance of meditation teachers and teachings to choose from, many of those who claim to be teachers are not rightly qualified. Some are pilgrims at the early stage of their own Self-Realization journey. They have progressed enough to get swept up by meditation's allure and to want to offer it to the world and make it their calling, but that does not mean they are ready to teach a path that can take you all the way to Self-Realization. And since there are no credible "Top Twenty" lists of meditation teachers or institutions, it can be challenging to find a teacher who is both qualified and right for you. Here is some guidance on how to go about your search and on the pitfalls you will want to avoid.

Investigate any path you are drawn to. Because meditation is an ancient discipline, many paths have been around for several decades—some for several centuries. What kind of energy does the teacher exude? Do you feel uplifted in their presence? What is their mission? How selfless is their motive? How long have they been teaching? What is it like to spend time in the company of this teacher's community of followers? What are the main pillars of their teaching, and how do those resonate with you? What is the philosophy behind their path? Your teacher does not have to be living or physically accessible to you. Their energy can emerge through their life story, their writings, their audiovisual records, and their followers. The most powerful way to experience a teacher's presence is within, as an intuitive feeling of their presence and their guidance.

If you feel drawn to a path, run an experiment by mindfully putting its teachings into practice in your life for some time, spending time in its community, and determining whether it is helping you make progress. Once you have found a path you wish to make your own, commit to it. You may find it more appealing to mix and match, to sample, to build your own path based on what works for you at any given moment. But think of it this way: How many athletes have become Olympians by charting their own course, patching together different coaches' ideas, without ever committing to a coach for a reasonable length of time?

Staying committed to your teacher helps tide you over during the dry periods—periods when you feel you are not progressing and start to lose motivation. In these times, doubts creep into your mind: "This path isn't working for me." If you give yourself the freedom to switch your teacher and path on a whim, you will feel like switching whenever you hit a dry phase. But then you'd never learn anything. Very few have made it to Self-Realization without a trusted teacher to whom they have been loyal.

Some of us may find it constrictive to follow a teacher. A true teacher would never ask you to blindly follow what they say; rather, they would guide you to discover your true nature and to heed your own inner voice. In yoga traditions, a true teacher is called a guru. The meaning of the word "guru" is "dispeller of darkness"; the guru liberates you by helping you discover your own light within. Your first responsibility, as a pilgrim on the path of Self-Realization, is to find the right path for yourself—one that will help you discover this light within.

HOW A SEEKER FOUND HIS PATH

Here is how Paul Brunton found his path during his search in "secret" India: "I wanted to gather the real facts about the yogis of today by the method of first-hand investigation. . . . Without that strict, scientific attitude I might have been led away into the wilderness of superstition. . . . I could never have done this did I not contain within my complex nature the two elements of scientific skepticism and spiritual sensitivity. . . . It is not easy to conjoin qualities which are usually held to be contradictory, but I sincerely tried to hold them in sane balance."

Along the way, he found

> well-intentioned fools, scriptural slaves, venerable know-nothings, money-seeking conjurers, jugglers with a few tricks, . . . pious frauds . . . and [self-styled] "divine teachers" who promise an ecstasy of the spirit, but give instead an exasperation of the mind. . . . I have met some men of remarkable attainments and fine character, as well as others who can do amazing things . . . but . . . I have no desire to become the depository of another man's doctrines; it is a living, first-hand, personal experience which I seek, a spiritual illumination entirely my own and not someone else's.

Dejected, Brunton prepared to return to Britain. Just three days before his ship was to sail from Mumbai, he experienced a strong inner pull to return to the premises of one of the yogis he had visited,

Ramana Maharshi. He canceled his departure and traveled back to south India to see the Maharshi.

At Maharshi's hermitage, he had hoped to engage in some form of intellectual inquiry on spiritual matters. Instead, Maharshi guided him to dive within. "The realization forces itself through my wonderment that all my questions are moves in an endless game, the play of thoughts which possess no limit to their extent; that somewhere within me there is a well of certitude which can provide me with all the waters of truth I require; and that it will be better to cease my questioning and attempt to realize the tremendous potencies of my own spiritual nature. So I remain silent and wait."

In these early strivings Brunton was seeking to access the interiorized mind. At one point, he expressed to Maharshi that he was losing hope of achieving any breakthroughs. Maharshi replied, "Every man is divine and strong in his real nature. What are weak and evil are his habits, his desires and thoughts, but not himself." Gradually, under Maharshi's guidance, Brunton started to achieve tangible gains.

> I slip quietly to the floor and straightway assume my regular meditation posture. In a few seconds I compose myself and bring all wandering thoughts to a strong center. An intense interiorization of consciousness comes with the closing of eyes. . . . The mental questionings which have marked most of my earlier meditations have lately begun to cease. . . . I want to dive into a place deeper than thought. I want to know what it will feel like to deliver myself from the constant bondage of the brain, but to do so with all my attention awake and alert. It is strange enough to be able to stand aside and watch the very action of the brain as though it were someone else's, and to see how thoughts take their rise and then die, but it is stranger still to realize intuitively that one is about to penetrate into the mysteries which hide the innermost recesses of [a person's] soul. . . . A perfectly controlled and subdued anticipation quietly thrills me.
>
> Finally it happens. Thought is extinguished like a snuffed candle.

In that magical moment, Brunton had entered his tranquil mind.

"How shall I record these experiences through which I next pass," Brunton wrote, "when they are too delicate for the touch of my pen? Scholars may burrow like moles among the growing piles of modern books and ancient manuscripts which line the walls of the house of learning, but they can learn no deeper secret than this, no higher truth than the supreme truth that man's very self is divine."

Perhaps this is why Daya Mata, the nun Elvis called his "spiritual mother," declared, "The nature of the soul is power, bliss, love. . . . Man runs after these things because he is unconsciously seeking to experience his own soul nature."

Chapter 13

LEADING WITH
SELF-REALIZATION

⤸⸱⸝

As human beings, our greatness lies not so much in
being able to remake the world . . . as in being able to
remake ourselves.

—*Gandhi*

HOW GANDHI SHOOK THE WORLD
BY GOING WITHIN

In 1888, Mohandas Gandhi traveled to London for the first time
at the age of eighteen and checked into a room at Victoria Hotel.
"I was quite dazzled by the splendor of the hotel. . . . I thought I
could pass a lifetime in that room." Gandhi had arrived in the city
with an important mission. His father had been the chief minister
of Porbandar state, a prominent position, until his death in 1885.
Gandhi grew up a timid and shy boy, and after being a mediocre student at school he had enrolled in college in India and explored the
idea of becoming a doctor, only to return home five months later after
failing his first set of classes. His older brother and he decided that
he should pursue a law degree in England and return to India as an
attorney. "The object of sending me to England," he later recounted

265

to his brother, "was that we . . . might thereby maintain the status of our father more or less, be well off and enjoy the good things of life."

Here he was, at the very seat of power of the British Empire, of which his nation, India, was the crown jewel. "[I was] all the time smiling within myself. . . . At that time, my only thought was to acquire all the accomplishments which make a gentleman." He took lessons in dancing, elocution, French, and the violin. He refashioned his wardrobe, wearing "a high silk hat top, a Gladstonian collar, stiff and starched . . . a morning coat, a double-breasted vest and dark striped trousers . . . boots . . . leather gloves . . . and a silver-mounted stick."

Fast-forward to 1931, when Gandhi returned for what would be his final visit to London. He was there to attend the Round Table Conference organized by the British government to discuss the future of colonial India. By now, he was one of the most famous people in the world. His next stop after London would be mainland Europe, and Italian educator Maria Montessori had remarked in anticipation, "Everybody knows him, even the smallest child, in every corner of Europe. Everyone, when he sees his picture, exclaims in his own language: That is Gandhi!" In India, people had started to call him Mahatma Gandhi instead of Mohandas Gandhi. The word "Mahatma" means "great soul."

This time, there was no Victoria Hotel. Gandhi accepted an invitation to be a houseguest in the low-income eastern district so he could interact with the city's poor. And this time, there was no "striped silk shirt" or "double-breasted vest." Gandhi arrived in London in the same garb he had begun to wear in India as a symbol of his kinship with the poor: sandals and a loincloth that left much of his body bare. When King George V asked to meet Gandhi, several Buckingham Palace officials fretted about Gandhi's dress. Gandhi responded after the meeting by noting that "the King was wearing enough for the both of us."

How did the mesmerized Gandhi become the mesmerizing Gandhi in between those two London visits?

After earning his law degree, Gandhi went back to India. He later wrote, "[I was] so much attached . . . to London and its environments;

for who would not be? London with its teaching institutions, public galleries, museums, theatres, vast commerce, public parks and vegetarian restaurants, is a fit place for a student and a traveler. . . . It was not without deep regret that I left London." Destiny awaited Gandhi on the other side—his initial meeting with Raychand, the diamond merchant, happened the day after his ship docked in Bombay. After a short stint in India, Gandhi left for South Africa to provide legal representation to an Indian client.

From South Africa, he wrote a letter to Raychand asking for his guidance on a set of hard questions: "What is the soul? Does it perform actions? Do past actions impede its progress or not? What is God? Is He the creator of the universe? If a claim is put forward that a particular religion is the best, may we not ask the claimant for proof? What will finally happen to this world? Will the world be morally better off in the future?" His fascination for late-Victorian London had started to fade as he became increasingly drawn to one goal, which he later described this way: "What I meant to achieve— what I have been striving and pining to achieve these thirty years—is self-realization." On another occasion he declared, "If I found myself entirely absorbed in the service of the community, the reason behind it was my desire for self-realization."

In the years that followed, Gandhi pursued Self-Realization not only by plumbing the depths of his consciousness to enter his Inner Core but also by guiding admirers and adversaries alike to discover their own Core. He saw the two actions as related. "[It is] my experiments in the spiritual field, which are known only to me . . . from which I have derived such power as I possess for working in the political field."

One of the first steps Gandhi took on his journey to Self-Realization was to implement a practice of silence. "I visited a Trappist monastery in South Africa. . . . Most of the inmates of that place were under a vow of silence. I inquired of the Father the motive of it and he said the motive is apparent: 'We are frail human beings. We do not know very often what we say. If we want to listen to the still small voice that is always speaking within us, it will not be heard if we continually speak.' I understood that precious lesson. I know the secret of silence."

As a youth, Gandhi had been uninterested in prayer. "I started with disbelief in God and prayer," he said, but then at a "late stage in life [I felt a] void." At thirty-six, he made prayer a regular practice. "Prayer has been the saving of my life," said he. "I have had my fair share of the bitterest public and private experiences. They threw me into temporary despair, but if I was able to get rid of it, it was because of prayer. . . . In spite of despair staring me in the face on the political horizon, I have never lost my peace. . . . That peace, I tell you, comes from prayer." On one occasion he announced, "I have so much to accomplish today that I must meditate for two hours instead of one." He also once reflected on how prayer can reshape our relationship with the world: "Prayer is the greatest binding force, making for the solidarity and oneness of the human family. If a person realizes his unity with God through prayer, he will look upon everybody as himself. The outer must reflect the inner."

In his early days, Gandhi embraced the racist sentiments prevalent in those times. In South Africa, this attitude initially made him distance himself from the black community, in part to demonstrate that Indians were closer in racial status to whites. As he grew in Self-Realization, he started to see the world very differently. In a speech in Johannesburg in 1908, he stated, "If we look into the future, is it not a heritage we have to leave to posterity that all the different races commingle and produce a civilization that perhaps the world has not yet seen?" It was this much-transformed Gandhi that left South Africa twenty-one years later. As Nelson Mandela later put it on a visit to India, "You gave us Mohandas; we returned him to you as Mahatma."

Soon after his return to India, Gandhi began to actively pursue social and political reform there. The strain the work placed on him made him at times feel he was "being torn to pieces." To rebuild his inner state, he decided to reserve Monday as a day of silence for himself. From then on, he never spoke on Mondays except during emergencies. At the Round Table Conference he attended in London, the first day happened to be a Monday; he participated without speaking a word. On Tuesday morning, he gave the address that led his personal secretary to observe to a British journalist that what Gandhi spoke, felt, thought, and did was always the same.

Gandhi strove to cultivate the tempered mind. The American journalist Louis Fischer, who spent time with Gandhi while penning a biography of him, wrote, "He had a violent nature and his subsequent mahatma-calm was the product of long training in temperament-control. He did not easily become an even-minded, desireless yogi. He had to remold himself Recognizing his deficiencies, he made a conscious effort to grow and change and restrain his bad impulses. He turned himself into a different person. He was a remarkable case of second birth in one lifetime."

Beyond temperance, Gandhi was seeking the tranquil mind, the stillness that goes beyond thought and feelings, a state he called "silent prayer." He wrote,

> True meditation consists in closing the eyes and ears of the mind to all else, except the object of one's devotion. . . . Emptying the mind of all conscious processes of thought and filling it with the spirit of God unmanifest brings one ineffable peace and attunes the soul with the Infinite. . . . [We should] make a serious effort to throw off the attachments of the world for a while . . . to make a serious endeavor to remain, so to say, out of the flesh. . . . The practice of complete withdrawal of the mind from all outward things, even though it might be only for a few minutes every day, will be found to be of infinite use.

In his later years, Gandhi was in a train going uphill when the coach became disconnected from the engine and started to roll downhill, gaining speed as it went. Passengers around him were terrified; the coach could at any moment derail and fall off the hill. But Gandhi continued dictating a note to an assistant, who exclaimed, "[Sir], do you know what is happening? We may not be alive. We are in-between life and death. The coach is moving backward with nothing to stop it, and it's gaining speed." Gandhi, unimpressed, replied,

"If we die, we die. But if we are saved, we would have wasted all this time." He guided his assistant to keep writing until the future resolved itself—and they did not die that day. In that moment, Gandhi was displaying the centered state that defines the peak of Self-Realization: the unshakable mind.

Gandhi once led a peace march in a riot-torn area of Bengal. While he was walking through a prominent Muslim section of the region, a fanatic rushed up to him, grabbed his throat, and threw him to the ground. Gandhi immediately started to recite verses he had memorized from the Quran, verses that invoked God's mercy and guidance. The man, Allahdad Khan Mondol, was startled to hear such a fine recital from his scripture. He apologized and eventually became one of Gandhi's followers. Gandhi's deep study of world scriptures had convinced him that they represent different paths to Self-Realization; in that life-threatening moment, his unshakable mind found the right path to awaken Mondol to the peace and love ever present in his Core.

Gandhi's greatest weapon in leading India's struggle for independence was his inner voice.

> There come to us moments in life when about some things we need no proof from without. A little voice within us tells us, "You are on the right track, move neither to your left nor right, but keep to the straight and narrow way." . . . The only tyrant that I accept in the world is the still small voice within me. . . . For me the voice [is] more real than my own existence. . . . The time when I learnt to recognize this voice was, I may say, the time when I started praying regularly. . . . It has never failed me, and for that matter, anyone else. And everyone who wills can hear the voice. It is within everyone.

The more Gandhi came face-to-face with his Inner Core, the more his awareness grew of its hidden presence in everyone. On this basis, he created a social and political reform movement named satyagraha—or soul force. We might think of it as Core Force. Its principles and tactics were nothing short of remarkable.

In 1922, Gandhi was arrested by the British government and tried for fomenting unrest in India. At his trial, he did not defend himself. He accepted the prosecutor's charges, and then made an impassioned case for how British colonial rule was morally degrading for the British and destructive for India, and why it was the duty of every Indian patriot to challenge unjust British policies and laws and seek India's independence. He ended by telling the Judge, "The only course open to you, the judge, is either to resign your post and thus disassociate yourself from evil, if you feel that the law you are called upon to administer is an evil and that in reality I am innocent; or to inflict on me the severest penalty, if you believe that the system and the law you are assisting to administer are good for the people of this country, and that my activity is therefore injurious to the public weal." Here, he was exercising a key principle of satyagraha—the idea that every individual has a conscience, and our only aspiration should be to help people awaken and follow their own inner voice. The judge was visibly moved, saying, "The law is no respecter of persons. Nevertheless, it will be impossible to ignore the fact that you are in a different category from any person I have ever tried or am likely to try." After sentencing Gandhi to six years in prison based on the law, he added, "And I should like to say in doing so that if the course of events in India makes it possible for the government to reduce the period and release you no one will be better pleased than I."

On his visit to London for the Round Table Conference, Gandhi asked to travel to Lancashire to visit its laid-off textile mill workers. As a colony, India had been forced by Britain to export cotton at low prices to British mills, where it was manufactured into cloth and sold back to Indians at a big premium—enriching Britain's coffers, but impoverishing India. So Gandhi had championed a movement in India to boycott British textiles, ultimately leading to the closure of Lancashire mills. The British government was concerned about

Gandhi visiting Lancashire on the assumption that the mill workers would be angry with him. But Gandhi, who saw the workers for their Core, was confident that he could, through dialog, win them over.

A large crowd was assembled to see him when he arrived. "Please listen to me for just a few minutes," Gandhi asked them quietly. "Give me a chance to present our point of view, and then, if you like, condemn me and my people. You tell me that three million people are out of employment here, have been out of employment for several months. In my country, three hundred million people are unemployed at least six months in every year. You say there are days when you can get only bread and butter for your dinner. But these people [in India] often go for days on end without any food at all."

By the end of their exchange, the mill workers were cheering for Gandhi, the man most responsible for their economic hardships. We sometimes write off our opponents when we feel they are taking an unjust position or when their interests are in conflict with our own. Gandhi's moment in Lancashire offers an action we can practice to build rapprochement: affirm the hidden Core in your opponents, and create a space for dialog where hearts are stirred and truth and solutions are mutually discovered.

Gandhi once described soul force as "gentle, it never wounds. It must not be the result of anger or malice. It is never fussy, never impatient, never vociferous. It is the direct opposite of compulsion. It was conceived as a complete substitute for violence." His goal was to show people that soul force—the capacity for heroic sacrifice to peacefully advance just causes in the world—was their native state, and that in small and silent ways, it already operated in their relationships at home and beyond. When a skeptic pointed to how there was no historical evidence of the existence or use of soul force in social transformation, Gandhi responded, "History, as we know it, is a record of the wars of the world . . . how kings played, how they became enemies of one another, how they murdered one another. . . . History is really a record of every interruption of the even working of the force of love or of the soul." He went on to highlight how soul force silently operates in everyday people's lives:

Two brothers quarrel: one of them repents and reawakens the love that was lying dormant within him; the two again begin to live in peace; nobody takes note of this. But if the two brothers through the intervention of [lawyers] or some other reason take up arms or go to the law—which is another form of the exhibition of brute force—their doings would be immediately noticed in the press, they would be the talk of their neighbors and would probably go down to history. And what is true of families and communities is true of nations There is no reason to believe that there is one law for families and another for nations.

But he also recognized that cultivating soul force required people to make a big investment in themselves. So he set up ashram communities in South Africa and later in India, where he welcomed people from around the world to live with him. The ashram routine included prayers, right diet, exercise, and other practices designed to help residents cultivate their Inner Core. Gandhi took a keen interest in the residents, tracking their individual progress, offering personal counsel, and maintaining a joyful environment. He wrote, "Just as physical training [needs] to be imparted through physical exercise, and intellectual through intellectual exercise, even so the training of the spirit [is] possible only through the exercise of the spirit. And the exercise of the spirit entirely depended on the life and character of the teacher."

To the people who had more limited contact with him at public rallies, his message was the same: go within and discover your true self. "If the crowd [at a rally] was loud or unruly, Gandhi would sit silently, for hours, until they were quiet. Then he would depart." What better way to be a messenger of peace than to guide people to the peace they possess in their Core?

In 1930, Gandhi wanted to build a nationwide civil disobedience movement against British rule. To the surprise of all, he decided to focus it on something as trite as salt. Britain's salt law prohibited Indians from producing their own salt so they would be required to buy the more expensive British salt. Jawaharlal Nehru, who later became India's first prime minister, recalled that when Gandhi proposed a protest against the salt law, "We were bewildered and could not fit in a national struggle with common salt." A leading newspaper, *The Stateman*, wrote, "It is difficult not to laugh, and we imagine that will be the mood of most thinking Indians." But Gandhi was unperturbed. His inner voice had led him to the idea of organizing a Salt March, during which he would walk with a group of followers all the way to the ocean and defy the law by simply drawing salt out of the water. "I had not the ghost of a suspicion how the breach of the salt law would work itself out," he declared. "But like a flash it came, and as you know, it was enough to shake the country from one end to the other."

The Salt March proved to be a stroke of genius, connecting the freedom struggle with the everyday experience of salt consumption that millions of poor people across the land could relate to. Gandhi took off from his ashram with seventy-eight followers and marched for several days to the oceanfront. He had astutely recruited ashram residents rather than political workers for the demonstration, since he recognized that it would call for strict adherence to the principles of satyagraha. Over the next few days, tens of thousands would greet the marchers along the way. Upon reaching the ocean, Gandhi raised a lump of salty mud and declared, "With this, I am shaking the foundations of the British Empire."

Mass civil disobedience broke out all over India, with millions defying the salt laws, boycotting British products, and refusing to pay taxes. The British government imprisoned over sixty thousand. One poignant instance of satyagraha involving twenty-five hundred marchers was described by a United Press correspondent: "The officers ordered [the protestors] to retreat but they continued to step forward. Suddenly . . . scores of native policemen rushed upon the advancing marchers and rained blows on their heads with their steel-shod [long batons]. Not one of the marchers even raised an arm to fend off the blows. They went down like ten-pins. Those struck down fell sprawling, unconscious or writhing with fractured skulls or broken shoulders. The survivors, without breaking ranks, silently and doggedly marched on until struck down. The raids and beatings continued for several days."

As people in Britain and the rest of the world read journalists' accounts of the events, their eyes were opened to the suffering of India's masses. International and domestic pressure started to grow on the British government to end its imperial rule. *Time* magazine named Gandhi its Man of the Year. Gandhi's equation of satyagraha was unfolding with near-mathematical precision. Even during the freedom struggle's worst setbacks, he had refused to believe that the British were evil; instead, he had projected that once the suffering of the oppressed became more visible, sooner or later, the humanity that lay hidden deep within the British people would come shining through, and they would reform. It was several years before India gained her outer freedom, but Gandhi's satyagrahis had already started to gain inner freedom by replacing bodily force—the tool of past revolutionaries—with soul force.

Most of the millions in India who followed Gandhi did not deeply study his philosophy. "I know that a whole people can adopt [non-violence] . . . without understanding its philosophy," Gandhi once wrote. "People generally do not understand the philosophy of all their acts." The Core intuitively knows what the intellect can sometimes not comprehend. Over time, as Gandhi's methods have been studied and replicated globally by other reformers, including Martin Luther King Jr. and other civil rights leaders in the United States, it has become clear that the emancipation of India was not Gandhi's final aim. He used India as a proof point to show humanity the hidden virtues that lie present in its Core. Attempting to assess Gandhi's impact on the world, Albert Einstein wrote, "Generations to come, it may be, will scarcely believe that such a one as this ever in flesh and blood walked upon the earth." Stafford Cripps, a member of Britain's War Cabinet who was sent by Churchill on a mission to win India's cooperation during World War II, later observed about Gandhi, "I know of no other man of any time or indeed of recent history who so forcefully and convincingly demonstrated the power of spirit over material things." Churchill had believed that "Man is spirit," and his emissary to India, Cripps, found the person whom he believed most exemplified this truth.

After Gandhi died, in January 1948, a foreign journalist asked an Indian friend to explain why the country was plunged into such an intense outpouring of grief over his death. The friend told him, "You know, the people feel that there was a mirror in the Mahatma in which they could see the greatest in themselves, and now they are afraid that mirror has been shattered."

What the diamond merchant Raychand had sparked in a youthful Gandhi is what he in turn sparked in hundreds of millions. Perhaps the central lesson from Gandhi's life is that our highest calling lies in awakening everyone to their Core identity—the peace, love, and joy that reside within—and that the surest way to do so is by first awakening to our own. And that is Self-Realization.

THE DESTINATION

～👁～

SRINIVASA RAMANUJAN WAS A COLLEGE DROPOUT WITH almost no formal training in mathematics. Yet, in his twenties, he discovered mind-bogglingly beautiful equations, like the one below.

$$\sqrt{\frac{\pi e}{2}} = \cfrac{1}{1+\cfrac{1}{1+\cfrac{2}{1+\cfrac{3}{1+\cfrac{4}{1+\cfrac{5}{1+\cfrac{6}{1+\cfrac{7}{1+\cfrac{8}{\ddots}}}}}}}}} + \left\{ 1 + \frac{1}{1\cdot3} + \frac{1}{1\cdot3\cdot5} + \frac{1}{1\cdot3\cdot5\cdot7} + \frac{1}{1\cdot3\cdot5\cdot7\cdot9} + \cdots \right\},$$

A prominent mathematician of the time, G. H. Hardy, acknowledged that he'd "never met [Ramanujan's] equal." One of the greatest unsolved mathematical mysteries of the twentieth century is the question of how the untutored Ramanujan arrived at these equations. He never proved the equations, leaving it to other mathematicians to determine if they were true or false. In one study of his final six hundred equations,

99 percent of them were proved, decades later, to be true. Ramanujan claimed that the equations were revealed to him in visions by a higher power. "An equation for me has no meaning," he said, "unless it expresses a thought of God." The number zero, he believed, represented absolute reality, and the number infinity represented the many manifestations of that reality.

Is it possible for you and me to reach a state where our every action, like Ramanujan's equations, "expresses a thought of God"?

What kind of civilization would we create if we lived and led with the understanding that we are all manifestations of the same absolute reality?

Chapter 14

TRANSCENDENCE

Let the mind be enlarged, according to its capacity,
to the grandeur of the mysteries, and not the mysteries contracted to the narrowness of the mind.

—*Francis Bacon*

THE THIRD TYPE OF INTUITION

Sammie told the following story in my class:

Once, when I was teenager, I was getting ready to go out with
my friends who were coming by to pick me up. I will never forget what happened next. My mother suddenly comes up to me,
quite agitated, and insists that I cancel my plans. I argued with
her heatedly, but she would not budge. "Sammie, you're *not*
going out today. For my sake." Finally, I relented, and told my
friends to go without me. That evening, they met with an accident. My mom later told me, "I just had this very bad feeling
about you going out that night, so I had to stop you."

Rohan, an executive MBA student, shared this:

I remember the day my daughter was born. I was in the hospital. Now please know that I am not a physician, and have no medical training or knowledge. And this was my first child, so I had no previous experience with childbirth. But that day, somehow, I had a very uncomfortable feeling arise within me. Something wasn't right. The nurse and the physicians assured me that all was fine with my daughter, but the feeling kept getting stronger in me. I urged the doctor to perform some tests to make sure things were fine. He finally acceded, and then discovered to his surprise that my daughter had low hemoglobin and needed a blood transfusion immediately. If they had not done that, she would have been at risk of dying. She is six months old now, and all is well with her. I am glad I trusted my feelings that day.

How did Sammie's mom and Rohan receive such remarkable and timely guidance from within?

Some of us think of our brain as a database. The more information we store in it over time, the more we know. Both expert and creative intuition, as discussed in the chapter "Living with Wisdom," help us draw out and integrate information from our memory database to deliver relevant insights. But this model of our brain doesn't allow us to explain Rohan's or Sammie's mom's experience. After all, they had no experience stored in their mental database that could have prompted their behavior.

There is another way to think of our brain——that it is not just a database, but a browser, a gateway to the "world wide web" of cosmic intelligence that we tune into under the right conditions. In the moments when we access guidance from this cosmic intelligence, we are practicing not expert or creative intuition but spiritual intuition.

If there is in fact a cosmic intelligence in the universe, and if there is a faculty of spiritual intuition that can bring us in touch with it, then our highest potential cannot reside within the circumscribed limits of our physical being. Could it be that when you arrive at your Inner Core and I arrive at mine, we will find that we have arrived at the same place, a Universal Core? Is this what the poet Tennyson meant when he wrote, "[We] are external manifestations of the Eternal Creative Spirit, differentiated into particular individualized forms"? And is it possible that this Universal Core is beyond anything we could ever imagine, like the sight of Yosemite Valley the day I woke up in its embrace?

SELF-TRANSCENDENCE

In 1949, the psychologist Abraham Maslow proposed that people's motivations were governed by a hierarchy of needs. At the bottom lie our basic hungers for food and shelter. In the middle lie our needs for security and love. And at the very top lies self-actualization, the desire to pursue one's full potential in a field of one's own choosing. But that was not all.

In his later years, Maslow revised his pyramid by adding another stage beyond self-actualization. He called it self-transcendence. "Transcendence refers to the very highest and most inclusive or holistic levels of human consciousness, [relating] to oneself, to significant others, to human beings in general, to other species, to nature, and to the cosmos," he wrote. "Practically every serious description of the 'authentic person' implies that such a person, by virtue of what he has become, assumes a new relation to his society and indeed, to society in general. He not only transcends himself in various ways; he also transcends his own culture."

The longing for transcendence, for a feeling of being connected to something much greater than yourself, is the highest of human hungers. Maslow investigated transcendence from the outside, interviewing people and formulating his ideas. But a tribe of truth-seekers has for thousands of years sought to cultivate transcendence from the inside, as a state to attain within themselves. These are the mystics, emerging out of a diversity of faiths and traditions, and united by their hunger to discover and connect with the potentialities that lie dormant within us all. They may trek different paths to ascend to the mountaintop of human potential, but all mystics follow similar principles to guide their view of life and its true purpose.

FIVE PRINCIPLES OF MYSTICISM

1. There is a force behind the universe; call it the Universal Core or what you may. This force is omnipresent (present everywhere), omniscient (knows everything), omnipotent (all-powerful), and all-loving. All human beings—and in fact, all life-forms—are individualized expressions of this Universal Core.

2. The purpose of life is to advance our consciousness so it can dissolve into the Universal Core. Higher consciousness isn't a reward to be earned in an afterlife for having lived virtuously, but a state to cultivate here and now, in this life, through the instrumentalities of our body and mind, with the right techniques and ways of living.

3. Our Inner Core, or soul, is our true, perfect nature, a pure reflection of the Universal Core from which we have emerged. When we awaken to qualities of spirit such as peace, wisdom, love, and joy, we transcend our individual self to feel a sense of unity with all life and all creation.

4. When we serve other people and other forms of life, it is the spirit in us serving the spirit in them. In those moments, we are serving our higher self. Service to others is therefore life's most natural calling.

5. The more we anchor ourselves in our Core, the more our spiritual intuition blossoms. Our thoughts and actions are then increasingly guided by the Universal Core, and our impact in the world grows. As Gandhi said, "There is a force in the universe, which, if we permit it, will flow through us and produce miraculous results."

WHO—OR WHAT—IS GOD?

A skeptic was visiting Self-Realization Fellowship Lake Shrine in Los Angeles—the same place Elvis took Priscilla. There he encountered a monk, Brother Vishwananda, and challenged him with a question: "You people are always talking about God. Tell me this. How do you define God?"

The monk peered into the skeptic's eyes. "God," he replied, "is your highest potential."

That is how mystics see it. God is spirit, and when you or I reach our highest potential, we become one with spirit. "You are all gods if you only knew it," said Yogananda. "Behind your waves of consciousness is the sea of God's presence." The Nobel Prize–winning physicist Erwin Schrödinger observed, "The mystics of many centuries, independently, yet in perfect harmony with each other (somewhat like the particles in an ideal gas) have described, each of them, the unique experience of his or her life in terms that can be condensed in the phrase: DEUS FACTUS SUM (I have become God)."

Religions sometimes portray God in human terms, possessed of a gender, a physical form, and a voice, seated on a throne in a heavenly kingdom, experiencing human emotions like anger and pleasure. Humanizing this force is a way to make a profound mystery more approachable. If that is the starting point in our relationship with God, that is fine. But if it becomes the end point, the relationship can sour or become distorted, because a human form can disappoint us if we feel that it judges or punishes us or doesn't care enough to intervene in our hour of need. Pure, loving spirit, in contrast, can never disappoint, for everything that happens to us is an invitation to come closer to our native land: cosmic consciousness. As Francis Bacon counseled in the quote at the start of this chapter, we need to expand our minds to take in the mystery, not contract the mystery to fit our minds. Mystics may bring the ineffable spirit down to a human level now and then, but they mostly strive to uplift their consciousness to a divine level. As the Jesuit priest Pierre Teilhard de Chardin observed, "We are not human beings having a spiritual experience. We are spiritual beings having a human experience."

THE MYSTIC IN US ALL

The founding father of modern psychology, William James, took a deep interest in mysticism. In his book *The Varieties of Religious Experiences*, he wrote, "There are two lives, the natural and the spiritual, and we must lose the one before we can participate in the other. . . . In mystic states we both become one with the Absolute and we become aware of our oneness. . . . The overcoming of all the usual barriers between the individual and the Absolute is the great mystic achievement."

William James's appreciation of mystic states stands in sharp contrast to the views of Sigmund Freud. Freud was dismissive of mystical experiences, suggesting that "the longing for spiritual union, which mystics so universally express, is really an unconscious desire to escape a harsh, disappointing reality by returning to the world of blissful unity and completeness we knew when we were babies." Despite his misconception of mysticism, Freud did direct us to an important part of our mind that lies beyond conscious awareness: the subconscious. Mystics direct us to another important part of our mind, one which also lies beyond conscious awareness but is very different from the subconscious: the *super* conscious.

Neuroscientist Andrew Newberg, a leading researcher in the emerging science of transcendence and mysticism, summed this up well in his book *Why God Won't Go Away: Brain Science and the Biology of Belief.* He points out that in the past, most scientists and psychologists regarded mystics as "the victims of damaged and deluded minds," but they are now recognizing that mystical experiences are radically different from schizophrenia and other psychotic states. Mystics describe their experiences as joyful; psychotics are often frightened and distressed by their hallucinations. Mystical states involve "a loss of pride and ego, a quieting of the mind, and an emptying of the self"; psychotics "often have feelings of religious grandiosity and inflated egotistical importance." Mystics can choose to withdraw from social engagement for a period of time and then return to function normally; psychotics' withdrawal is less voluntary and often long-lasting. People who experience mystical states have been found to "enjoy much higher levels of psychological health than the public at large, in terms of better interpersonal relationships, higher self-esteem, lower levels of anxiety, clearer self-identity, an increased concern for others, and a more positive overall out look in life."

Within each of us is a mystic, waiting to be awakened. Brain scan studies show how transcendence can be approached. Newberg reports,

> Sometimes when a person is deeply immersed in an intense prayer, meditation, or spiritual practice, there will be a sudden and dramatic decrease in neural activity in the frontal and parietal lobes. This is when our subjects are most likely to describe incredible shifts of perception and experiences of unity consciousness . . . [which give] you the sense that "you" are dissolving and becoming one with everything else in the world, even God. . . . When your frontal lobe activity drops suddenly and significantly, logic and reason shut down. Everyday consciousness is suspended, allowing other brain centers to experience the world in intuitive and creative ways. . . . Our Buddhist subjects described the sensation as becoming one with pure consciousness. The Franciscan nuns in our study felt a sense of unity and connectedness with Jesus or God. These are two entirely different practices, but the unity experience affected the same areas in everyone's brains.

THE MAGIC IN EVERY MOMENT

On an African safari in Botswana a few years ago, my spirit danced with joy each time we encountered wildlife—zebras, giraffes, lions, elephants, rhinos, and more. But every now and then we would drive through barren terrain littered with mounds of mud. In those moments, I urged our guide John to keep moving to look for more interesting places. Then one time, I decided to inquire about the mounds. "Ah, I was wondering if you'd ask," John said conspiratorially, as if he'd been holding on to a secret that was now ripe for sharing. "These are termite mounds." He stopped our jeep next to one of them and continued, "Let me tell you some things about them." What followed was a revelation.

I learned that millions of termites contribute to making a mound, which is among the largest structures built by *any* animal. After hearing my guide's introduction to the subject, I discovered Amia Srinivasan's wonderful article "What Termites Can Teach Us," in which she describes how a mound's interior is "an intricate structure of interweaving tunnels and passageways, radiating chambers, galleries, archways, and spiral staircases. . . . It is not so much a building as a body, a self-regulating organic process that continuously reacts to its changing environment, building and unbuilding itself. . . . Termites appear to do all this without any centralized planning: there are no architects, engineers, or blueprints. . . . [While] individual termites are not particularly intelligent, lacking memory and the ability to learn . . . put enough termites together, in the right conditions, and they will build you a cathedral."

Einstein's words came to my mind that day in Botswana: "There are two kinds of people. Those who believe everything is a miracle, and those who believe nothing is a miracle." As I listened to the guide I felt as though Einstein were directly admonishing me. "Hitendra, if you had brought just a bit of curiosity to what you saw as dull, dead mounds, they would have left you awestruck, for they are shrines to nature's genius." I remembered how, as a child, I used to lie on our home lawn at night and look up at the sky in wonderment, trying to fathom the vast reach of the universe, feeling a kinship with every star I set my eyes on. And now here I was, feeling the same wonderment looking down at the ground I was standing on. "The real voyage of discovery," Marcel Proust said, "consists not in seeking new landscapes, but in having new eyes."

Researchers have found that "experiencing awe often puts people in a self-transcendent state, where they focus less on themselves and feel more like a part of a larger whole." So let us make time to cultivate awe, to see the miracle in everything. Because, as Walt Whitman once wrote, "A leaf of grass is no less than the journey-work of the stars."

THE FLOW OF SPIRIT IN CREATIVE MINDS

Many great writers, artists, scientists, reformers, and other creative minds throughout history have operated with a near mystic connection with their craft, their work guided by their spiritual intuition in moments when they stepped back to let spirit flow.

I remember the moment vividly, sitting at the Metropolitan Opera in New York City watching Giacomo Puccini's *Madame Butterfly*, the plaintive strains of the aria "Un bel dì" piercing the auditorium. I felt transported to a higher realm, and was reminded of a conversation Puccini had with the writer Arthur Abell:

> "The great secret of all creative geniuses," remarked Puccini, "[is the] conscious, purposeful appropriation of one's own soul forces." . . . He proceeded to describe how he would first cultivate "the burning desire and the intense resolve to create something worthwhile." He would then make a "fervent demand for and from the Power that created me" coupled with "the full expectation that this higher aid will be granted." He believed "this perfect faith" opened the way for the "inspired ideas" to be born in his consciousness.
>
> "Was that the process when you were composing [Madama] Butterfly?"
>
> "It was. . . . The music of this opera was dictated to me by God; I was merely instrumental in putting it on paper and communicating it to the public. . . .
>
> "We mortals here on this earth are partners of the Creator. . . . [A composer] must acquire by laborious study and application

the technical mastery of his crafts, but he will never write anything of lasting value unless he has Divine aid also. There is a vast
amount of good music paper wasted by composers who don't
know this great truth. We are dealing in this domain with higher
spiritual laws.

"Dante, Rafael, Stradivarius all drew on that same Omnipotent Power. The inspiration from above stimulates the intellect
and the emotions. An inspired person sees things in a totally different light from one who is not inspired. Inspiration is an awakening, a quickening of all of man's faculties, and it is manifested
in all high artistic achievements. . . . It is a Divine influence."

Johannes Brahms once remarked to Abell in response to a similar inquiry, "When I feel the urge, I begin by appealing directly to my
Maker. . . . I immediately feel vibrations that thrill my whole being. . . .
Straightaway the ideas flow in upon me, directly from God, and not
only do I see distinct themes in my mind's eye, but they are clothed in
the right forms, harmonies, and orchestration. Measure by measure,
the finished product is revealed to me. . . . All great creative geniuses
do this, although some of them do not seem to be as conscious of the
process as others."

Picasso described his creative process in this manner: "Painting
is stronger than I am. It makes me do what it wants. [At the start of
any work] there is someone who works with me." Einstein discussed
his process of discovery as follows: "The intellect has little to do
on the road to discovery. There comes a leap in consciousness . . .
and the solution comes to you and you do not know how or why.
All great discoveries are made in this way." He also said, "The finest
emotion of which we are capable is the mystic emotion. . . . Everyone
who is seriously involved in the pursuit of science becomes convinced that a spirit is manifest in the laws of the universe. . . . I
want to know His thoughts; the rest are details." When Ramanujan
had his visions, he was clearly operating more as a mystic than as a
mathematician.

Were these creative minds burrowing a tunnel from their individual intelligence to a cosmic intelligence, turning their brains into browsers to search for universal inspiration for their creative projects? "Spirit," wrote Yogananda, "pushes Itself out into visible manifestation as soon as a channel is opened through which It can flow."

INNER SURRENDER

Success, to a mystic, is simply being in tune with spirit. Mother Teresa described herself as a little pencil in God's hands: "God is writing his love letter to the world in this way, through works of love. . . . The essential thing is not what we say but what God says to us and through us." Lincoln described himself as an "instrument" of a larger power, charged with "so vast, so sacred a trust." Gandhi was once asked by an American journalist, Vincent Sheean, why he felt so certain when the inner voice spoke to him. "Others," said Sheean, "have inner voices and are not sure." He asked, "Does the certainty precede the [surrender]?" In other words, did Gandhi surrender to its guidance only once he was sure it was the voice of God? Gandhi replied, "No, the [surrender] precedes the certainty." Sheean reports that "the words were said with vivacity, as if I had misunderstood something vital." Gandhi was telling Sheean that it was only when he had "reduce[d] myself to a zero" by surrendering his own desires that he could be certain that the inner guidance he was receiving was not a projection of his ego, but of spirit. Great leaders are great followers. They strive to surrender their own attachments and hungers so they can gain guidance from the universe through their inner voice.

"God's will be done. I am in His hands," Lincoln told his friends when they spoke about their fears of his being assassinated. When asked how he felt about the risk of being assassinated, Gandhi replied that God "would save [my life] if He needs it for further service in this body," and that "when my time is up, no one . . . can stand between Him and me." Both Lincoln and Gandhi were ultimately assassinated, in each case merely a few months after their crowning achievement—for Lincoln, the end of the Civil War and the passing of a constitutional amendment to ban slavery, and for Gandhi, India's transition from British imperial rule to self-government through a nonviolent revolution.

Perhaps it is because they practiced such exquisite surrender in their lives and such attunement to their inner voices that Gandhi and Lincoln were each able to walk into their final act on the stage of life with both premonition and grace.* Gandhi's niece Manu described how events transpired on January 30, 1948. Gandhi had been wrapped up in a long meeting, and when it ended he was told that two other Indian leaders had come to meet him. Conscious that he was late for his public prayer service, he told Manu, "Tell them that, if I remain alive, they can talk to me after the prayer on my walk." Gandhi went out to greet the public and make his way to his seat; a few seconds later, he was dead, felled by an assassin's bullet.

On April 15, 1865, President Lincoln was speaking with William Crook, a bodyguard at the White House who ultimately worked there for fifty years, serving twelve presidents. As Lincoln and his wife were leaving to visit a theater, the president said, "Good-bye, Crook." Crook later recalled, "It was the first time that he neglected to say 'Good-night' to me, and it was the only time that he ever said 'Good-bye.'" That evening, it was not the president but his bullet-ridden body that returned from the theater.

WHEN THE CURTAIN FALLS

What exactly will that moment be like when we are taking our last bow? We will not know until we get there, but we can gain valuable insights from the accounts of people who have come very close to taking their final bow and then returned to tell their story. Scientists call this a near-death experience (NDE): an individual sustains a physical

---

* Martin Luther King Jr.'s soaring "I've Been to the Mountaintop" speech drops hints of the premonition he, too, had of his imminent demise; he was assassinated the day after he made this speech.

trauma, like an accident or a heart attack, which renders them unconscious and puts them at the brink of dying, and then recovers. What
distinguishes NDEs from other scenarios in which people come close
to dying is that those who have gone through NDEs have a clear and
conscious recollection of all they experienced during the time they
were, medically speaking, unconscious.

Scientists have analyzed thousands of NDEs over the years.
Although the experiences related are highly varied and personal, they
contain remarkable parallels—parallels that cut across race, gender,
social class, age, nationality, religious beliefs, and personality traits.
Tom's story, which is quite typical, was related in *After*, a book written
by one of the leading NDE researchers, Dr. Bruce Greyson, professor
emeritus of psychiatry and neurobehavioral sciences at the University
of Virginia School of Medicine. I paraphrase his account below:

Growing up, Tom had a hot temper. One day when he was
nineteen, while driving his pickup truck he almost ran into a man
crossing the street. When he told the man that he should have been
using the crosswalk, the man reacted by reaching through the window and slapping him, whereupon Tom got out of his truck and beat
the man almost to death before leaving him lying on the street and
driving away.

Fifteen years later, Tom had propped his pickup truck on jacks
and was underneath the vehicle working on it when the asphalt under
one of the jacks gave way, causing the truck to fall onto Tom and
crush him. Unable to breathe, Tom lost consciousness. He ultimately
survived and later described what had happened while he was unconscious. His whole life flashed in front of him—every feeling, every
thought, every word, every action. Greyson quotes him as saying, "My
life review was absolutely, positively, everything basically from the
first breath of life right through the accident. It was that panoramic
view. It was everything." Among the many incidents he reexperienced
was the fight with the man he had attacked so brutally years before.
Survivors of NDEs commonly report life reviews. As they near death,
they stand witness to their whole life, including all the parts they had
forgotten. Every detail.

If this were all there was to Tom's story, it would be powerful enough. For it suggests that when the moment comes for life to recede from us, everything that we have been and done will flash before us, inviting us to review it.

But there is more. In the replay of the reel of Tom's life, when it came to this fight as well as all his other misdeeds, Tom experienced them not just as himself but also as his victims. About the man he had beaten, Tom is quoted as saying,

> I never knew that man either before we had the altercation or after. But in the life review I came to know that he was in a drunken state and that he was in a severe state of bereavement for his deceased wife. . . . I . . . experienced seeing [the] fist come directly into my face. And I felt the indignation, the rage, the embarrassment, the frustration, the physical pain. . . . I felt my teeth going through my lower lip. . . . I was in that man's body, seeing through that man's eyes. . . . And for the first time I saw what an enraged Tom not only looked like but felt like. . . .
>
> During this life review I watched everything uncondition-ally. It wasn't judgmental or negative. . . . I wish that I could tell you how it really felt and what the life review is like, but I'll never be able to do it accurately. Will you be totally devas-tated by the crap you've brought into other people's lives? Or will you be equally enlightened and uplifted by the love and joy that you have shared in other people's lives? Well, guess what? It pretty much averages itself out. You will be responsible for your-self, judging and reliving what you have done to everything and everybody in very far-reaching ways.

Tom's description isn't unique; about half of NDE survivors who go through a life review report the same phenomenon of witnessing and experiencing their life not just from their own perspective but also from the perspective of the people they interacted with. They are experiencing the embodiment of the Golden Rule: "Do unto others as you would want them to do unto you." They realize that, as

Greyson says, this rule is not "a moral guideline we should strive to follow, but a description of how the world works, a law of nature as inescapable as gravity."

Greyson has described how the near-death experience changes people afterward:

> They typically return with a sense that we are all part of something greater. They seem to have increased compassion and concern for others and a sense of connection to—and desire to serve—other people, which often leads to more altruistic behavior. Experiencers tend to see themselves as integral parts of a benevolent and purposeful universe, in which personal gain, particularly at someone else's expense, is no longer relevant. . . . Among the experiencers I've studied, 90 percent said their attitudes and beliefs changed as a result of their NDEs, and more than half said that the effects of their NDEs continued to increase over time. Two-thirds said they felt better about themselves as a result of their NDEs. Experiencers return from NDEs with a new or strengthened belief in life after death, a feeling of being loved and valued by some higher power, increased self-esteem, and a new sense of purpose or mission.

Dr. Kenneth Ring, another preeminent NDE researcher, says that those who have undergone NDEs realize that "I was the very people that I hurt, and I was the very people I helped to feel good." Like Greyson, he notes that experiencers "become less materialistic and less concerned with success in conventional terms. They lose their ambition to achieve by ordinary criteria for a successful life. Instead they may be very interested in helping others. [They start] to live more fully in the present moment, rather than dwell in the past or dream of the future."

Most experiencers, reports Dr. Greyson, even those without a particular religious faith, say that since their NDEs "they've been aware of the presence in their lives of *something* sacred or divine." He goes on to report that "more than four out of five described having a stronger belief in a higher power and an inner sense of divine presence" in which "they consistently describe feeling peaceful, calm, tranquil, 'at home,' grateful, and, most of all, loved." Further, he writes, "Many experiencers use the analogy of a wave in the ocean to describe this condition. The wave is one small part of the vast ocean and is composed of the same water as the rest of the ocean, yet it maintains its integrity as a distinct wave with its own properties—at least for a while."

SHAKESPEARE'S RIDDLE

Shakespeare frequently used his characters—even those who were rather flawed—to slip deep insights about human nature into his audience members' minds. His most powerful verse for me is from *Hamlet*:

> *This above all: to thine own self be true,*
> *And it must follow, as the night the day,*
> *Thou canst not then be false to any man.*

"To thine own self be true" is the central theme of this book. Shakespeare is not inviting you to be true to every habit, thought, desire, or emotion, but to your highest potential. When you nurture your five Core Energies and strive to operate from your Inner Core, it is then that you are being true to yourself—your true self.

But how is it that, when you are true to yourself, "Thou canst not then be false to any man"? When you operate from your Core, you will be honest, wise, respectful, and caring. You will then be true to others because you will approach all relationships with integrity and good intentions.

That makes sense. But there is another truth to these words. When you operate from your authentic self, you start to see how much purity, beauty, and grace exist unconditionally within you, and you are naturally led to ponder, "If this is what exists within me, despite my foibles and failings, then it must exist within every human being." You begin to recognize others not simply for who they show up as on the outside, but for who they are at their Core. You strive to draw out the best in them, thus helping them come closer to their true self. As Goethe said, "The way you see people is the way you treat them, and the way you treat them is what they become."

And there is an even deeper truth to Shakespeare's words. When you reach your Inner Core, you will have arrived at the Universal Core that underlies creation. You will have transcended your human identity to experience the kind of state Tom did during his near-death experience: seeing yourself in everyone you encounter. Humanity, then, will be experienced by you as your own higher self; you will find the same spirit flowing through us all. You will only be true to yourself when you are true to all of humanity. This is the way of the mystic.*

THE DAY THE UNIVERSE SPOKE

I remember my first meditation upon finally receiving Yogananda's lessons on the technique of Kriya Yoga. It was the moment I had been waiting for all my life—to begin, in great earnest, my quest for Self-Realization; to have my consciousness one day merge into the infinite, into ever-new, ever-conscious bliss.** Now I had the teaching that I knew would eventually take me there.

On that day, as I performed my first practice of the Kriya technique, I was struck by a sudden, surprising revelation:

Hitendra, welcome. The rewards that await you are beyond compare. Before we begin, let me ask you this. Imagine that you have come to that place of bliss that you have long hungered

---

* Was Shakespeare a mystic? In *Shakespeare's Window into the Soul: The Mystical Wisdom in Shakespeare's Characters*, the scholar Martin Lings sheds light on how the Bard's writings show a "keen understanding of the passage the soul must make to reach its final sacred union with the divine."

** My favorite word for God, among the many in Sanskrit, the language of India's scriptures, is Sat-Chit-Ananda: ever-existing, ever-conscious, ever-new bliss. Who wouldn't want to merge with that?

for. Would you actually be perfectly happy if any of your family members were hurting?

And your friends?

And other human beings?

And all other living beings?

Would there not be a part of you that would hurt if any of them were still hurting?

A feeling swept over my heart: I will only be fully in joy when every living being is in joy. Until that happens, a part of me will always want to help others arrive at the same state that I myself am striving for.

NAMASTE

While watching newsreels on India's independence struggle, Albert Einstein noticed that Gandhi folded his hands when meeting others. Gandhi was using the traditional Indian form of greeting. Einstein wrote to Gandhi inquiring about the meaning of the gesture. Gandhi shared the following explanation with Einstein. Now that we have arrived at our destination, let this, dear reader, be my own departing message to you:

"Namaste. I honor the place in you where the entire universe resides . . . a place of light, of love, of truth, of peace, of wisdom. I honor the place in you where when you are in that place and I am in that place there is only one of us."

AUTHOR'S NOTE

My attempt in this book has been to lay out universal truths about human nature that can help us succeed in our pursuit of happiness, health, high performance at work, and harmony in relationships.

The full promise of the truths we've explored lies in activating and expressing the five Core Energies in our everyday moments and in building enduring habits. To help you in this quest, I offer you the following resources, available at www.hitendra.com/inner-core-book.

1. An Inner Mastery, Outer Impact survey to help you assess how you are activating the five Core Energies and expressing them in actions that bring out the best in yourself and others—and the gaps you may want to work on

2. An Inner Mastery, Outer Impact toolkit for pursuing the five-stage path of Purpose, and of Wisdom, Growth, Love, and Self-Realization

3. Access to Mentora Digital, where you will obtain practical guidance and tools to help you live and lead with the five Core Energies

4. Opportunities to build growth connections with other readers of this book who are journeying to their Inner Core

5. A library of personal-journey stories from other readers, and the opportunity to share your own

Whichever path you take to your Core, I wish you boundless success, inner and outer.

ACKNOWLEDGMENTS

My work, and thus this book, has benefited immeasurably from the engagement, ideas, questions, and personal journeys of students, client executives, and other participants in Mentora Institute workshops and my class at Columbia. My work has been further enriched by the insights, stories, and presence of a number of inspiring guest speakers in my Personal Leadership class at Columbia, including Ferose S.V., Craig Boyan, Joe Zhou, Magda Wierzycka, Candace Lightner, Brother Govindananda, Apolo Ohno, Jan Petrie, Josh Waitzkin, David Burns, Henry Grossman, Melissa James, Rahul Varma, Raghu Krishnamurthy, Josh Davis, Adam Bryant, Rhonda Morris, David Greenspan, Jen Kluczkowski, Louisa Serene, and Prince Ea. A number of Personal Leadership teaching and research assistants have made treasured contributions to this work over the years.

The encouragement and support I received from Kamel Jedidi, Joel Brockner, and Nayla Bahri were pivotal in getting my work on Personal Leadership off the ground. The Marketing Division at Columbia graciously gave me license to indulge in this newfound passion back in 2007. Dean Glenn Hubbard and his office took a big leap by agreeing to partly sponsor an MBA Personal Leadership retreat, which became a pivotal part of the class experience. Columbia's MBA Academic Affairs team, Kelley Blanco and her EMBA team, Troy Eggers, Mike Malefakis, Pierre Yared, and their team at CBS Executive Education, and the business school team at Hong Kong University have been a joy to work with. Paul Ingram, Todd Jick, and Bruce Craven have given me great encouragement and insights at every stage of my Personal Leadership work at

Columbia. I also received much warmth and support for my work from Kathy Phillips, who tragically left the stage of life at the peak of her life and career, just before the seeds of collaboration we had sown could sprout. I am grateful as well for the early support I received from Michael Morris and Casey Ichniowski.

Twelve years ago, David Burns allowed me to walk up to him at one of his seminars through a throng of his psychotherapist fans to introduce myself and explore a way to bridge his work into the business world. Since then, he's become a valued counselor, a source of inspiration, and a treasured friend. I have learned so much from David about our emotions, thoughts, beliefs, words, and how they impact our happiness and our relationships. Dan Siegel's passion for the human condition, and for integrating multiple streams of insight and inspiration to advance our understanding on this topic, had a formative influence on my early work in this area. But it is also the care and presence that he and Caroline Welch bring to all their interactions that have deeply moved and instructed me. Both through how they think and how they lead, Raghu Krishnamurthy and Rahul Varma have solidified my conviction about how central inner mastery is to success in executive roles. Carol Dweck was an early cheerleader as I sought to bring the latest psychological findings into the business school classroom fifteen years ago. I will forever cherish the kindness and grace with which she welcomed me at Stanford and offered thought partnership in the early, exploratory, somewhat fragile years of my forays into Personal Leadership. Dorian Ralston and Hara Marano took an early bet on me by researching my path to Personal Leadership and sharing it with the world through a cover story in *Psychology Today*. Arthur Brooks has helped me in many formal and informal ways to find my place in the world as a writer; one of life's special gifts is when you can see someone you deeply admire and look up to as your friend, and that's what Arthur is to me.

Petra Nemeth has been a steadying light for me all through the conception, writing, and publication of this book. Natasha Gill, Simran Bhui, Cara Fernandes, and more recently Anushka Mimani conducted some of the biographical and autobiographical research on inspiring leaders, found source material, and provided invaluable feedback on early drafts of book chapters. Andrea Miller and Jerry Foulkes have, over the years, offered much wisdom and encouragement on moving my work from the classroom to the camera, and now to a book. Achala Punja researched and wrote ten beautiful essays on iconic leaders that helped me form my own thinking on these luminous lives. Preeti Srinivasan became a valued research associate and thought partner in my early days of writing, and, over time, a dear friend. Sabina Beri provided such warm-spirited and selfless support in guiding my early thinking on the path to publishing. Pam Krauss has been a treasured guide through the topsy-turvy ride down the publishing lane. Lauren Landress was especially helpful in helping me link my mental library of Yogananda's words with published sources. Eleanor Campbell provided me a much-valued opportunity to learn how this book might be experienced by today's college going youth, and to chip away at a few rough edges in my writing before it was too late. Brad Stulberg, Austin Smith, and other kindred spirits have given me great counsel on how to prepare myself for a book launch.

Beth Rashbaum was the first individual beyond me to cast eyes on the book manuscript, and I am so glad for that because her editing helped take it to a whole new level. I have deeply appreciated the candor and care in every one of Beth's remarks and her capacity to push, pull, and pivot. Dan Burrier gave me rich inputs on an early draft of the manuscript and brought a brand marketer's eye to polishing my ideas and phrasings of things. He's been a constant, caring, and committed presence in the unfoldment of my work over many years. Jan Petrie has been a treasured spiritual sister and guide from the day I first met her, and I have benefited so much from her perspectives in the writing of this book. I also owe a lifetime debt to her for bringing me closer to Mother Teresa's life, work, and spirit.

Lauren Marino has been a wonderful editorial partner. This book would have been a much lesser contribution to the world without Lauren's encouragement and support, and as important, her push to have me create the right balance in the book between living and leading. Mollie Weisenfeld so dedicatedly kept us organized, connected, and marching toward our milestones. Fred Francis brought much patience, grace, and care to stewarding me through all stages of the publication process. Kelley Blewster showed me how the path to editorial perfection is paved for a book, where every atom in one's creation is in sync with every other atom. Amanda Kain designed us a cover that was so beautiful that I had to work twice as hard to write a book that might do justice to it; you will be the judge. Quinn Fariel and Lauren Rosenthal have been a real joy to work with in taking our message to the market.

Nathaniel Jacks and Richard Pine took an early bet on me, for which I will owe them a lifelong debt. They have shown a boundless capacity to both understand and accept me and to challenge and change me as I've wandered around in search of the right passage for my ideas to make their way out of the maze of my mind and into yours.

Judy Calabrese has been the most wonderful assistant I could have hoped to have, always warm, happy, positive, and patient with every twist and turn my career, life, and spirits have taken over these last twelve years. I would be nowhere on this journey without our team at Mentora Institute and the collective contributions they have made to advance our methods, serve our clients, and build an amazing digital platform.

The love and understanding I've received from the monks and nuns of Self-Realization Fellowship and Yogoda Satsanga Society are silent forces that have nurtured me and inspired my work.

Much of this book took form during immersive spells of writing at some of my favorite cafés—Chalait, Irving Farm, and Daily Oven in New York City; Intelligentsia, Copa Cafe, and Republik Coffee Lounge in Pasadena; and Society Café in Bath, UK. I'm so grateful to their teams for having adopted me.

My parents inspired many of the ideas in this book through the precepts they chose to direct their lives. "I knew very early, I am quite sure of it, that through them another Being concerned himself with me and even addressed himself to me." Jacques Lusseyran's sentiments for his parents ring true to me for my own.

Through our animated discussions, Mrinalini helped me sharpen and extend my thinking on several topics to arrive at a deeper understanding of human nature, and its full potential. She and Renu showed infinite grace in giving me the time to work on this endeavor, shared astute critiques of draft materials I read to them, and challenged me to go beyond codifying and teaching the principles in this book to coming a bit closer to living them.

SOURCES

Introduction

xiii **"To other countries":** Lawrence Dunbar Reddick, "Account by Lawrence Dunbar Reddick of Press Conference in New Delhi on 10 February 1959," Stanford University, The Martin Luther King, Jr. Research and Education Institute, accessed November 26, 2021, https://kinginstitute.stanford.edu/king-papers/documents/account-lawrence-dunbar-reddick-press-conference-new-delhi-10-february-1959.

xvi **if you bring a role model to mind:** J. Shah, "Automatic for the People: How Representations of Significant Others Implicitly Affect Goal Pursuit," *Journal of Personality and Social Psychology* 84 (2003): 661–681.

Chapter 1: A Life Well Lived

3 **The newspapers reported him dead:** "Alfred Nobel," *Encyclopedia Britannica,* accessed December 2, 2021, www.britannica.com/biography/Alfred-Nobel.

4 **A palliative care nurse:** Bronnie Ware, "Regrets of the Dying," accessed November 26, 2021, https://bronnieware.com/blog/regrets-of-the-dying/.

7 **"The big question about how people behave" and "[My dad] was a hundred percent":** Alice Schroeder, *The Snowball: Warren Buffett and the Business of Life* (New York: Bantam, 2008).

7 **"As you move along in your career":** "Notes from the Meeting Dr. George Athanassakos and Ivey MBA and HBA Students Had with Mr. Warren Buffett," Ivey Business School, University of Western Ontario, February 27, 2015, www.ivey.uwo.ca/media/2953339/buffett-interview-2015.pdf.

7 **he didn't succumb to the temptation:** Andy Serwer and Julia Boorstin, "The Oracle of Everything, Warren Buffett, Has Been Right About the Stock Market, Rotten Accounting, CEO Greed, and Corporate Governance. The Rest of Us Are Just Catching On," CNN Money, November 11, 2002, https://money.cnn.com/magazines/fortune/fortune_archive/2002/11/11/331843/index.htm.

7 **And he has donated:** Carol Loomis, "Warren Buffett Gives Away His Fortune," *Fortune,* June 25, 2006.

Chapter 2: The Pursuit of Success

9   **"After he had finished":** Eknath Easwaran, *Gandhi the Man*, 4th ed. (Tomales, CA: Nilgiri Press, 2011).

11   **"During Gen. Burnside's command of the Army":** James M. McPherson, *Tried by War: Abraham Lincoln as Commander in Chief* (New York: Penguin Press, 2008).

12   **many of these letters were unsigned and unsent:** Douglas L. Wilson, *Lincoln's Sword* (New York: Knopf Doubleday, 2006).

15   **Babette, an organic chemist:** David Burns, *Feeling Good Together* (New York: Broadway Books, 2008).

24   **"The writer has conversed with multitudes of men":** J. G. Holland, "Life of Abraham Lincoln, by J. G. Holland," 1887, published online by Abraham Lincoln Association, accessed December 2, 2021, https://quod.lib.umich.edu/l/lincoln2/abx9856.0001.001?rgn=main;view=fulltext.

24   **"His pursuit of the truth":** William H. Herndon and Jesse W. Weik, *Abraham Lincoln*, vol. 2 (Delhi, India: Lector House, 2019).

27   **both were, of their own confession, indifferent students:** Nelson Mandela, *Conversations with Myself* (Basingstoke, UK: Pan Macmillan, 2010); M. K. Gandhi, *An Autobiography, or The Story of My Experiments with Truth* (Ahmedabad, India: Navajivan Trust, 1927).

29   **in Gandhi's presence:** See, for instance, Gandhi and Mondol story in Chapter 13, "Leading with Self-Realization."

29   **In Mother Teresa's presence:** David C. McClelland and Carol Krishnit, "The Effect of Motivational Arousal Through Films on Salivary Immunoglobulin A," *Psychology and Health* 2, no. 1 (1988): 31–52.

29   **In Steve Jobs's presence:** "It was a self-fulfilling distortion. You did the impossible, because you didn't realize it was impossible." Debi Coleman, quoted in Walter Isaacson, *Steve Jobs* (New York: Simon and Schuster, 2011).

29   **In Churchill's presence:** "'Nobody left his presence without feeling a braver man' was said of Pitt; but it is no less true of [Churchill]." John Martin, quoted in Martin Gilbert, *Winston S. Churchill: Finest Hour, 1939–1941* (New York: RosettaBooks, 2015).

29   **In Mandela's presence:** See stories of Mandela with Niël Barnard and General Constand Viljoen in Chapter 7, "Leading with Wisdom."

29   **"Oh sure. It's not a faith in technology":** Jeff Goodell, "Steve Jobs in 1994: The Rolling Stone Interview," *Rolling Stone*, published online January 17, 2011, www.rollingstone.com/culture/culture-news/steve-jobs-in-1994-the-rolling-stone-interview-231132/.

29   **"I think Steve felt a vindication" and "will sense the care":** Brent Schlender and Rick Tetzeli, *Becoming Steve Jobs: The Evolution of a Reckless Upstart into a Visionary Leader* (New York: Crown, 2015).

34   **"The stunning variety of living systems":** Jeremy M. Berg et al., *Biochemistry*, 5th ed. (New York: W. H. Freeman, 2002).

35   **Winston Churchill always sought:** Carlo D'Este, *Warlord: A Life of Winston Churchill at War, 1874–1945* (New York: HarperCollins, 2009).

35   **He once gave skin:** Valentine Low, "How Winston Churchill Went Under Knife to Save Soldier," *The Times*, September 9, 2017.

36   **"Man is spirit":** Jon Meacham, *Franklin and Winston: An Intimate Portrait of an Epic Friendship* (New York: Random House, 2003).

Chapter 3: Ways of Knowing

37   **"Truth resides in every human heart":** William Borman, *Gandhi and Non-Violence* (Albany: State University of New York Press, n.d.).

42   **psychology has been going through a "replication crisis":** Ed Yong, "Psychology's Replication Crisis Is Running Out of Excuses," *The Atlantic,* November 20, 2018.

43   **the studies that have failed replication:** Marta Serra-Garcia and Uri Gneezy, "Nonreplicable Publications Are Cited More than Replicable Ones," *Scientific Advances* (May 2021).

43   **"Half of what we are going to teach you":** "Past Deans of the Faculty of Medicine," Harvard Medical School, accessed November 26, 2021, https://hms.harvard.edu/about-hms/office-dean/past-deans-faculty-medicine.

47   **"My home situation was very congenial":** Clayborne Carson, ed., *The Autobiography of Martin Luther King, Jr.* (New York: Grand Central Publishing, 1998). Unless otherwise specified, all biographical information about and quotes from Martin Luther King Jr. that appear in this chapter come from this source or can be easily located online.

47   **"My memories are of the friction":** Malcolm X as told to Alex Haley, *The Autobiography of Malcolm X* (New York: Random House, 1965). Unless otherwise specified, all biographical information about and quotes from Malcolm X that appear in this chapter come from this source or can be easily located online.

48   **"I don't think anybody ever got more":** Manning Marable, *Malcolm X: A Life of Reinvention* (New York: Penguin, 2011).

50   **"Occasionally he stumbled over the truth":** Winston Churchill, *The Irrepressible Churchill: Stories, Sayings and Impressions of Sir Winston Churchill* (London: Robson, 1987).

51   **"What if you could ride alongside a beam of light?":** Walter Isaacson, "The Light-Beam Rider," *New York Times*, October 30, 2015.

51   **a banker convicted of a crime and a dictator:** Bill Donohue, *Unmasking Mother Teresa's Critics* (Manchester, NH: Sophia Institute Press, 2016).

53   **"Both read the same Bible":** Ronald C. White, *Lincoln's Greatest Speech: The Second Inaugural* (New York: Simon and Schuster, 2002).

54   **"There is a fundamental difference":** Ki Mae Heussner, "Stephen Hawking on Religion: 'Science Will Win,'" ABC News, June 4, 2010, https://abcnews.go.com/WN/Technology/stephen-hawking-religion-science-win/story?id=10830164.

54   **"All religions, arts and sciences":** Albert Einstein, *Out of My Later Years: The Scientist, Philosopher, and Man Portrayed Through His Own Words* (New York: Philosophical Library/Open Road, 1950).

55 *Time slows down as you speed up*: Alexandra Witze, "Einstein's 'Time Dilation' Prediction Verified," *Scientific American*, September 22, 2014.

55 *An electron is both a particle and a wave*: Robert Matthews, "How Can an Electron Be Both a Particle and a Wave?," *BBC Science Focus Magazine*, accessed December 2, 2021, www.sciencefocus.com/science/how-can-an-electron-be-both-a-particle-and-a-wave/.

55 *One cannot measure both*: This is Heisenberg's well-known uncertainty principle.

55 *It is impossible for a mathematical system*: From Gödel's well-known incompleteness theorems, published in 1931.

55 *Matter is in fact condensed energy*: Brian Koberlein, "How Are Energy and Matter the Same?," Universe Today, November 26, 2014, www.universetoday.com/116615/how-are-energy-and-matter-the-same/.

55 **"The general notions about human understanding"**: Fritjof Capra, *Tao of Physics* (London: Bantam Books, 1977).

56 **"the science of the soul"**: Introduction to the Self-Realization Fellowship Lessons, "Highest Achievements Through Self-Realization," Self-Realization Fellowship, accessed December 2, 2021, https://yogananda.org/lessons.

57 **Gandhi himself was deeply influenced**: M. K. Gandhi, *An Autobiography, or The Story of My Experiments with Truth* (Ahmedabad, India: Navajivan Trust, 1927).

57 **Gandhi began an active correspondence**: M. K. Gandhi, *All Men Are Brothers* (London: A & C Black, 2005).

57 **In addition to his deeply held Christian beliefs**: Leo Tolstoy, *A Confession* (Anaheim, CA: Golgotha Press, 2011).

61 **I discovered that my spiritual teacher**: Daya Ma, *Only Love*, e-book ed. (Los Angeles: Self-Realization Fellowship, 2017).

62 **"thousands of people of different races," "A man should not be judged," "There is no greater serenity of mind," and "In my thirty-nine years"**: Marable, *Malcolm X*.

Chapter 4: Living with Purpose

72 **our happiness in achieving a goal is short-lived:** Jonathan Haidt, *The Happiness Hypothesis* (New York: Basic Books, 2006).

73 **The happiness treadmill:** Haidt, *The Happiness Hypothesis*. Psychologists call it the hedonic treadmill.

73 **"After climbing a great hill":** Nelson Mandela, *Long Walk to Freedom: The Autobiography of Nelson Mandela* (New York: Little, Brown and Company, 1995). Unless otherwise specified, all quotes from Mandela appearing in this chapter come from this source.

76 **activates strong motivation from within:** Daniel Pink, *Drive* (New York: Riverhead Books, 2011).

76 **We wake up each day feeling inspired:** Jodi L. Berg, "The Role of Personal Purpose and Personal Goals in Symbiotic Visions," *Frontiers in Psychology* (April 2015), www.frontiersin.org/articles/10.3389/fpsyg.2015.00443/full.

76   **We happily take on even the most mundane tasks:** Amy Wrzesniewski and
      Jane E. Dutton, "Crafting a Job: Revisioning Employees as Active Crafters
      of Their Work," *Academy of Management Review* 26 (2001): 179–201, www
      .researchgate.net/publication/211396297_Crafting_a_Job_Revisioning
      _Employees_as_Active_Crafters_of_Their_Work.

76   **after a three-month meditation retreat:** Daniel Goleman and Richard
      Davidson, *Altered Traits: Science Reveals How Meditation Changes Your Mind,
      Brain, and Body* (New York: Avery, 2017).

78   **"I cared so much about the paper":** Katharine Graham, *Personal His-
      tory* (New York: Knopf Doubleday, 1998). Unless otherwise specified, all
      quotes from Katharine Graham appearing in this chapter come from this
      source.

82   **Alexander of Macedon was told by his mother:** Donald L. Wasson, "Alex-
      ander the Great as a God," *World History Encyclopedia*, July 28, 2016, www
      .worldhistory.org/article/925/alexander-the-great-as-a-god/.

82   **This prophecy did come to pass:** Colette Hemingway and Seán Heming-
      way, "The Rise of Macedonia and the Conquests of Alexander the Great,"
      Metropolitan Museum of Art, October 2004, www.metmuseum.org/toah
      /hd/alex/hd_alex.htm.

82   **The quotes and narrative below:** J. W. McCrindle, *Ancient India as Described
      by Megasthenes and Arrian* (New Delhi: Munshiram Manoharlal, 2000); and
      Richard Stoneman, *The Legends of Alexander the Great* (London: I. B. Tauris,
      2011).

85   **persuaded another yogi, Kalanos, to join him:** Sylvano Borruso, *A History
      of Philosophy for (Almost) Everyone* (Nairobi: Paulines Publications Africa,
      2007).

85   **Ashoka, like Alexander, ascended to power:** Kristin Baird Rattini, "Who
      Was Ashoka?," *National Geographic*, April 2019.

85   **"declares that a king's true glory":** Joshua J. Mark, "The Edicts of Ashoka
      the Great," *World History Encyclopedia*, June 29, 2020, www.worldhistory
      .org/Edicts_of_Ashoka/.

88   **Your son's school is quite dysfunctional:** Walter Isaacson, *Steve Jobs* (New
      York: Simon and Schuster, 2001).

89   **"You will know," you reply:** Ellis Hamburger, "Steve Jobs Despised
      'Bizarro' Rich People, Plus 10 More Facts from Walter Isaacson's 60 Min-
      utes Interview," *Business Insider*, October 13, 2011, www.businessinsider
      .com/walter-isaacson-steve-jobs-60-minutes-2011-10.

89   **"Look at the memory chips":** Isaacson, *Steve Jobs*.

90   **Andras Grof was born in Budapest:** Walter Isaacson, "Andrew Grove: Man
      of the Year," *Time*, December 29, 1997, https://time.com/4267448/andrew
      -grove-man-of-the-year/.

90   **Milada Horáková was born in Prague:** RoBoT, "JUDr. Milada Horáková,"
      Valka.cz, accessed December 2, 2021, www.valka.cz/13681-JUDr-Milada
      -Horakova; and Veronika Lehovcová Suchá, "Eight Years in Prison for
      Judicial Murder from 1950," Aktuálně.cz, November 2, 2007, https://
      zpravy.aktualne.cz/eight-years-in-prison-for-judicial-murder-from-1950
      /r~i:article:512908/.

90   **On the day of her execution:** Wilma A. Iggers, "Women of Prague" (Providence, RI: Berghahn Books, 1995).

91   **He developed a struggle-truce-struggle format:** B. Surendra Rao, "Marching to His Own Beat," *The Hindu*, May 21, 2012; and Bipin Chandra et al., *India's Struggle for Independence, 1857–1947* (New York: Penguin, 1989).

92   **In a study of janitors:** David Zax, "Want to Be Happier at Work? Learn from These 'Job Crafters,'" *Fast Company*, June 3, 2013, www.fastcompany.com/3011081/want-to-be-happier-at-work-learn-how-from-these-job-crafters.

93   **The BBC once profiled a Somalian immigrant:** "Somali Refugee Turned TV Journalist," audio recording, *Outlook*, BBC, August 13, 2013, www.bbc.co.uk/programmes/p01drjhx.

93   **"No work is insignificant":** Martin Luther King Jr., *The Measure of a Man* (Overland Park, KS: Digireads Publishing, 2020).

95   **"Zindzi says her heart is sore":** Nelson Mandela, *The Prison Letters of Nelson Mandela* (New York: Liveright, 2018).

95   **Mahatma Gandhi was once racing:** H. H. Sant Rajinder Singh Ji Maharaj, "Lessons from the Mahatma's Book of Life," *New Indian Express*, October 2014.

96   **When she posted her payment for her grocery bills:** Lynn Sherr, *Failure Is Impossible: Susan B. Anthony in Her Own Words* (New York: Crown, 2010).

96   **While vacationing in Florida:** Joseph Lash, *Eleanor and Franklin* (New York: Norton, 1971).

97   **Steve Jobs's sister, Mona:** Mona Simpson, "A Sister's Eulogy for Steve Jobs," *New York Times*, October 30, 2011.

Chapter 5: Leading with Purpose

99   **When you are inspired by some great purpose:** Quoted in Wayne W. Dyer, *Wisdom of the Ages: 60 Days to Enlightenment* (New York: Harper, 1998).

99   **"I am now the most miserable man living":** Katie Bacon, "Commander in Grief," *The Atlantic*, October 2005.

100   **"Oh how hard it is to die":** Joshua Wolf Shenk, *Lincoln's Melancholy: How Depression Challenged a President and Fueled His Greatness* (Boston: Mariner Books, 2006).

100   **"I am naturally anti-slavery":** Abraham Lincoln, "Letter to Albert G. Hodges," Abraham Lincoln Online, accessed December 2, 2021, www.abrahamlincolnonline.org/lincoln/speeches/hodges.htm.

100   **"I used to be a slave":** Sidney Blumenthal, "Abraham Lincoln on His Illinois Childhood: 'I Used to Be a Slave,'" *Newsweek*, May 7, 2016, www.newsweek.com/abraham-lincoln-childhood-slave-456333.

100   **In Lincoln's day, a child was required by law:** Michael Schuman, "History of Child Labor in the United States, Part 1: Little Children Working," Monthly Labor Review, US Bureau of Labor Statistics, January 2017, www.bls.gov/opub/mlr/2017/article/history-of-child-labor-in-the-united-states-part-1.htm.

100   **"Say to him that if we could meet now":** Abraham Lincoln, letter to John D. Johnston, 1851, published online by Abraham Lincoln Association,

accessed December 2, 2021, https://quod.lib.umich.edu/l/lincoln/lincoln2/1:150.1?rgn=div2;view=fulltext.

101 **"Public sentiment is everything"**: John M. Hay and John G. Nicolay, *Abraham Lincoln*, vol. 2 (Charleston, SC: Nabu Press, 2010).

101 **Lincoln witnessed a series of violent events**: Michael Burlingame, "Abraham Lincoln: Life Before the Presidency," Miller Center, University of Virginia, accessed December 2, 2021, https://millercenter.org/president/lincoln/life-before-the-presidency.

101 **"[America's founding fathers] aspired to display before an admiring world"**: Abraham Lincoln, "Lyceum Address," Abraham Lincoln Online, accessed December 3, 2021, www.abrahamlincolnonline.org/lincoln/speeches/lyceum.htm.

101 **rail-splitter, boatman, manual laborer, store clerk**: Burlingame, "Abraham Lincoln."

101 **"not among those who"**: Eric Foner, *The Fiery Trial: Abraham Lincoln and American Slavery* (New York: Norton, 2012).

102 **Matson contended that they still belonged to him**: Charles R. McKirdy, *Lincoln Apostate: The Matson Slave Case* (Jackson: University Press of Mississippi, 2011).

102 **"that spirit which desired the peaceful extinction of slavery"**: Foner, *The Fiery Trial.*

102 **"Twenty-two years ago Judge Douglas"**: Abraham Lincoln, "Letter to George Robertson," Abraham Lincoln Online, accessed December 3, 2021, www.abrahamlincolnonline.org/lincoln/speeches/robert.htm.

103 **Douglas argued that America's new territories**: Abraham Lincoln and Stephen A. Douglas, "Debates of Lincoln and Douglas: Carefully Prepared by the Reporters of Each Party at the Times of Their Delivery" (1860), published online by Perseus Digital Library, Tufts University, accessed December 2, 2021, www.perseus.tufts.edu/hopper/text?doc=Perseus%3Atext%3A2001.05.0024%3Achapter%3D14%3Apage%3D225.

103 **"I think the authors of that notable instrument"**: "Lincoln Interprets the Declaration of Independence," published online by the National Park Service, rev. September 11, 2003, accessed December 2, 2021, www.nps.gov/parkhistory/online_books/source/sb2/sb2j.htm.

103 **"a beacon to guide" not only everyone in his time**: Abraham Lincoln, "Speech at Lewistown, Illinois," 1858, published online by Abraham Lincoln Association, accessed December 2, 2021, https://quod.lib.umich.edu/l/lincoln/lincoln2/1:567?rgn=div1;view=fulltext.

103 **"I now sink out of view"**: Abraham Lincoln, "To Anson G. Henry," 1858, published online by Abraham Lincoln Association, accessed December 2, 2021, https://quod.lib.umich.edu/l/licoln/lincoln3/1:56?rgn=div1;view=fulltext.

103 **But the *Evening Post* opined**: Doris Kearns Goodwin, *Leadership: Lessons from the Presidents for Turbulent Times* (London: Penguin Publishing Group UK, 2018).

104 **A year after Lincoln's loss, he received an invitation**: Abraham Lincoln, "Cooper Union Address," Abraham Lincoln Online, accessed December 3, 2021, www.abrahamlincolnonline.org/lincoln/speeches/cooper.htm.

105   **Remarkably, Lincoln barely spoke in public:** Harold Holzer, "The Sound of Lincoln's Silence," *New York Times*, November 23, 2010, https://opinion ator.blogs.nytimes.com/2010/11/23/the-sound-of-lincolns-silence/.

105   **"It was not so at the beginning":** Harold Holzer, *Lincoln as I Knew Him: Gossip, Tributes, and Revelations from His Best Friends and Worst Enemies* (Chapel Hill, NC: Algonquin Books, 1999).

105   **A Union army general issued:** Michael Fellman, "The First Emancipation Proclamation," *New York Times*, August 29, 2011, https://opinionator .blogs.nytimes.com/2011/08/29/the-first-emancipation-proclamation.

106   **Douglass announced that:** Frederick Douglass, "The State of the War," *Douglass' Monthly*, February 1862, Vol. IV, No. IX.

106   **"Though I was not entirely satisfied":** Frederick Douglass, *The Life and Times of Frederick Douglass, from 1817-1882* (United Kingdom: Christian Age Office, 1882).

106   **After a bloody battle at Gettysburg:** James L. Cotton Jr., *The Greatest Speech Ever* (Palisades, NY: History Publishing Company, 1999).

106   **"Ah! You surprise me, gentlemen":** "The President's Habeas Corpus Proclamation and the Act of Congress on the Subject," *New York Herald*, September 18, 1863.

107   **The further Lincoln progressed in his presidency:** Holzer, *Lincoln as I Knew Him.*

107   **Lincoln knew what he wished for:** "Lincoln's Evolving Thoughts on Slavery, and Freedom," *Fresh Air*, National Public Radio, October 11, 2010, www .npr.org/2010/10/11/130489804/lincolns-evolving-thoughts-on-slavery -and-freedom.

107   **His initial vision of a post–Civil War country:** Foner, *The Fiery Trial.*

108   **"his re-election was an impossibility":** Joel Achenbach, "The Election of 1864 and the Last Temptation of Abraham Lincoln," *Washington Post*, September 11, 2014, www.washingtonpost.com/national/health-science /the-election-of-1864-and-the-last-temptation-of-abraham-lincoln /2014/09/11/e33f99aa-345b-11e4-9e92-0899b306bbea_story.html.

108   **"I am a beaten man, unless we can have some great victory":** Joseph A. Fry, *Lincoln, Seward, and US Foreign Relations in the Civil War Era* (Lexington: University Press of Kentucky, 2019).

109   **"promoted, prolonged, and profited":** Anne Farrow et al, *Complicity: How the North Promoted, Prolonged, and Profited from Slavery* (New York: Ballantine Books, 2005).

109   **"With malice toward none":** "Lincoln's Second Inaugural Address," National Park Service, April 18, 2020, https://www.nps.gov/linc/learn /historyculture/lincoln-second-inaugural.htm.

109   **"Mr. President, that was a sacred effort":** Andrew Delbanco et al, *The Abolitionist Imagination* (Germany: Harvard University Press, 2012).

109   **He bent the law in carefully calculated ways:** "President Lincoln's Suspension of Habeas Corpus Is Challenged," History.com, November 13, 2009, www.history.com/this-day-in-history/lincolns-suspension-of-habeas-corpus -is-challenged.

109   **As a Union victory in the Civil War became a near certainty:** Richard Carwardine, *Lincoln: A Life of Purpose and Power* (New York: Vintage, 2007).

109 **"Viewed from the genuine abolition ground":** David W. Blight, *Frederick Douglass: Prophet of Freedom* (New York: Simon and Schuster, 2018).

110 **"I am proud, in my passing speck of time":** Abraham Lincoln, "Fragment on the Struggle Against Slavery," 1858, published online by Abraham Lincoln Association, accessed December 12, 2021, https://quod.lib.umich.edu /l/lincoln/lincoln2/1:521.1?rgn=div2;view=fulltext.

110 **"the right to rise":** Niles Anderegg, "'The Right to Rise' and Lincoln's Support of the Homestead Act," *President Lincoln's Cottage Blog*, March 2, 2010, https://lincolncottage.wordpress.com/2010/03/02/the-right-to-rise-and -lincolns-support-of-the-homestead-act/.

Chapter 6: Living with Wisdom

114 **"myside bias":** Keith E. Stanovich, *The Bias That Divides Us: The Science and Politics of Myside Thinking* (Cambridge: MIT Press, 2021).

115 **An ancient Indian epic, the Katha Upanishad, provides an apt metaphor:** Swami Ambkinanda Saraswati, *The Katha Upanishad* (London: Frances Lincoln Publishers, 2001).

116 **"Let's not forget that the little emotions":** Vincent van Gogh, "To Theo van Gogh. Saint-Rémy-de-Provence, Sunday, 14 or Monday, 15 July 1889," published online by Van Gogh Museum, accessed December 2, 2021, http:// vangoghletters.org/vg/letters/let790/letter.html.

116 **People who have a high propensity for anger:** "From Irritated to Enraged: Anger's Toxic Effect on the Heart," Harvard Health Publishing, December 6, 2014, www.health.harvard.edu/heart-health/from-irritated -to-enraged-angers-toxic-effect-on-the-heart.

116 **"As heat conserved is transmuted into energy":** "Young India (September 1920)," South Asian American Digital Archive, accessed December 3, 2021, https://www.saada.org/item/20111027-433.

117 **They are happier people:** Martin E. P. Seligman, *Learned Optimism* (New York: Knopf Doubleday, 2006).

117 **Research studies that have tracked people over several decades:** Deborah D. Danner, David A. Snowdon, and Wallace V. Friesen, "Positive Emotions in Early Life and Longevity, Findings from the Nun Study," *Journal of Personality and Social Psychology* 80 (2001), www.apa.org/pubs/journals /releases/psp805804.pdf.

118 **An emotion like anxiety can alert you:** Katharina Star, "The Benefits of Anxiety and Nervousness," Verywell Mind, September 17, 2020, www .verywellmind.com/benefits-of-anxiety-2584134; and Kendry Cherry, "Understanding the Optimism Bias," Verywell Mind, May 10, 2020, www .verywellmind.com/what-is-the-optimism-bias-2795031.

118 **Otherwise, science shows, your behavior and decision-making at work will be influenced:** Francesca Gino, "Don't Let Emotions Screw Up Your Decisions," *Harvard Business Review*, May 6, 2015, https://hbr.org/2015/05/dont -let-emotions-screw-up-your-decisions.

121 **My favorite distortions:** David Burns, *Feeling Good: The New Mood Therapy* (New York: Harper, 2008).

123 **Distorted thoughts typically have a whiplash effect:** Burns, *Feeling Good.*

130 **Joseph Campbell studied myths:** Joseph Campbell, *The Hero with a Thousand Faces: The Collected Works of Joseph Campbell* (New York: Perseus Books Group, 2008).

133 **Its author, William Henley, suffered from tuberculosis:** "William Ernest Henley," Poetry Foundation, accessed November 26, 2021, www.poetry foundation.org/poets/william-ernest-henley.

133 **"It matters not how strait the gait":** William Ernest Henley, *Book of Verses* (Charleston, SC: Nabu Press, 2010).

133 **"A smooth life," Yogananda noted, "is not a victorious life":** "The Help and Blessings of an Ever-Living Guru: Selections from the Wisdom-Legacy of Paramahansa Yogananda," *Self-Realization Magazine*, Spring 2002.

137 **Larry Ellison, the founder of Oracle Corporation, has described:** Lawrence J. Ellison, "2016 Commencement Address," University of South California, May 13, 2016, https://about.usc.edu/history/commencement/2016-commencement-address/.

138 **On another occasion, Larry said:** Ina Fried, "Larry Ellison Says We Already Know What Apple Without Jobs Will Look Like," All Things Digital, August 12, 2013, https://allthingsd.com/20130812/larry-ellison-says-we-already-know-what-apple-without-jobs-will-look-like/.

138 **We free our mind to do its best work:** Jason Kelly, "Performance Anxiety," *University of Chicago Magazine*, Nov.–Dec. 2011, accessed December 2, 2021, https://mag.uchicago.edu/science-medicine/performance-anxiety.

138 **We don't feel the need to keep showing:** Nonattachment makes us less focused on proving that we're smart, so we can more actively embrace the growth mindset. People with a growth mindset are more open to stepping out of their comfort zone to learn new skills. See Carol Dweck, *Mindset: The New Psychology of Success* (New York: Ballantine Books, 2007). See also D. Vandewalle et al., "The Influence of Goal Orientation and Self-Regulation Tactics on Sales Performance: A Longitudinal Field Test," *Journal of Applied Psychology* 84 (1999): 249–259.

139 **We are comfortable taking an unpopular stand:** See, for instance, how Warren Buffett benefited from remaining calm in the face of criticism over the fact that he did not invest in internet/telecom stocks just before the bubble burst in 2002. Andy Serwer, "The Oracle of Everything Warren Buffett Has Been Right About the Stock Market, Rotten Accounting, CEO Greed, and Corporate Governance. The Rest of Us Are Just Catching On," *CNN Money*, November 11, 2002, https://money.cnn.com/magazines/fortune/fortune_archive/2002/11/11/331843/index.htm.

139 **We are not limited by a particular definition of success:** One of the main causes of the failure of startups is that they don't change their definition of success by pivoting in a new direction. See, for instance, G2 Consultores, "Failure to Pivot Can Lead Your Startup to Death," *Entrepreneur*, November 27, 2020, www.entrepreneur.com/article/360506.

139 **we are no longer trapped:** This relates again to the pitfall of myside bias, discussed earlier in the chapter.

139 **"God is on our side":** Francis Bicknell Carpenter, *Six Months at the White House with Abraham Lincoln* (Carlisle, MA: Applewood Books, 2008).

139 **Many players are surprised to learn that in 27 years at UCLA:** Rafael Aguayo, *Dr. Deming: The American Who Taught the Japanese About Quality* (New York: Touchstone, 1991).

141 **"Don't aim at success":** Viktor E. Frankl, *Man's Search for Meaning* (Boston: Beacon Press, 1962).

142 **"Coming back to America":** Walter Isaacson, *Steve Jobs* (New York: Simon and Schuster, 2011).

142 **"Words and language":** David G. Myers, *Intuition* (New Haven, CT: Yale University Press, 2002).

142 **"I believe in intuitions and inspirations":** Einstein in an interview with George Sylvester Viereck, "What Life Means to Einstein," *Saturday Evening Post,* October 26, 1929, accessed November 27, 2021, www.saturday eveningpost.com/wp-content/uploads/satevepost/einstein.pdf.

143 **Expert intuition works in contexts:** Myers, *Intuition,*

145 **Science is showing that although we cannot predict:** Linda Johnson, *Intuition—Your Most Powerful Tool: How to Make Decisions You Won't Regret* (Brooklyn, NY: Angelico Press, 2013).

146 **Science has shown this first-thing-upon-waking-up time:** Deirdre Barrett, *The Committee of Sleep: How Artists, Scientists, and Athletes Use Dreams for Creative Problem Solving—and How You Can Too* (Berlin: Oneiroi Press, 2001).

Chapter 7: Leading with Wisdom

149 **He later reflected on how he drove around the country:** Rian Malan, "What a Lost Prison Manuscript Reveals About the Real Nelson Mandela," *The Spectator,* January 18, 2014.

149 **"Wolfie, one day I am telling you":** Wolfie Kodesh, interview by John Carlin, "The Long Walk of Nelson Mandela," *Frontline,* accessed November 27, 2021, www.pbs.org/wgbh/pages/frontline/shows/mandela /interviews/kodesh.html

149 **"is an ideal place to learn to know yourself":** "A Letter from Nelson Mandela to Winnie Mandela," February 1, 1975, website of Pan Macmillan, posted November 5, 2015, www.panmacmillan.com/blogs/general/a-letter -from-nelson-mandela-to-winnie-mandela.

150 **A prison official, Lieutenant Prins:** Nelson Mandela, *Long Walk to Freedom: The Autobiography of Nelson Mandela* (New York: Little, Brown and Company, 1995).

150 **"When you heard some of his utterances":** Richard Stengel, "Mandela: His 8 Lessons of Leadership," *Time,* July 9, 2008.

150 **The inmates watched a documentary on the Hells Angels:** Mandela, *Long Walk to Freedom.*

151 **"I like friends who have independent minds":** Nelson Mandela, website of Nelson Mandela Foundation, 2005, www.nelsonmandela.org/images /uploads/LWOM.pdf.

151 **"He thinks things through very carefully":** Neville Alexander, interview by John Carlin, "The Long Walk of Nelson Mandela," *Frontline,* accessed November 27, 2021, https://www.pbs.org/wgbh/pages/frontline/shows /mandela/interviews/alexander.html.

151   **"when reason had extinguished passion":** Patti Waldmeir, *Anatomy of a Miracle: The End of Apartheid and the Birth of the New South Africa* (New Brunswick, NJ: Rutgers University Press, 1998).

151   **"Our emotion said":** Nelson Mandela, "Oprah Winfrey's 2000 Interview with Nelson Mandela," video, accessed November 27, 2021, https://abcnews.go.com/GMA/video/nelson-mandela-dead-oprah-winfreys-2000-interview-civil-21122480.

151   **"He said to me, Mac . . . if you don't know your opposite":** Alec Russell, "Full Transcript: Mac Maharaj on Mandela, Zuma and South Africa," *Financial Times*, July 26, 2015, www.ft.com/content/061882b4-338b-11e5-bdbb-35e55cbae175.

151   **"you don't address their brains":** John Carlin, "Nelson Mandela: The Freedom Fighter Who Embraced His Enemies," *The Guardian*, December 7, 2013.

152   **Some of them even started to ask Mandela:** Barbara Jones and Christo Brand, *Mandela: My Prisoner, My Friend* (New York: Thomas Dunn Books, 2014).

152   **"Mandela became like a father to me":** Christian Arthur, "Nelson Mandela 'Like a Father to Me,' Former Prison Guard Tells UMass Boston Audience," UMass Boston, December 4, 2014, www.umb.edu/news/detail/nelson_mandela_like_a_father_to_me_former_prison_guard_tells_umass_boston_a.

152   **was a "rugby nut":** Richard Stengel, *Mandela's Way: 15 Lessons on Life, Love and Courage* (New York: Crown Archetype, 2010).

152   **"Despite the lack of contact":** Justice Malala, "The Nelson Mandela I Knew," *The Guardian*, December 6, 2013.

152   **"seen as a dark and demonic figure":** John Carlin, *Invictus: Nelson Mandela and the Game That Made a Nation* (New York: Penguin, 2009).

155   **"Good afternoon Mr. President":** "Making Peace with Your Enemy: Nelson Mandela and His Contributions to Conflict Resolution" (transcription), Saltman Center for Conflict Resolution, William S. Boyd School of Law Thomas, and Mack Moot Courtroom, November 1, 2014, https://scholars.law.unlv.edu/cgi/viewcontent.cgi?article=1661&context=nlj.

155   **"I immediately regretted [this]":** Mandela, *Long Walk to Freedom*.

156   **"He offered Constand a cup of tea":** Carlin, *Invictus*.

157   **"Of course I was afraid":** Stengel, *Mandela's Way*.

157   **"Mandela is not a saint":** Erin Conway-Smith, "Mandela Was No Saint, Says de Klerk," *Independent.ie*, April 10, 2012.

157   **"I am not a saint":** Lydia Polgreen, "Mandela's Death Leaves South Africa Without Its Moral Center," *New York Times*, December 5, 2013, www.nytimes.com/2013/12/06/world/africa/nelson-mandela.html.

Chapter 8: Living with Growth

159   **"I learned to play a little bit":** Kevin Crouch and Tanja Crouch, *The Gospel According to Elvis* (London: Bobcat Books, 2012).

160   **"I feel so alone now":** Ray Connolly, *Being Elvis* (London: Orion, 2016).

160 **"I need a long rest":** Alice Vincent, "Uneasy Lies the Head," *Calgary Herald,* April 14, 2018, www.pressreader.com/canada/calgary-herald/2018 0414/282248076146174.

160 **"The goal is not to be the richest man in the cemetery":** Jeff Goodell, "Steve Jobs in 1994: The Rolling Stone Interview," *Rolling Stone,* January 17, 2011, www.rollingstone.com/culture/culture-news/steve-jobs-in-1994-the -rolling-stone-interview-231132/.

160 **So Steve made a trip to India:** Brent Schlender and Rick Tetzeli, *Becoming Steve Jobs: The Evolution of a Reckless Upstart into a Visionary Leader* (New York: Crown, 2015).

160 **"put a dent in the universe":** Chunka Mui, "How Will You Put a Dent in the Universe? Here's My Plan," *Forbes,* September 18, 2019

160 **"computers and society, [which were] out on a first date":** Mike Langberg, "1999: The Apple Revolution—Jobs, Wozniak Made Technology Attractive to the Average Consumer," *Mercury News,* August 29, 2014.

161 **"At 30, I was out":** Schlender and Tetzeli, *Becoming Steve Jobs.*

162 **"[In] every block of marble I see a statue":** Stephen Houlgate and Michael Baur, *A Companion to Hegel* (Hoboken, NJ: John Wiley and Sons, 2011).

162 **"He was almost mystical in his approach":** Kareem Abdul-Jabbar, "Back-Talk; Appreciating the Wisdom of Wooden," *New York Times,* December 10, 2000.

164 **"We must have a proper picture":** Richard L. Johnson, *Gandhi's Experiments with Truth: Essential Writings By and About Mahatma Gandhi* (Lanham, MD: Lexington Books, 2005).

165 **"The outer storm was to me a symbol of the inner":** M. K. Gandhi, *An Autobiography, or The Story of My Experiments with Truth* (Ahmedabad, India: Navajivan Trust, 1927).

165 **"I must say that no one else has ever made":** M. K. Gandhi, *The Essential Writings* (Oxford, UK: Oxford University Press, 2008).

166 **From the hills around Florence:** "David, by Michelangelo," Michelangelo .org, accessed December 2, 2021, www.michelangelo.org/david.jsp.

166 **One day, twenty-six-year-old Michelangelo:** "Michelangelo's David," Florence Museum, accessed December 2, 2021, www.florence-museum.com /michelangelo-david.php.

167 **In large part, our ability to grow is influenced by our mindset:** Carol Dweck, *Mindset: The New Psychology of Success* (New York: Ballantine Books, 2007).

167 **Neuroscience is providing a physiological understanding:** Norman Doidge, *The Brain That Changes Itself* (New York: Penguin, 2007).

168 **Gandhi once stole money from his father:** M. K. Gandhi, *An Autobiography, or The Story of My Experiments with Truth,* Epub ed. (Ahmedabad, India: Navajivan Publishing House, 2017).

169 **Mandela once drove around his country:** Rian Malan, "What a Lost Prison Manuscript Reveals About the Real Nelson Mandela," *The Spectator,* January 18, 2014.

169 **Early in Lincoln's political career:** David Herbert Donald, *Lincoln* (New York: Simon and Schuster, 1996).

169 **We can, for instance, be an ambivert:** Bryan Lufkin, "Why Ambiverts Are Better Leaders," BBC, March 23, 2021, www.bbc.com/worklife/article /20210319-why-ambiverts-are-better-leaders.

169   **We can even exhibit opposing qualities:** A. Peter McGraw and Jeff Larsen, "The Case for Mixed Emotions," *Social and Personality Psychology* (2014); Jonathan Adler and Hal Hershfield, "Mixed Emotional Experience Is Associated with and Precedes Improvements in Psychological Well-Being," *PLOS One*, April 23, 2012; Hal E. Hershfield et al., "When Feeling Bad Can Be Good: Mixed Emotions Benefit Physical Health Across Adulthood," *Journal of Personality and Social Psychology* (April 30, 2012).

169   **"In my own life and in the life of a person":** Clayborne Carson, ed., *The Autobiography of Martin Luther King, Jr.* (New York: Grand Central Publishing, 1998).

169   **leading voices in psychology are recognizing:** Walter Mischel and Yuichi Shoda, "A Cognitive-Affective System Theory of Personality: Reconceptualizing Situations, Dispositions, Dynamics, and Invariance in Personality Structure," *Psychological Review* (1995).

169   **look for bright spots:** Chip Heath and Dan Heath, *Switch: How to Change Things When Change Is Hard* (New York: Random House, 2010).

169   **Research reveals that if you recognize:** Nick Benett, "Being at Ease with Yourself Means Being Accepting of Others," *Courier Mail,* July 9, 2016.

169   **you will feel *more true* to yourself:** A. B. Cooper et al., "Feeling Good and Authentic: Experienced Authenticity in Daily Life Is Predicted by Positive Feelings and Situation Characteristics, Not Trait State Consistency," *Journal of Research in Personality* 77 (2018): 57–69.

173   **"Michelangelo phenomenon":** Stephen M. Drigotas et al., "Close Partner as Sculptor of the Ideal Self: Behavioral Affirmation and the Michelangelo Phenomenon," *Journal of Personality and Social Psychology* (1999), https:// psycnet.apa.org/record/1999-03699-005.

174   **Research shows that our emotions, values, and behavior:** Agneta H. Fischer, Ruud Zaalberg, and Anthony Manstead, "Social Influences on the Emotion Process," *European Review of Social Psychology* (January 2003); and Harvard Medical School, "Happiness Is 'Infectious' in Network of Friends: Collective—Not Just Individual—Phenomenon," ScienceDaily, December 5, 2008, www.sciencedaily.com/releases/2008/12/081205094506.htm.

174   **"Why am I doing this?":** *Enron: The Smartest Guys in the Room*, dir. Alex Gibney, based on the book by Bethany McLean and Peter Elkind (Jigsaw Productions, 2005).

175   **Research shows that when solitude is forced:** Jane E. Brody, "The Surprising Effects of Loneliness on Health," *New York Times*, December 11, 2017.

175   **when you intentionally cultivate solitude:** Richard M. Ryan and Edward L. Deci, "Solitude as an Approach to Affective Self-Regulation," *Journal of Personality and Social Psychology* (December 2017).

175   **"In the attitude of silence":** Mahatma Gandhi, *The Way to God: Selected Writings from Mahatma Gandhi* (Berkeley, CA: North Atlantic Books, 2011).

175   **"Although I am a typical loner":** Albert Einstein, "My Credo," 1932, published online by Albert Einstein in the World Wide Web, accessed December 3, 2021, www.einstein-website.de/z_biography/credo.html.

175   **Keith LaMar understands this well:** Keith Lamar as told to Samantha Michaels, "I've Spent 27 Years in Solitary Confinement. Here Are Some

Tips on Making the Best Use of Time Alone," *Mother Jones*, March 24, 2020.

177 **introduced me to the Examen:** See for example, James Martin, *Learning to Pray* (San Francisco: HarperOne, 2021), for a beautiful chapter on the daily Examen.

178 **"interiorly nudge":** Inspired by the phrase "interiorly nudging" in George A. Aschenbrenner, *Consciousness Examen*, Sew ed. (Chicago: Loyola Press, 2007).

180 **"For the past 33 years":** "'You've Got to Find What You Love,' Jobs Says," *Stanford News*, June 14, 2005, https://news.stanford.edu/2005/06/14/jobs-061505/.

180 **"spontaneously sensitive when important things happen":** Thomas Green, *Experiencing God: The Three Stages of Prayer* (Notre Dame, IN: Ave Maria Press, 2010).

180 **"Lincoln gladly profited by the teaching":** B. Eugene Griessman, Gene Griessman, and Abraham Lincoln, *The Words Lincoln Lived By: 52 Timeless Principles to Light Your Path* (New York: Touchstone, 1998).

181 **"I'm the most miserable man you've ever seen":** Crouch and Crouch, *The Gospel According to Elvis.*

181 **"Elvis had been searching his entire life":** David Ritz, *Elvis: By the Presleys* (New York: Crown, 2005).

181 **"I'm not a man. I'm not a woman":** Larry Geller, *Leaves of Elvis' Garden* (Beverly Hills, CA: Bell Rock Publishing, 2010).

181 **"I have this picture in my mind":** Ritz, *Elvis: By the Presleys.*

182 **"When he came to Mother Center to see me":** Geller, *Leaves of Elvis' Garden.*

182 **"You must go slow with this process":** Ritz, *Elvis: By the Presleys.*

182 **"There's no hiding from her, Lawrence":** Geller, *Leaves of Elvis' Garden.*

183 **Elvis is buried in the meditation garden:** Jenny Desborough, "Elvis Presley death: Where is Elvis Presley buried?," Express (October 7, 2020).

183 **he had started to supplement his inner strivings:** Schlender and Tetzeli, *Becoming Steve Jobs.*

183 **"fairer and wiser":** Ed Catmull and Amy Wallace, *Creativity, Inc.* (New York: Random House, 2014).

184 **"he was a changed man":** Jeff Goodell, "The Steve Jobs Nobody Knew," *Rolling Stone*, October 27, 2011, www.rollingstone.com/culture/culture-news/the-steve-jobs-nobody-knew-71168/.

184 **"Then why are you working?":** Connie Guglielmo, "Untold Stories About Steve Jobs: Friends and Colleagues Share Their Memories," *Forbes*, October 3, 2012.

184 **"Relentless Steve—the boorish, brilliant":** Catmull and Wallace, *Creativity, Inc.*

184 **"The Steve that I met in early '98":** Schlender and Tetzeli, *Becoming Steve Jobs.*

185 **"Late last year, Jobs called me":** Goodell, "The Steve Jobs Nobody Knew."

185 **"organized the speakers, the attendees and the performers":** Laurie Segall, "Steve Jobs' Last Gift," *CNN Business*, September 10, 2013, https://money.cnn.com/2013/09/10/technology/steve-jobs-gift/index.html.

Chapter 9: Leading with Growth

187   **"Character building begins":** Eleanor Roosevelt, *You Learn by Living: Eleven Keys for a More Fulfilling Life* (Louisville, KY: Westminster John Knox Press, 2009).

187   **"You have no looks":** Robin Gerber, *Leadership the Eleanor Roosevelt Way: Timeless Strategies from the First Lady of Courage* (New York: Penguin, 2003).

187   **"Mine was a very miserable childhood":** Harold Ivan Smith, *Eleanor: A Spiritual Biography: The Faith of the 20th Century's Most Influential Woman* (Louisville, KY: Westminster John Knox Press, 2017).

188   **"I often felt that I'd like to have":** Joseph Persico, *Franklin and Lucy* (New York: Random House, 2008).

188   **"Will you tell her [that] her father is so sorry":** Smith, *Eleanor: A Spiritual Biography*.

188   **"far and away the most impressive and fascinating person":** Blanche Wiesen Cook, *Eleanor Roosevelt, Volume 1: The Early Years, 1884–1933* (New York: Penguin, 1993).

188   **"You must cultivate curiosity":** Eleanor Roosevelt and Nancy Woloch, ed., *Eleanor Roosevelt: In Her Words: On Women, Politics, Leadership, and Lessons from Life* (New York: Black Dog and Leventhal, 2017).

188   **"For the first time in all my life all my fears left me":** Ann Atkins, *Eleanor Roosevelt—Unleashed: Life of Soul Searching and Self Discovery* (Paoli, PA: Flash History Press, 2011).

188   **"It may seem strange, but no matter how plain a woman may be":** Persico, *Franklin and Lucy*.

189   **"a certain kind of orthodox goodness was my ideal and ambition":** Eleanor Roosevelt, *The Autobiography of Eleanor Roosevelt* (New York: Harper Perennial Modern Classics, 2014).

189   **"I left everything to my mother-in-law and my husband":** Russell Freedman, *Eleanor Roosevelt: A Life of Discovery* (Boston: Houghton Mifflin Harcourt, 1993).

189   **"Your mother only bore you":** Doris Kearns Goodwin, *No Ordinary Time: Franklin and Eleanor Roosevelt: The Home Front in World War II* (New York: Simon and Schuster, 1995).

189   **"had no sense of values whatsoever":** Gerber, *Leadership the Eleanor Roosevelt Way*.

189   **"In return for the privilege of loving":** Joseph P. Lash, *Eleanor and Franklin* (New York: Norton, 2014).

189   **Most Admired Woman in Gallup's US polls:** "Most Admired Man and Woman, 1946–2020," table, Gallup, accessed November 27, 2021, https://news.gallup.com/poll/1678/most-admired-man-woman.aspx.

189   **ranked ninth among the "most admired" people:** "Gallup's List of Widely Admired People," as of December 1999, Wikipedia, accessed November 27, 2021, https://simple.wikipedia.org/wiki/Gallup%27s_List_of_Widely_Admired_People.

189   **"For the first time I was going to live on my own":** Victoria Garrett Jones, *Eleanor Roosevelt: A Courageous Spirit* (New York: Sterling Publishing, 2006).

189 **"I was learning to have a certain confidence in myself"**: Eleanor Roosevelt, *This Is My Story* (New York: Harper and Brothers, 1937).

190 **"I became," she wrote, "more determined to try for certain ultimate objectives"**: Hazel Rowley, *Franklin and Eleanor: An Extraordinary Marriage* (New York: Farrar, Straus and Giroux, 2010).

190 **After the death of her third child in infancy**: Smith, *Eleanor: A Spiritual Biography.*

190 **"I learned that the ability to attain this inner calm"**: Roosevelt, *You Learn by Living.*

190 **"I took it for granted that men were superior creatures**: Russell Freedman, *Eleanor Roosevelt: A Life of Discovery* (New York: Clarion Books, 1997).

190 **"There are times, I think, in everyone's life"**: Lash, *Eleanor and Franklin*

191 **"filled with a passion for politics"**: Gerber, *Leadership the Eleanor Roosevelt Way.*

191 **"Nothing ever happens to us except"**: Roosevelt, *You Learn by Living.*

191 **"drifting far afield from the old influences"**: Gerber, *Leadership the Eleanor Roosevelt Way.*

191 **"the first (and only) First Lady to hold regular press conferences"**: Lewis L. Gould, *American First Ladies: Their Lives and Their Legacy* (Abingdon -on-Thames, UK: Routledge, 1996).

191 **In 1938, as First Lady, Eleanor attended a conference**: Jeremy Gray, "In 1938 Birmingham, Eleanor Roosevelt Faced Bull Connor's Wrath," AL.com, April 24, 2019, www.al.com/news/2019/04/in-1938-birmingham -eleanor-roosevelt-defied-bull-connor.html.

192 **"Courage is more exhilarating than fear"**: Roosevelt, *You Learn by Living.*

192 **"interest people and bring about discussion"**: Eleanor Roosevelt and David Emblidge, *My Day: The Best of Eleanor Roosevelt's Acclaimed Newspaper Columns, 1936–1962* (London: Hachette UK, 2009).

192 **"When I say that she inspected those hospitals"**: Paul M. Sparrow, "A First Lady on the Front Lines," Franklin D. Roosevelt Library and Museum, August 25, 2016, https://fdr.blogs.archives.gov/2016/08/25/a-first-lady -on-the-front-lines/.

192 **On that trip, she traveled twenty-six thousand miles**: *American Experience: Eleanor Roosevelt* (PBS Home Video, WGBH Educational Foundation, and Ambrica Productions, 2000).

193 **"You must be interested in anything that comes your way"**: Roosevelt, *You Learn by Living.*

193 **"I think that I am the most uninteresting fellow"**: Gerber, *Leadership the Eleanor Roosevelt Way.*

193 **"I'd rather be hung than seen"**: Atkins, *Eleanor Roosevelt—Unleashed.*

193 **During World War II, she personally followed up on visas**: Blanche Wiesen Cook, *Eleanor Roosevelt: Volume 2, The Defining Years, 1933–1938* (New York: Penguin, 2000).

193 **"she was at first a person of her times"**: Warren Boroson, "Eleanor Roosevelt and the Jews," *Jewish Standard,* July 26, 2013, https://jewishstandard .timesofisrael.com/eleanor-roosevelt-and-the-jews/.

194 **She brought to the task her own convictions:** Rebecca Adami, *Women and the Universal Declaration of Human Rights* (Abingdon-on-Thames, UK: Routledge, 2019).

194 **President Truman called Eleanor Roosevelt the "First Lady of the World":** "First Lady of the World: Eleanor Roosevelt at Val-Kill," National Park Service, November 5, 2012, www.nps.gov/teachers/classrooms/26valkill.htm.

194 **"perhaps the greatest woman [of] our time":** "Roosevelt, (Anna) Eleanor," Martin Luther King, Jr. Research and Education Institute, Stanford University, accessed December 2, 2021, https://kinginstitute.stanford.edu/encyclopedia/roosevelt-anna-eleanor.

194 **"The influence you exert":** Gerber, *Leadership the Eleanor Roosevelt Way.*

194 **"We all create the person we become":** Roosevelt, *You Learn by Living.*

194 **"It is useless to resent anything in this world":** Smith, *Eleanor: A Spiritual Biography.*

Chapter 10: Living with Love

195 **as the eight hundred students:** Elizabeth Chuck, "Authorities: Georgia Shooting Suspect Had Nearly 500 Rounds of Ammunition," NBC News, August 22, 2013, www.nbcnews.com/news/us-news/authorities-georgia-shooting-suspect-had-nearly-500-rounds-ammunition-flna6c10968110.

195 **"You . . . want me to tell them to come on in now?":** "911 Call Captures School Employee Talking Down Gunman," NPR, August 22, 2013, www.npr.org/2013/08/22/214576953/911-call-captures-school-employee-talking-down-gunman.

196 **"I was terrified":** Anderson Cooper, "Interview with School Shooting Hero and the 911 Operator," CNN Transcripts for August 22, 2013, https://transcripts.cnn.com/show/acd/date/2013-08-22/segment/01.

196 **"I saw this 20-year-old man standing in front of me":** Moni Basu, "She Saved a School from a Gunman. Hear What She Thinks About Arming Teachers," CNN, March 1, 2018, https://edition.cnn.com/2018/03/01/us/antoinette-tuff-school-shootings/index.html

196 **"When he got to telling me":** Cooper, "Interview with School Shooting Hero and the 911 Operator."

196 **"I had tried to commit suicide myself":** Julie Wolfe and WXIA, "Antoinette Tuff Reflects on 1 Year Since McNair Shooting," 11 Alive, August 20, 2014, www.11alive.com/article/news/local/decatur/antoinette-tuff-reflects-on-1-year-since-mcnair-shooting/85-253219542.

198 **Jupiter is like a protective shield:** Andrew Fazekas, "See Jupiter Take One for the Solar System," *National Geographic*, March 31, 2016.

198 **The moon helps to stabilize the Earth's axis:** Nola Taylor Redd, "Earth's Stabilizing Moon May Be Unique Within Universe," Space.com, July 29, 2011, www.space.com/12464-earth-moon-unique-solar-system-universe.html.

199 **Abraham Lincoln was traveling in a coach:** J. E. Gallaher, *Best Lincoln Stories, Tersely Told* (Glasgow, UK: Good Press, 2019).

202 **"Love is very patient, very kind":** 1 Corinthians 13:4–8 (James Moffatt New Testament).

203   **Research shows that people who practice compassion:** "How Sharing Kindness Can Make You Healthier and Happier," Mayo Clinic, November 1, 2018, www.mayoclinic.org/healthy-lifestyle/stress-management/in-depth /how-sharing-kindness-can-make-you-healthier-happier/art-20390060.

203   **After helping others, people report feeling calmer:** Christine L. Carter, "What We Get When We Give," *Psychology Today*, February 19, 2010, www.psychologytoday.com/us/blog/raising-happiness/201002/what-we -get-when-we-give.

203   **The practice of Love also makes us healthier:** Steve Siegle, "The Art of Kindness," Mayo Clinic, May 29, 2020, www.mayoclinichealthsystem.org /hometown-health/speaking-of-health/the-art-of-kindness.

205   **"When I hire somebody really senior":** Betsy Morris, "What Makes Apple Golden," *Fortune*, March 17, 2008, https://fortune.com/2008/03/17/what -makes-apple-golden/

205   **"It is quite easy for me to think of a God of love":** Clayborne Carson, ed., *The Autobiography of Martin Luther King, Jr.* (New York: Grand Central Publishing, 1998).

205   **Research shows that when children receive strong love:** Amir Levine and Rachel Heller, *Attached: The New Science of Adult Attachment and How It Can Help You Find—and Keep—Love* (New York: Penguin Publishing Group, 2011).

206   **Research shows that when you view a photo:** Emre Selcuk and Vivian Zayas, "Mental Representations of Attachment Figures Facilitate Recovery Following Upsetting Autobiographical Memory Recall," *Journal of Personality and Social Psychology* (April 2012); Mario Mikulincer and Phillip R. Shaver, "Boosting Attachment Security to Promote Mental Health, Prosocial Values, and Inter-Group Tolerance," *Psychological Inquiry* (December 2007): 139–156.

207   **"What I have seen, and experienced":** Malcolm X as told to Alex Haley, *The Autobiography of Malcolm X* (New York: Random House, 1965).

207   **"I feel like I am on my back":** Alice Schroeder, *The Snowball: Warren Buffett and the Business of Life* (New York: Bantam, 2008).

208   **Science shows that these actions will increase your happiness:** "Giving Thanks Can Make You Happier," Harvard Health Publishing, August 14, 2021, www.health.harvard.edu/healthbeat/giving-thanks-can-make-you -happier.

211   **On December 30, 2006, an old man woke up:** Will Bardenwerper, *The Prisoner in His Palace: Saddam Hussein, His American Guards, and What History Leaves Unsaid* (New York: Scribner, 2017).

212   **A short while later, pandemonium broke loose:** Jacob Silverman, "The American Soldiers Who Grieved for Saddam Hussein," *New Republic*, June 2, 2017.

212   **their feelings for him changed:** Bardenwerper, *The Prisoner in His Palace*.

214   **as Gandhi wrote, "To a pure heart, all hearts are pure":** Mahatma Gandhi, *The Collected Works of Mahatma Gandhi*, vol. 30 (New Delhi: Publications Division, Ministry of Information and Broadcasting, Government of India, 2000).

215   **Hitler started by hating the Jews:** Robert Gellately, *Social Outsiders in Nazi Germany* (Princeton, NJ: Princeton University Press, 2018).

215 **Hitler issued a decree:** "Sealing the Third Reich's Downfall: Adolf Hitler's 'Nero Decree,'" National WWII Museum, March 18, 2020, www.national ww2museum.org/war/articles/sealing-third-reichs-downfall-adolf-hitlers -nero-decree; Albert Speer, *Inside the Third Reich* (London: Orion, 2015).

215 **Research shows that the feeling many people experience:** Vivian Zayas and Yuichi Shoda, "Love You? Hate You? Maybe It's Both: Evidence That Significant Others Trigger Bivalent-Priming," *Social Psychological and Personality Science* (July 2014).

216 **When couples who are in an unhappy relationship:** John Gottman and Nan Silver, *The Seven Principles for Making Marriage Work* (New York: Crown, 1999).

216 **But every time you hate, you train your brain's neural circuitry:** University College London, "Brain's 'Hate Circuit' Identified," *Science Daily*, October 29, 2008, www.sciencedaily.com/releases/2008/10/081028205658.htm.

216 **Forgiveness has many benefits:** Frederic Luskin, *Forgive for Good* (New York: HarperCollins, 2002).

216 **Research shows that when we learn to let go of grudges:** Luskin, *Forgive for Good*; "Interview with Robert D. Enright About the Forgiving Life," American Psychological Association, 2011, www.apa.org/pubs/books /interviews/4441016-enright; "Forgiveness: Letting Go of Grudges and Bitterness," Mayo Clinic, November 13, 2020, www.mayoclinic.org/healthy -lifestyle/adult-health/in-depth/forgiveness/art-20047692; S. O'Beirne, A. M. Katsimigos, and D. Harmon, "Forgiveness and Chronic Pain: A Systematic Review," *Irish Journal of Medical Science* 189 (2020): 1359–1364, https://doi.org/10.1007/s11845-020-02200-y.

217 **"the policy of an-eye-for-an-eye-for-an-eye-for-an-eye":** Louis Fischer, *The Life of Mahatma Gandhi* (New York: Signet Classics, 2010).

220 **As with hatred, when we judge others:** Jennifer Frei and Philip Shaver, "Respect in Close Relationships," *Personal Relationships* 9 (2002); see also the discussion on contempt in Gottman and Silver, *The Seven Principles for Making Marriage Work*.

221 **"I just want to wish you people good luck":** Nelson Mandela, *Long Walk to Freedom: The Autobiography of Nelson Mandela* (New York: Little, Brown and Company, 1995).

222 **when people in a marital relationship report that they experience no conflicts:** John Gottman, "The Roles of Conflict Engagement, Escalation, and Avoidance in Marital Interaction: A Longitudinal View of Five Types of Couples," *Journal of Consulting and Clinical Psychology* (1993); and John Gottman, "A Theory of Marital Dissolution and Stability," *Journal of Family Psychology* (1993).

222 **Research also shows that people who are kind and helpful:** Adam Grant, *Give and Take: Why Helping Others Drives Our Success* (New York: Penguin, 2013).

228 **Eleanor Roosevelt once talked of her aunt Bye:** Robin Gerber, *Leadership the Eleanor Roosevelt Way: Timeless Strategies from the First Lady of Courage* (New York: Penguin, 2003).

230 **"Well, to be honest with you":** Cooper, "Interview with School Shooting Hero and the 911 Operator."

Chapter 11: Leading with Love

231 **Father Leo Maasburg has shared the following story:** Leo Maasburg, *Mother Teresa of Calcutta* (San Francisco: Ignatius Press, 2015).

233 **Agnes's brother once asked their mother:** Kathryn Spink, *Mother Teresa*, rev. ed. (San Francisco: HarperOne, 2011).

233 **"I'm not going to pay for electricity":** Maasburg, *Mother Teresa of Calcutta.*

233 **"Home," Mother Teresa would later say, "is where the mother is":** Spink, *Mother Teresa.*

234 **Gradually, the nuns came:** "66 Years of Mother Teresa's Missionaries of Charity: Facts You Should Definitely Know on the Charity," *India Today*, October 7, 2016.

234 **in a 1999 Gallup poll:** Frank Newport, "Mother Teresa Voted by American People as Most Admired Person of the Century," Gallup, December 31, 1999, https://news.gallup.com/poll/3367/mother-teresa-voted-american -people-most-admired-person-century.aspx.

234 **She performed the most humble tasks:** Spink, *Mother Teresa.*

235 **"You will, I am sure, ask me":** *Mother Teresa*, documentary film, produced and directed by Jeanette and Anne Petrie (1986).

235 **The Harvard newspaper reported:** "Mother Teresa Speaks Her Mind," *Harvard Magazine*, April 25, 2011, www.harvardmagazine.com/2011/04 /greatest-hits-mother-teresa.

235 **when Prime Minister Margaret Thatcher sought to reassure:** Bill Donohue, *Unmasking Mother Teresa's Critics* (Manchester, NH: Sophia Institute Press, 2016).

235 **One day some protestors gathered outside:** Spink, *Mother Teresa.*

235 **"We often encountered very seriously handicapped children":** Maasburg, *Mother Teresa of Calcutta.*

236 **"She took my hand and a beautiful smile appeared" and "It was late in the day":** Mother Teresa, *Mother Teresa: In My Own Words* (Barnhart, MO: Liguori Publications, 1996).

236 **"One year I wanted to do something special":** Mother Teresa, *In the Heart of the World: Thoughts, Stories and Prayers* (Novato, CA: New World Library, 2010).

237 **"If you judge someone":** Maasburg, *Mother Teresa of Calcutta.*

237 **"Some people feel that you're almost like a living saint":** *Mother Teresa*, documentary film.

238 **"You cannot give," she said, "what you do not have":** Spink, *Mother Teresa.*

238 **"My secret is quite simple. I pray":** Susan Conroy, *Mother Teresa's Lessons of Love and Secrets of Sanctity* (Huntington, IN: Our Sunday Visitor, 2003).

238 **"Every time you smile at someone":** Gwen Costello, *Spiritual Gems from Mother Teresa* (New London, CT: Twenty-Third Publications, 2008).

238 **"The amazing thing about her":** John B. Izzo, *Second Innocence: Rediscovering Joy and Wonder: A Guide to Renewal in Work, Relationships, and Daily Life* (Oakland, CA: Berrett-Koehler Publishers, 2004).

238 **"She radiated an inner joy":** Maasburg, *Mother Teresa of Calcutta.*

239 **"do small things with great love":** Brian Kolodiejchuk, *Mother Teresa: Come Be My Light* (New York: Crown, 2007).

Chapter 12: Living with Self-Realization

241 **"one heard much of certain so-called holy men":** Paul Brunton, *A Search in Secret India: The Classic Work on Seeking a Guru* (London: Rider, 2003).

242 **On the surface of the Earth:** Briann Clegg, "Earth's Core: What Lies at the Centre and How Do We Know?," *Science Focus*, July 30, 2021.

242 **Danish seismologist Inge Lehmann:** John P. Rafferty, "Inge Lehmann," *Britannica*, last edited May 9, 2021, www.britannica.com/biography/Inge -Lehmann.

243 **Hindu scriptures written by nameless authors:** Constance Jones and James D. Ryan, *Encyclopedia of Hinduism* (New York: Infobase Publishing, 2006).

243 **three-thousand-year-old seals:** Brishti Guha, "How Ancient Is Yoga? Seals Recovered from Indus Valley Civilisation Sites Tell a Fascinating Story," *Times of India*, June 20, 2019.

243 **Kabbalah practices of contemplation:** Steven A. Fisdel, *The Practice of Kabbalah: Meditation in Judaism* (Lanham, MD: Jason Aronson, 1996).

243 **Evidence of Taoist meditation practices:** Livia Kohn, *Taoist Meditation and Longevity Techniques* (Berkeley, CA: Centre for Chinese Studies Publication, 1989).

243 **Two thousand years ago, Buddha:** "Becoming the 'Buddha': The Way of Meditation," The Pluralism Project, Harvard University, 2020, https:// hwpi.harvard.edu/files/pluralism/files/becoming_the_buddha-the_way _of_meditation_1.pdf.

243 **The desert mothers and fathers in early Christianity:** Benedicta Ward, *The Sayings of the Desert Fathers: The Alphabetical Collection* (Collegeville, MN: Cistercian Publications, 1984).

243 **Saint Teresa of Avila:** Saint Teresa of Avila, *Interior Castle* (Mineola, NY: Dover Publications, 2012).

243 **Sufism evolved as a contemplative movement:** "Jalaluddin Rumi," BBC, revised September 1, 2021, www.bbc.co.uk/religion/religions/islam/art /rumi_1.shtml.

243 **"the most practical science in the world":** "Paramahansa Yogananda, *Metaphysical Meditations* (Los Angeles: Self-Realization Fellowship, 1967).

244 **Meditation has an all-around positive impact:** Daniel Goleman and Richard Davidson, *Altered Traits: Science Reveals How Meditation Changes Your Mind, Brain, and Body* (New York: Avery, 2017).

244 **Meditation slows down the aging process:** Jo Marchant, "How Meditation Might Ward Off the Effects of Ageing," *The Guardian*, April 24, 2011, www.theguardian.com/lifeandstyle/2011/apr/24/meditation-ageing -shamatha-project.

244 **Meditators' brains age more slowly:** Brigid Schulte, "Harvard Neuroscientist: Meditation Not Only Reduces Stress, Here's How It Changes Your Brain," *Washington Post*, May 26, 2015, www.washingtonpost.com/news /inspired-life/wp/2015/05/26/harvard-neuroscientist-meditation-not-only -reduces-stress-it-literally-changes-your-brain/.

244 **Meditation trains our mind to pull away:** Goleman and Davidson, *Altered Traits*.

245 **Meditation strengthens and stabilizes our feeling of self-worth:** Christopher Pepping, Analise O'Donovan, and Penelope Davis, "The Positive Effects of Mindfulness on Self-Esteem," *Journal of Positive Psychology* (September 2013); and Casey Lindberg, "More than Just Relaxing, Meditation Helps Improve Self-Image of Anxiety Sufferers," *Stanford News*, June 3, 2009, news.stanford.edu/news/2009/june3/meditate-060309.html.

245 **Research shows that with meditation, you learn to honor both:** "An improved ability to regulate attention accompanies some of the beneficial impact of meditation." Goleman and Davidson, *Altered Traits*.

245 **This capacity to swiftly and authentically move in and out:** Tara Bennett, *Emotional Alchemy: How the Mind Can Heal the Heart* (New York: Harmony Books, 2002).

245 **Meditation helps you operate with intention rather than instinct:** How Meditation Helps with Depression, Harvard Health Publishing, February 12, 2021, www.health.harvard.edu/mind-and-mood/how-meditation-helps-with-depression.

246 **"For most people, concentration takes mental effort":** Goleman and Davidson, *Altered Traits*.

246 **"During time-outs, the players are often so revved up":** Phil Jackson and Hugh Delehanty, *Sacred Hoops: Spiritual Lessons of a Hardwood Warrior* (New York: Hyperion, 2006).

246 **"One of the secrets of using your time well":** Eleanor Roosevelt, *You Learn by Living: Eleven Keys for a More Fulfilling Life* (Louisville, KY: Westminster John Knox Press, 2009).

247 **"your mind just slows down":** Walter Isaacson, *Steve Jobs* (New York: Simon and Schuster, 2011).

247 **"I've been [practicing meditation] for 44 years":** Marcus Baram, "Ray Dalio, Hedge Fund Genius, Says Meditation Is the Secret to His Success," *International Business Times*, November 12, 2013, www.ibtimes.com/ray-dalio-hedge-fund-genius-says-meditation-secret-his-success-1466108.

248 **"First of all, the girls must have the spirit of joy":** *Mother Teresa*, documentary film, produced and directed by Jeanette and Anne Petrie (1986).

248 **"Joy is not simply a matter of temperament":** Mother Teresa, *In the Heart of the World: Thoughts, Stories and Prayers* (Novato, CA: New World Library, 2010).

249 **"portable paradise":** Paramahansa Yogananda, *God Talks with Arjuna* (Los Angeles: Self-Realization Fellowship, 1999).

249 **"Seek the unconditioned, indestructible pure Bliss within yourself":** Paramahansa Yogananda, *The Divine Romance* (Los Angeles: Self-Realization Fellowship, 1986).

249 **"This joy is not an abstract quality of mind":** Paramahansa Yogananda, "How to Perceive the Infinite Christ," *Self-Realization Magazine*, Winter 1996.

250 **Research shows that executives overuse their strengths at work:** Robert Kaplan and Robert Kaiser, "Stop Overdoing Your Strengths," *Harvard Business Review*, February 2009.

250 **life expectancy in the developed world:** Max Roser, Esteban Ortiz-Ospina, and Hannah Ritchie, "Life Expectancy," Our World in Data, October 2019, https://ourworldindata.org/life-expectancy.

250 **is demonstrating a higher average IQ:** Psychologists call it the Flynn Effect, named after the person who first documented and promoted awareness of the significant increases in IQ over time. "Flynn Effect," Wikipedia, last edited November 27, 2021, https://en.wikipedia.org /wiki/Flynn_effect.

251 **In January 2017, British prime minister Theresa May:** Ceylan Yoginsku, "U.K. Appoints a Minister for Loneliness," *New York Times*, January 7, 2018, www.nytimes.com/2018/01/17/world/europe/uk-britain-loneliness.html.

251 **Science shows that loneliness is a disease:** John T. Cacioppo and William Patrick, *Loneliness: Human Nature and the Need for Social Connection* (New York: Norton, 2008).

252 **"Divine joy outlasts everything":** Paramahansa Yogananda, Self-Realization Fellowship website, accessed December 2, 2021, https://yogananda.org /kriya-yoga-path-of-meditation-overview.

256 **"If you just sit and observe":** Walter Isaacson, *Steve Jobs* (New York: Simon and Schuster, 2011).

256 **"conscious sleep":** Paramahansa Yogananda, *The Science of Religion* (Los Angeles: Self-Realization Fellowship, 2016).

257 **"We too are called to withdraw":** Mother Teresa, *Everything Starts from Prayer: Mother Teresa's Meditations on Spiritual Life for People of All Faiths* (Ashland, OR: White Cloud Press, 2009).

258 **"in the world, but not of the world":** Paramahansa Yogananda, *The Second Coming of Christ* (Los Angeles: Self-Realization Fellowship, 2008).

258 **"A Self-realized master":** Paramahansa Yogananda, *Autobiography of a Yogi* (Los Angeles: Self-Realization Fellowship, 1946).

258 **"Our mental stages fluctuate":** Goleman and Davidson, *Altered Traits*.

260 **"when people new to meditation practiced":** Goleman and Davidson, *Altered Traits*.

262 **"I wanted to gather the real facts":** Brunton, *A Search in Secret India*.

264 **"The nature of the soul is power, bliss, love":** Daya Mata, *Only Love: Living the Spiritual Life in a Changing World* (formerly *Qualities of a Devotee*) (Los Angeles: Self-Realization Fellowship, 2004).

Chapter 13: Leading with Self-Realization

265 **"As human beings, our greatness":** Eknath Easwaran, *Gandhi the Man: How One Man Changed Himself to Change the World* (Tomales, CA: Nilgiri Press, 2011).

265 **"I was quite dazzled by the splendor of the hotel":** M. K. Gandhi, *An Autobiography, or The Story of My Experiments with Truth*, Epub ed. (Ahmedabad, India: Navajivan Publishing House, 2017).

265 **"The object of sending me to England":** Stephen Hay, *The Making of a Late-Victorian Hindu: M. K. Gandhi in London, 1888–1891* (Bloomington: Indiana University Press, 1989), www.jstor.org/stable/3827899.

266 **"[I was] all the time smiling within myself":** "Gandhi in Britain," History Extra, February 1, 2018, www.historyextra.com/period/20th-century /gandhi-in-britain/.

266 **He took lessons in dancing, elocution:** Susanne Hoeber Rudolph, "The New Courage: An Essay on Gandhi's Psychology," 1963, published online by Cambridge University Press, July 18, 2011, https://doi.org/10 .2307/2009253.

266 **"Everybody knows him, even the smallest child":** Sarvapelli Radhakrishnan, "Mahatma Gandhi: Essays and Reflections on His Life and Work," *Jaico Publishing House* (2013).

266 **This time, there was no Victoria Hotel:** "Second Round Table Begins," India Video, accessed November 20, 2021, www.indiavideo.org/text /second-round-table-conference-138.php.

266 **"the King was wearing enough for the both of us":** Pramod Kapoor, "MK Gandhi's Most 'Indelicate' Gift for Queen Elizabeth (and Other Stories About Khadi)," *Scroll.in*, October 2, 2017, https://scroll.in/article /852143/mk-gandhi-s-most-indelicate-gift-for-queen-elizabeth-and-other -stories-about-khadi.

266 **"[I was] so much attached":** Jad Adams, *Gandhi: Naked Ambition* (London: Quercus Books, 2010).

267 **"What is the soul? Does it perform actions?":** "Shrimad Rajchandra's Reply to Gandhiji's Questions," Shrimad Rajchandra Ashram, accessed December 2, 2021, www.mkgandhi.org/ebks/shrimad-rajchandra-gand hiji-questions-answers.pdf.

267 **"What I meant to achieve":** Gandhi, *An Autobiography, or The Story of My Experiments with Truth.*

267 **"[It is] my experiments in the spiritual field":** Mahatma Gandhi and Louis Fischer, *The Essential Gandhi: An Anthology of His Writings on His Life, Work, and Ideas* (New York: Vintage, 2002).

267 **"I visited a Trappist monastery in South Africa":** M. K. Gandhi and R. K. Prabhu, *Truth Is God (Gleanings from the Writings of Mahatma Gandhi Bearing on God, God-Realization and the Godly Way)* (Ahmedabad, India: Navajivan Mudranalaya, 1955).

268 **"I started with disbelief in God and prayer":** M. K. Gandhi, *Prayer* (Ahmedabad, India: Navajivan Publishing House, 1977), www.mkgandhi.org/ebks /prayer.pdf.

268 **"I have so much to accomplish today":** Will Williams, *The Effortless Mind: Meditation for the Modern World* (New York: Simon and Schuster, 2018).

268 **In his early days, Gandhi embraced the racist sentiments:** E. S. Reddy, *Gandhiji's Vision of a Free South Africa: A Collection of Articles* (New Delhi: Sanchar Publishing House (1995).

268 **"If we look into the future":** Javed Majeed and Isabel Hofmeyr, *India and South Africa* (Abingdon-on-Thames, UK: Routledge, 2017).

268 **"You gave us Mohandas; we returned him to you as Mahatma":** A. S. Padmanabhan, "From Mahatma to Mohandas," *The Hindu*, October 1, 2020, www.thehindu.com/books/from-mohandas-to-mahatma/article16372 839.ece1.

268 **"being torn to pieces":** Gandhi and Fischer, *The Essential Gandhi.*

269   **"He had a violent nature":** Louis Fischer, *Gandhi: His Life and Message for the World* (New York: Penguin, 2010).

269   **"True meditation consists in closing the eyes and ears of the mind":** Gandhi, *Prayer.*

269   **"[Sir], do you know what is happening?":** "The Untold Stories of Mahatma Gandhi," The Art of Living, April 3, 2013, www.artofliving.org /untold-stories-mahatma-gandhi.

270   **"There come to us moments in life":** R. K. Prabhu and U. R. Rao, *Mind of Mahatma Gandhi* (Ahmedabad, India: Navajivan Mudranalaya, 1960).

271   **"The only course open to you":** M. K. Gandhi, *The Selected Works of Mahatma Gandhi*, vol. 6, *The Voice of Truth* (Ahmedabad, India: Navajivan Mudranalaya, 1968).

271   **On his visit to London for the Round Table Conference:** Nandini Rathi, "Gandhi Jayanti 2018 Special: When Mahatma Gandhi Was Welcomed by Textile Mill Workers of Lancashire," *Indian Express*, October 2, 2018.

272   **"Please listen to me for just a few minutes":** Easwaran, *Gandhi the Man.*

272   **By the end of their exchange:** Rathi, "Gandhi Jayanti 2018 Special."

272   **"gentle, it never wounds":** M. K. Gandhi, *Harijan Vol. 1: 1933–1934* (Ahmedabad, India: Navajivan Trust, 2013).

272   **"History, as we know it, is a record":** Mahatma Gandhi, "17. Passive Resistance," *The Selected Works of Mahatma Gandhi*, vol. 3, *Basic Works*, MKGandhi.org, accessed December 2, 2021, www.mkgandhi.org/hinds waraj/chap17_passiveresistance.htm.

273   **So he set up ashram communities:** Gandhi, *An Autobiography, or The Story of My Experiments with Truth.*

273   **"If the crowd [at a rally] was loud or unruly":** John Dear, *Mahatma Gandhi: Apostle of Non-Violence*, accessed December 2, 2021, http://johndear.org /pdfs/mahatmagandhiapostleofnonviolence.pdf.

274   **"We were bewildered and could not fit in":** Gopalkrishna Gandhi, "The Great Dandi March—Eighty Years After," *The Hindu*, April 6, 2010.

274   **"I had not the ghost of a suspicion":** Arvind Sharma, *Gandhi: A Spiritual Biography* (New Haven, CT: Yale University Press, 2013).

274   **The Salt March proved to be a stroke of genius:** Peter Ackerman and Jack DuVall, *A Force More Powerful: A Century of Non-violent Conflict* (New York: St. Martin's Griffin, 2000).

274   **"With this, I am shaking the foundations of the British Empire":** Dennis Dalton, *Gandhi: Selected Political Writings* (Indianapolis: Hackett Publishing Company, 1996).

274   **Mass civil disobedience broke out:** R. Krithika, "Marching to Freedom," *The Hindu*, March 28, 2019, www.thehindu.com/children/marching -to-freedom/article26661034.ece.

274   **"The officers ordered [the protestors] to retreat":** Webb Miller, *I Found No Peace: A Journey Through the Age of Extremes* (Liverpool, UK: deCoubertin Books, 2011).

275   *Time* **magazine named Gandhi:** "Mahatma Gandhi: Man of the Year," *Time*, January 5, 1931.

275   **"I know that a whole people can adopt":** Rudrangshu Mukherjee, ed., *The Penguin Gandhi Reader* (New Delhi: Penguin Books, 1993).

275 **"Generations to come"**: R. R. Ramchandani, *Gandhi in South Africa: A Study in Social Accounting* (Thousand Oaks, CA: SAGE Publications, 1993), www.jstor.org/stable/45072593.

275 **"I know of no other man of any time"**: Louis Fischer, *The Life of Mahatma Gandhi* (New York: Signet Classics, 2010).

276 **"You know, the people feel that there was a mirror"**: Easwaran, *Gandhi the Man*.

Part Three Introduction

277 **99 percent of them were proved, decades later, to be true:** John Noble Wilford, "Mathematician's Final Equations Praised," *New York Times*, June 9, 1981, accessed December 2, 2021, www.nytimes.com/1981/06/09/science/mathematician-s-final-equations-praised.html

Chapter 14: Transcendence

281 **"[We] are external manifestations"**: Arthur Abell, *Talks with Great Composers* (Secaucus, NJ: Carol Publishing Group, 1998).

281 **He called it self-transcendence:** Mark E. Koltko-Rivera, "Rediscovering the Later Version of Maslow's Hierarchy of Needs: Self-Transcendence and Opportunities for Theory, Research, and Unification," *Sage Journals* (December 1, 2006), https://doi.org/10.1037/1089-2680.10.4.302.

281 **"Transcendence refers to the very highest"**: Richard H. Cox, Betty Ervin-Cox (ed.), and Louis Hoffman, *Spirituality and Psychological Health* (Denver: Colorado School of Professional Psychology Press, 2005).

283 **"You are all gods if you only knew it"**: Paramahansa Yogananda, *The Divine Romance* (Los Angeles: Self-Realization Fellowship, 1986).

283 **"The mystics of many centuries"**: Erwin Schrödinger, *What Is Life?*, reprint ed. (Cambridge, UK: Cambridge University Press, 2012).

284 **"the longing for spiritual union"**: Andrew Newberg and Eugene G. D'Aquili, *Why God Won't Go Away: Brain Science and the Biology of Belief* (New York: Ballantine Books, 2008).

286 **Amia Srinivasan's wonderful article:** Amia Srinivasan, "What Termites Can Teach Us," *New Yorker*, September 17, 2018.

287 **"experiencing awe often puts people in a self-transcendent state"**: Summer Allen, *The Science of Awe* (Greater Good Science Center, UC Berkeley, September 2018).

287 **"The great secret of all creative geniuses"**: Abell, *Talks with Great Composers*.

288 **"Painting is stronger than I am"**: David Myers, *Intuition* (New Haven, CT: Yale University Press, 2002).

288 **He also said, "The finest emotion of which we are capable"**: Alice Calaprice, *Dear Professor Einstein: Albert Einstein's Letters to and from Children* (Buffalo, NY: Prometheus Books, 2002).

289 **"Spirit," wrote Yogananda, "pushes Itself out into visible manifestation"**: Paramahansa Yogananda, "Creating Prosperity Consciousness," *Self-Realization Magazine*, Spring 2009.

289   **"God is writing his love letter to the world":** Kathryn Spink, *Mother Teresa* (New York: HarperOne, 2011).

289   **"instrument" of a larger power:** Abraham Lincoln, "July 4, 1861: July 4th Message to Congress," University of Virginia, Miller Center, accessed November 28, 2021, https://millercenter.org/the-presidency/presidential-speeches/july-4-1861-july-4th-message-congress.

289   **Gandhi was once asked by an American journalist:** Vincent Sheean, *Lead, Kindly Light: Gandhi and the Way to Peace* (n.p.: Borodino Books, 2018).

289   **"reduce[d] myself to a zero":** Jag Parvesh Chander, *The Teachings of Mahatma Gandhi* (Lahore, Pakistan: Indian Printing Works, 1945).

289   **"God's will be done. I am in His hands":** Joshua Wolf Shenk, "Lincoln's Great Depression," *The Atlantic*, October 2005.

289   **"would save [my life] if He needs it for further service":** R. K. Prabhu and U. R. Rao, *The Mind of Mahatma Gandhi* (Ahmedabad, India: Navajivan Publishing House, 1967).

290   **Gandhi's niece Manu described how events transpired:** Tridip Suhurud, *The Diary of Manu Gandhi* (Oxford, UK: Oxford University Press, 2019).

290   **On April 15, 1865, President Lincoln was speaking:** Margarita Spalding Gerry and William Henry Crook, *Lincoln's Last Day* (Glasgow, UK: Good Press, 2020).

291   **Growing up, Tom had a hot temper:** Bruce Greyson, *After: A Doctor Explores What Near-Death Experiences Reveal About Life and Beyond* (New York: St. Martin's Essentials, 2021).

293   **"I was the very people that I hurt":** Evelyn Elsaesser Valarino and Kenneth Ring, *Lessons from the Light: What We Can Learn from the Near-Death Experience* (Needham, MA: Moment Point Press, 2006).

293   **"become less materialistic":** Kenneth Ring, *Life at Death: A Scientific Investigation of the Near-Death Experience* (New York: Coward-McCann, 1980).

296   **While watching newsreels:** Mark Albion, *Making a Life, Making a Living* (New York: Hachette Book Group, 2000).